THE OUTSIDER:
The Life of
Pierre Elliott Trudeau

Michel Vastel
translated by Hubert Bauch

Macmillan of Canada
A Division of Canada Publishing Corporation
Toronto, Ontario, Canada

Canadian Cataloguing in Publication Data
Vastel, Michel
    The outsider

Translation of: Trudeau le Québécois.
Includes bibliographical references.
ISBN 0-7715-9100-4

1. Trudeau, Pierre Elliott, 1919-   . 2. Trudeau, Pierre Elliott, 1919-   —Relations with French-speaking Canadians.*   3. Quebec (Province)— Politics and government—1960-   . 4. Canada— Politics and government—1963-1984.*   5. Prime ministers—Canada—Biography. I Title.

FC626.T78V3813 1990   971.064'4'092   C90-094461-7
F1034.3.T78V3813 1990

Cover design by Craig Allen
Cover photo by Jean-Marc Carisse

Macmillan of Canada
A Division of Canada Publishing Corporation
Toronto, Ontario, Canada

1 2 3 4 5   FP   94 93 92 91 90

Printed in Canada

Table of Contents

To Geneviève,
Anne, Violaine, and Marie,
who willingly shared
a whole summer of my life with "him."

Preface

This book was first an idea, then a title, in the mind of Francine Montpetit of Les Editions de l'Homme.

Writing about Trudeau, even after eleven years spent covering Parliament and national affairs in Ottawa, is still a pretty rash undertaking, akin to writing about God in first-year theology.

But the idea was nevertheless appealing. None of Trudeau's biographers, official or otherwise, has thus far concentrated on the particular aspect of his career dealt with in this book—his relations with Quebec and with his fellow Quebeckers. No one had taken the trouble to dig through the archives at Brébeuf college or the University of Montreal for Trudeau's early writings. Nor has anyone sought to trace the source of Trudeau's political thought by way of a systematic analysis of his articles written during the 1950s.

Such an extended analysis of the life and career of Trudeau the outsider revealed a perseverance, a coherence and consistency of ideas about the man that make him endlessly fascinating.

Pierre Trudeau politely declined to collaborate in the preparation of this book. His friends and former colleagues were, for the most part, forthcoming, though too often on the condition that they remain anonymous, and some agreed only after they had asked his permission. Many of his enemies didn't have to be asked. Still others said they are saving their reminiscences for their own memoirs. If they are to be taken at their word, we are in store for an orgy of Trudeau testimonials—when he will no longer be around to corroborate or correct the facts.

In any case, Trudeau has written so much, and spoken so much, in a manner so clear, absolute, and definitive, that the only question that remains is why he was never willing to revise, even the slightest bit, his opinions about Quebec.

I owe a special thanks to *Le Devoir*'s former publisher Benoît Lauzière, who generously freed me from my obligations as parliamentary correspondent in Ottawa, as well as to Manon Cornellier, who ably assisted me in my research in the parliamentary archives. A number of my colleagues, notably Jean Paré and Pierre Godin, encouraged me to plunge ahead into this adventurous undertaking.

The staff at the Library of Parliament responded to my endless requests with exceptional persistence and patience. In the Quebec college libraries, in particular the one at Montreal's Brébeuf college, I came across buried treasures that the Quebec Cultural Affairs Department should have an interest in bringing to light.

One forgets that a journalist is not a writer. This book would not have achieved the quality I had hoped for at the outset had it not been for the literary sensibilities of my wife Genevieve and her attentive reading of the French manuscript, as well as the personal recollections and comments contributed by Nicolle Forget. I am also in debt to Jean Bernier, literary director at Les Editions de l'Homme, for his sage advice.

As for this English version, I am deeply indebted to Macmillan of Canada, which decided that this book on Trudeau and Quebec was worth sharing with English-Canadian readers.

Its reading would not be so pleasant, however, were it not for the lively style of my translator and colleague, Hubert Bauch, and the patient revisions and useful comments of Kathryn Dean, freelance editor, and Philippa Campsie, editor-in-chief of Macmillan.

In accordance with the traditional formula, I take complete responsibility for my work. I have taken care to verify facts and quotations. In particular, the words and writings of Trudeau himself have been taken from official transcriptions of press conferences and interviews and from the official biography by George Radwanski.

Ottawa, June 1990

Prologue

A Taste for Paradox

*It is wonderful to be despised, if, deep down,
we know we are right.*
                    Pierre Elliott Trudeau, May 1939

April 6, 1968. For more than seven hours now, during ballot count after ballot count, the 2,366 delegates to the Liberal party leadership convention had been milling around in the overheated confines of Ottawa's Civic Centre, chanting two words that would be heard around the world in the sixteen years to come: "Trudeau, Canada!"

Trudeau himself, looking more mysterious than ever, let his gaze drift out absently over the crowd, his regard lighting for an instant on the familiar face of a friend, or lingering briefly, as though for a moment of relaxation, on a pretty woman. He ate slowly from a handful of raisins, chewing them distractedly. Now and then, even with the TV cameras focussed on him at all times, he would toss a peanut in the air and deftly catch it in his mouth.

"Pierre Trudeau, one thousand two hundred and three . . . "

The roar of the crowd drowned out the party president's voice and seemed to carry the man of the hour above the heads and shoulders of the deliriously cheering Liberal faithful and the sea of bobbing placards to the red-and-white-draped podium.

"Trudeau, Canada! Trudeau, Canada! Trudeau, Canada!"

The country had finally found its Kennedy: a man with a brilliant mind, often surrounded by pretty women, with an athletic air even though he was on the verge of turning fifty. A very different man from the unfathomable Mackenzie King, the plodding Louis St. Laurent, the cantankerous John Diefenbaker, or the austere Lester Pearson.

Canada was entering its second century in pursuit of the same dream that inspired its birth and growth as a nation. The dream of Sir John A. Macdonald and of Sir Wilfrid Laurier. "Trudeau, Canada!" It was a ringing cry of confidence. It was the beginning of everything, or so it was thought.

Everything was already in place.

The Royal Commission on Bilingualism and Biculturalism had wrapped up its tour of the country and come to a disturbing conclusion. "All that we have seen and heard has convinced us that Canada is undergoing the most crucial period in its history since Confederation. We believe that things have reached a crisis: the time has come for decisions and real change."

Pierre Trudeau, as minister of justice, had already proposed a constitutional reform package, including a declaration of the rights of man, a new amending formula, better guarantees to ensure the recognition of both official languages, and Supreme Court reform.

Nonetheless the co-chairman of the Commission on Bilingualism and Biculturalism, André Laurendeau, had whispered to his secretary, Neil Morrisson: "I consider Trudeau to be an enemy."

For its part, Quebec's intelligentsia deplored the rise to power of a man who called the thesis of special status for Quebec "bullshit" and "a huge intellectual joke." Claude Ryan, then publisher of *Le Devoir*, had already sensed in this man anointed by English Canada as "the Quebecker we need," "an instinctive rigidity, a latent hostility toward important elements of Quebec opinion, and the dogmatism and insecurity which mark a man cut off from the milieu he is supposed to represent." Ryan wrote this less than thirty months after Trudeau had left Montreal.

By then François Aquin had become the first separatist member to sit in the Quebec National Assembly. On November 18, 1967, René Lévesque slammed the door of the Liberal party behind him, breaking with his colleagues in Jean Lesage's *"équipe du tonnerre"* (Lesage's "A-team" of young, bright politicians and bureaucrats) to found the Sovereignty-Association Movement.

"There is no reason to suppose that the separatists are very strong, or that they have the support of the people," remarked

Canada's new prime minister in a scathing tone. "We shall see. . . . Let them prove themselves, let them get themselves elected. Then we'll discuss it."

In celebrating the discovery of its new saviour, the country failed to hear the echo of its cry of "Trudeau, Canada!" which was already rolling down the valley of the St. Lawrence and developing into a resounding crescendo of "*Lévesque, Québec!*"

Trudeau was forty-nine years old; Lévesque, forty-six. An entire generation, adolescent during the Depression and grown to adulthood during the war years, had flexed its muscles during a revolution that wasn't nearly as quiet as it seemed.

And yet another generation was rising from the sixties, which had seen democracy restored in Quebec, and Trudeau allowed to carry out his own revolution in Ottawa. Robert Bourassa, thirty-four, was preparing his campaign to succeed Lesage and putting distance between himself and the federal Liberals. One Brian Mulroney, twenty-nine, was beginning to make a name for himself as an organizer for the "*bleus*" in Quebec.

Trudeau-Lévesque, Bourassa-Mulroney: the principal actors in the "crisis" foreseen by André Laurendeau and his colleagues on the B&B Commission were in place. "The province of Quebec has no opinions, only emotions," Laurier had said. Soon it would be called on to make a choice.

Too busy celebrating the springtime of the "Northern Magus," the rest of Canada was blissfully unaware of all this. In the wake of the convention in Ottawa, the newspapers were at a loss to explain "the Trudeau enigma." "The prime minister will not resemble the Trudeau we have known up to now," promised the man himself.

He was right. The "three doves," as the "three wise men" were known in French—Jean Marchand, Gérard Pelletier, and Pierre Trudeau—would not stay meekly in the federal coop for long. One of them was already growing the claws of a hawk. Though he was brought into politics by Marchand and Pelletier, Trudeau would turn to Marc Lalonde and Michael Pitfield as his mainstays in power.

"I entered federal politics precisely to say 'no!'" Trudeau had the nerve to say.

The single sour note in the joyful symphony of Trudeaumania was sounded by Father Roger Marcotte, who had studied philosophy with Trudeau. It appeared in a short piece that Marcotte wrote about his former Jean-de-Brébeuf classmate:

" . . . In the delicate negotiations between men, between oneself and others, Pierre luckily holds a trump card that he has already found very useful: a natural aptitude for shaking up 'an idea that has been around too long,' as the French poet Paul Valéry said, a penchant for the type of prank that a man uses to distance himself, even at the risk of looking foolish, when tension or misunderstanding bring men to the edge of ridicule or tragedy."

God knows the pranks and pirouettes Pierre Trudeau has pulled in his lifetime. Behind the Queen's back at Buckingham Palace; on an airport runway on an official visit abroad; at the doors of the National Press Building in Ottawa. The way he thumbed his nose at Joe Clark, or gave the one-fingered salute to the good folk of Salmon Arm, B.C.

"A perfect balance between the scholar and the fool," wrote Pierre Trudeau's classmates in their newspaper in 1938. "In fact it is hard to tell when he is one or the other. What is certain is that he is at once one *and* the other . . . Philosopher, man of science, tragedian, comedian, savage, social animal, student, and athlete . . . these are the paradoxes of our vice-president. Simple where others are conceited, and fanciful where others are simple."

Intellectually, the pirouette became almost a game, a means of distancing himself, as Father Marcotte said. So it was that, a few moments after he had finally attained his goal, after nine provincial premiers had resigned themselves to accepting a charter of rights and freedoms and the patriation of the Constitution with a new amending formula, Trudeau let slip that it was "an abject failure."

Those who were in the National Press Theatre that day thought they saw him smile before he ducked behind the heavy curtains. But eight years later, his adversaries still take him at his word.

It is difficult to get a fix on this man who can deal with a crisis without revealing whether he wants to laugh or to cry.

In 1941 the whole world was wracked by violence and genocide. Pierre Elliott Trudeau, renaming himself "Le Chevalier True de la Roche-Ondine" (a pun on his name that made him sound like a medieval knight) in the pages of *Quartier latin*, the University of Montreal's student paper, threw himself into histrionics and scolded those of his fellow students who had dared to oppose Canada's mobilization.

Was this the same Pierre Trudeau who, on November 25, 1942, on the stage of the auditorium of the Ecole Lajoie in Outremont, denounced conscription and supported a certain Jean Drapeau, "the candidate of the conscripts" for the House of Commons? "Enough cataplasms, it's time for cataclysms!" Pierre Trudeau distanced himself without really saying whether he thought the war was foolish or tragic.

He has always been elusive, behind that oriental mask of his with its high cheekbones, prominent nose that crinkles, mouth that purses, and a voice that climbs into his nose when he gets excited. Only the look in his eyes, continually altered by myopia, sometimes as blurred as a distant horizon, sometimes as precise as a razor blade, occasionally betrays him. As though his soul, behind those deep eyes, cannot conceal a wave of tenderness or a flash of anger.

"I was a very sensitive child," Trudeau explained to his official biographer, George Radwanski. "I guess when you are that way, you have to develop a strong suit of armour to be sure that you are not buffeted by every frown and elated at every smile. I think that's a very known and visible part of my makeup, that access to my inner self is not very easy for anybody. I know I can be hurt as anyone, and therefore I don't, I never did, let just anybody in."

Trudeau was going on fifty when he entered politics in the footsteps of Wilfrid Laurier. No opinions, only emotions? On a wall in the prime minister's official residence, Trudeau hung a tapestry that read, in French, "*La raison avant la passion*": Reason over passion. Was it to keep himself in line? Perhaps he distrusted the Québécois blood coursing through his veins.

September 1989. Roger Marcotte teaches comparative religion and philosophy to Pierre Trudeau's sons at Collège Jean-de-Brébeuf in Montreal, Trudeau's own alma mater. On registration day, Trudeau patiently waited in line with all the other parents, declining an invitation from the principal to go ahead of everyone else.

"Here he was again, just as we knew him back then," sighed the Brébeuf Jesuits, somewhat moved. "The timid boy who didn't flaunt his privileges."

Yet that same summer, when he wanted to take his three sons to Asia, Trudeau asked Canadian Airlines to give him the four airline tickets for the trip. So much for modesty and simplicity . . .

Who, then, is the real Pierre Trudeau? The one adored by his friends and abhorred by his enemies, sometimes with the same blindness. Always pirouetting off, slipping away before anyone can completely catch hold of him. As a result, people can choose to see only those aspects of his character they happen to like.

Sometimes charming, sometimes rude, sometimes mischievous, often arrogant, and always distant, the bohemian young man nick-named Piotr, the rather annoying Pierre-Philippe who came to call himself Pierre Elliott, whom the English call by his initials PET, and whose enemies simply call Trudeau, the man so many women surely couldn't have known long enough to call "Pierre," whose children call him "Dad," and who signed his official correspon-dence as prime minister "Pierre-E. Trudeau," has rarely been simply Pierre Elliott Trudeau.

Transplanted to Ottawa, Trudeau the Québécois has teased the sophists, donned the mask of arrogance, and occasionally allowed himself to lash out with an iron fist. Was it to hide his real nature? One thing is certain: he would never have become what he did if English Canada had not discovered him. Was it just to use him? Or was it the other way around?

Trudeau spent only twenty years on the west side of the Ottawa River, when he was in the full prime of his life. When he could at last take the time to watch his children grow, he "returned" to Quebec, without knowing for sure if Justin, Sacha, and Michel would ever, in the paternal language they were finally learning, call themselves "Québécois," "French Canadians," "Canadians," or "citizens of the world."

The society that Pierre Trudeau never wanted to be "distinct" shows itself to be more and more "distant." He was booed when he went to pay homage to the late René Lévesque as he lay in state, the old adversary whom he no doubt respected, even while he was struggling to defeat him. And many of his disciples, somewhat embarrassed, no longer dare talk to him about this new Quebec where they are living quite comfortably.

He feels betrayed, he who has so often been called "the traitor." He clings to the last shred of power within his grasp, the Liberal Party of Canada. He begs Marc Lalonde to take it in hand again, and lays his conditions before Jean Chrétien. In the twilight of his life, he fears that he will once again have to be the one to say "No!"—to his party, to his friends, to his fellow Québécois. The last one . . .

When Trudeau finds himself short of arguments, he readily cites great minds, like the turn-of-the-century French writer Charles Péguy, for example, whom he quoted in 1938: "I don't judge a man on what he says, but on the way he says it."

Well, Trudeau has said many things. In many different ways.

Part One

The Dilettante (1919-1949)

" . . . my competitiveness was born of a fear of being left behind, rather than from the desire to surge ahead."

1

Bourgeois Jokes

When Gérard Pelletier described the candidate to the leadership of the Liberal Party of Canada as "Pierre Trudeau, a Canadian Quebecker," on February 16, 1968, he did not mention Trudeau's age. And with good reason — at the time no one knew for sure how old he was.

Suzette, sister of the justice minister and leadership candidate, claimed that he was born in 1919. Charles, the youngest in the Trudeau family, said he thought it was more like 1920. And Trudeau's official biography in the *Parliamentary Guide* stated that he was born in Montreal on October 18, 1921.

In the end a researcher from *Time Canada* had to dig through the baptismal register of St. Viateur Parish in Outremont to get to the bottom of this little mystery: after having shaved two years off his age as he approached 50, the Prime Minister of Canada finally admitted that he was born in 1919, not 1921. "I don't like to be too precise about my age," he explained. "That way I don't have to reply to birthday cards, and I don't read the horoscopes." Trudeau, by the way, is a Libra.

The official biography of the Liberal Party of Canada was subsequently adjusted to read: "Long before becoming the object of a royal commission, bilingualism and biculturalism reigned in a comfortable home on McCulloch Street in Outremont in the city of Montreal. Into this bicultural milieu Pierre Trudeau was born on October 18, 1919, the first son in a family of three children."

Pierre Trudeau may have tried to make himself younger in this way because, in the early years of his life, he was hardly a child prodigy. He was "kind of puny," said his classmates. His sister recalled that he was "timid," and he himself said that his health was delicate. He was more of a slogger than a natural when it came to schoolwork. "I always had to work harder in order not to be left behind." Indeed, admission to the Bar at age twenty-four is hardly a sign of genius.

In October 1919 the world was digging itself out of the rubble of World War I and Canada had attained international sovereignty by virtue of having signed the Treaty of Versailles. On the home front, the "unionist" coalition headed by Arthur Meighen in Ottawa was beginning to fall apart. Wilfrid Laurier had died in February, and Mackenzie King, who had already succeeded him as party leader, was preparing to bring the Liberals back to power.

Quebec, which was shut out of power in Ottawa and was having difficulty adjusting to a peacetime economy, turned in on itself. Thirty years later, in a masterful analysis entitled, "The Province of Quebec at the Time of the Asbestos Strike," which constituted an eighty-one-page introduction to the history of the asbestos strike, Trudeau explained: "A people which had been defeated, occupied, decapitated, pushed out of commerce, driven from the cities, reduced little by little to a minority, and diminished in influence in a country which it had nonetheless discovered, explored, and colonized, could adopt few attitudes that would enable it to preserve its identity. This people devised a system of security, which became overdeveloped; as a result, they sometimes overvalued all those things that set them apart from others, and showed hostility to all change (even progress) coming from without.

"That is why our nationalism, to oppose a surrounding world that was English-speaking, Protestant, democratic, materialistic, commercial, and later industrial, created a system of defence which put a premium on all the contrary forces: the French language, Catholicism, authoritarianism, idealism, rural life, and later the return to the land."

In 1919, however, Jean-Charles Emile Trudeau (Charlie to his poker friends, and simply Charles to his family) was an exception to the situation later described by his son. The descendant of a farming family from St. Michel de Napierville, he was the first to attend university and go into law and business. "The bourgeoisie doesn't go very far back with Trudeau," noted his childhood friends who remembered how much he used to enjoy visiting his paternal grandparents' farm.

The Automobile Owners' Association that Charles Trudeau had founded in Montreal in 1927 had grown, five years later, to 15,000 members and 30 service stations. Along with gas, the cooperative offered free road maps, towing in case of breakdowns, and cut-rate quarts of oil, all for a $10 membership fee. The business prospered, and Champlain, a subsidiary of Imperial Oil, bought it out. So it was that in 1933 Charles Trudeau emerged from the Great Depression a millionaire.

He invested in mines (Hollinger), smelters (Algoma), recreation (Belmont Park), and even sports, buying a share of the old Montreal Royals baseball team.

"He was a man I admired very much in everything because, at least in the eyes of the world I lived in, he was a successful man," explained Trudeau. "He had a lot of friends. The house was always full of friends."

But he was also a French Canadian who frequented the francophone St. Denis Club, rather than the anglophone St. James, and who bought a house in Outremont rather than on the Westmount side of the mountain. He was something of a bon vivant, who would often go out at night for poker parties with his pals, after supervising the children's homework. On weekends he would take the family to Mont Tremblant in the Laurentians, where he introduced his sons to boxing and hunting.

His wife, Grace Elliott, on the other hand, came from an old Scottish family. Her mother was French Canadian and had taught her to speak French, but she had been influenced by her education at boarding school in Dunham in the Eastern Townships, and retained the manners of Montreal's well-to-do English bourgeoisie.

Her brother, who lived in France, had introduced her to the painter Georges Braque, one of the inventors of cubism. From Europe she brought back several small paintings that she hung on the old oak picture rails of the large brick house at 84 McCulloch Street in Outremont. Visitors to the house remember it as being austere and somewhat intimidating. "It was all brown and there was lace everywhere," recalled Margaret Trudeau, "a mahogany grand piano and chairs covered with needlepoint."

Delicate, "spiritual, and blessed with a solid sense of humour," according to Gérard Pelletier, who saw her often, Grace Elliott imparted to her son a taste for literature and adventure. She also introduced young Pierre to the long canoe trips of which he became so fond.

Her eldest child, Suzette, studied at the Couvent du Sacré Coeur, an institution run by French-speaking nuns and attended by young girls from good families. She sometimes quarrelled with Pierre, the elder of the two sons and his father's favourite. Young Pierre liked to show off his knowledge and, already a bit of a chauvinist, tried to demonstrate to his sister that he knew more than she did. One day he took apart her doll to find out how on earth the wretched thing was able to speak.

Charles Junior, a year younger than Pierre, lived somewhat in his shadow, particularly at Collège Brébeuf. He was "the other Trudeau," who always kept himself far removed from his brother's public life. An architect by profession, he retired early and settled in the Laurentian town of Morin Heights.

Pierre Elliott first attended classes in the English section of the small elementary school on Querbes Street in Outremont. "I punched him out once or twice," recalled radical labour leader Michel Chartrand, who attended the French section of the school. Until adolescence, Pierre Trudeau would alternate between French and English.

He is, in fact, one or the other, often because he feels like making others mad at him.

"When I got to college," he told Peter Gzowski in 1962, "there was another Pierre Trudeau there, so I added one of my baptismal names, Philippe, to my signature. But later I started to use Elliott, which was my mother's name and another of my baptismal names, and I confess it was in part to annoy the nationalists. You have to remember that the thirties were a time of great patriotic fervour. The teacher would read to us, with all due pathos, the triumphant passages from our history, and when he would get to the choice bits, like the battle of Carillon, the students would applaud. I found this amusing, and when we studied the battles won by the English, it would be my turn to applaud."

When the young Pierre Trudeau visited Germany with his parents in 1932, his father sent him to a hotel to ask if there were any rooms available. Instinctively he mixed English, rather than French, in with German when addressing the desk clerk: "Well, look, *haben Sie drei Zimmer frei*?" Yet the Germans had already invaded France, and were preparing to do so again. If there was a language they had a chance to know, it was French, not English.

His childhood friends remember him as a "weak, timid, emotional" little guy. It didn't take much to make him cry. A compliment would make him blush. And they remember how funny his long skinny legs looked in the short pants of the college uniform.

His schoolyard fights soon convinced the little Trudeau, whom even his father found somewhat frail, that he "needed physical discipline to be as healthy as the boy next door." So every morning he would conscientiously do his 5BX air cadet exercises.

"From that, I think, developed my interest in sport and perhaps from there my physical prowess," he said later. "Wanting to learn how to box—being weak I'd have to be able to defend myself more than the next guy. Or learning how to wrestle or being good at tumbling."

The delicate boy, whose father taught him boxing to make him shape up a bit, turned into a brawler. A schoolmate who insisted on calling him "Toto" got his nose broken in the middle of a Latin class.

In an essay that he wrote after taking a canoe trip from Montreal to Hudson Bay, Trudeau extolled the joys of physical exertion: "It's not spiritual satisfaction that pushes the body to hard labour. That satisfaction is often mixed with pride, and the body never fails to wreak revenge on it. On a long, difficult portage, I have often felt my reason desert me shamefully, even as my legs and back held me to the task. The verses I chanted through clenched teeth at the beginning become brutish grunts. There is nothing attractive in this bestial search for that wonderful feeling of lightness that always marks the end of a portage."

Condescendingly, Pierre Trudeau claimed that there was "perhaps only a chance distinction" between ordinary people who spent Sunday afternoons canoeing on a pond in Parc Lafontaine in midtown Montreal and those like him "who dare to cross a lake, make a portage, spend the night under a tent and return, exhausted, under the paternal eye of the guide." But his position as a millionaire's son in the midst of the Great Depression made him one of the privileged few. A chauffeur drove the Trudeau brothers up Côte St. Catherine to Collège Brébeuf in their father's limousine while some of their friends, like Michel Chartrand, would walk several kilometres to save the three-and-a-half-cent bus fare.

At the beginning of the school year, remembers Chartrand, the students would "count those who were missing, as at the end of a long war." Families could be ruined overnight, and the children would have to leave school to go back to the farm or to work in a factory. But Pierre Trudeau would return from his holidays with memories exceptional for the time, such as the trip to faraway Europe, the dream of all children of his generation.

When he visited Italy in the summer of 1932, it was already under Mussolini's absolute dictatorship, and Germany was on the verge of electing Hitler, the head of the National Socialists, as federal chancellor. The rise of fascism must have made a significant impression on the still-adolescent Pierre Trudeau. When he returned to school it was not the balkanization of Canada that he talked about to his schoolmates at Brébeuf, but that of Europe. "He was always talking about Silesia [partitioned between Poland and Germany in 1921], saying that nationalism leads to the disintegration of states," remembered Roger Marcotte.

One year later, in 1933, while attending the Montreal Royals' spring training camp in Florida, Jean-Charles Emile Trudeau came down with a severe case of pneumonia and died suddenly. Young Pierre was devastated.

It was a different Trudeau who rejoined his schoolmates at Brébeuf after several days' absence. He took to shocking his fellow students by wearing eccentric outfits or by interrupting the drone of boring teachers with nasty rejoinders. He threw himself into overcoming his timidity. "But it was too obvious, too excessive to look unforced," recalled Roger Marcotte.

"He astonished us with his cubist ties and his brush cuts," his school friends wrote in the June 1940 issue of *Le Brébeuf*, the college paper. "Trudeau's 'don't-give-a-damn' attitude stems from a philosophy of life that reduces public opinion to its true value."

The Trudeau of the time was, above all, a nonconformist. In 1939, in an essay entitled "Rehabilitating Pascal" (whom the Brébeuf Jesuits did not greatly care for) the Philosophy I student declared: " . . . originality is none other than the rare effect of a real personality . . . "

"*A priori*, [extravagant] originality cannot be rare, because we are all sufficiently intelligent to do bizarre things for no particular reason from time to time: clearly we have to get used to appearing crazy if we are to do things that are frankly honest."

Pierre Trudeau was never short of attention-getting ideas. He would suggest that his friends try going around wearing a bootlace instead of a tie, or wearing shorts when they were not the fashion (which he did in his thirties when he wore them before the picket line of striking miners at Murdochville in the Gaspé peninsula), or by shaving their heads or growing beards.

Trudeau has always had a flair for a witticism, hurtful at times, but without malice. This was long before he became a hardened politician who sought to injure with his repartee. At the age of twenty, Trudeau wasn't trying to crush people. All he wanted was attention.

When a teacher was waxing overly pretentious, Trudeau would get up and open a window, as if to indicate that it was all so much hot air. He wilfully rebelled against the Jesuit fathers' code of discipline. One day, the weight of discipline heavy on his shoulders — even though he was already sprouting tufts of a beard on his chin — he dipped his pen in vinegar and wrote: "The timid make bad firemen. They're all for using fire engines, hoses, and big ladders to extinguish a match . . . "

The only discipline he would accept was the discipline he imposed on himself. "Deciding to be my own man, and seek for approval in myself," he told his biographer, "I suddenly began to take a kind of perverse pleasure at being what in those days we used to call 'un original,' in dress, in manner of speaking, in my readings, in artistic taste."

He went from being an original to systematically flouting convention and glorying in nonconformist behaviour. And he censured those who would not readily follow his contentious path. "We are too stupid to realize that our own judgements are dictated by and dependent on newspaper headlines, snippets of conversation, and hearsay. We see the whole of humanity adopt ridiculous lifestyles and thoughts, on the pretext that it is easier to do the wrong thing with a crowd, than to react alone."

The Pierre Trudeau who, according to his classmates, represented "the perfect balance between the scholar and the fool," dappled, as he said, his writing with humour, poetry, and sophisms, but rarely put forward his own views. For a philosophy student, in times that could at best be described as troubled, he expressed himself as eccentrically in his writing as he did in his way of dressing.

"Better to have a jagged pen than a dried-out one," he said by way of excuse.

"Have you no ideas?" the editor of *Le Brébeuf*, the college's student paper, wrote to his fellow students. "Then go and make some up. You can't make up any? Then borrow some; the truth is up to you. You don't want to borrow? What the hell, write without ideas. People will take you for a poet, or an editor-in-chief, or a politician."

The student who finished first in his class and won all the Latin prizes — versification, translation, prose composition — as well as prizes for literature, history, English, and physics, who was accorded an honourable mention by the City of Montreal Savings Bank "for his sense of order and economy," pointedly rejected any suggestion that he was an intellectual pedant. "Thinkers, you see, are people who take everything seriously," he wrote in 1938, "and worse, they take themselves seriously. Unfortunately, when they hear themselves say 'weighty and profound,' they refuse to understand 'thick and hollow.'"

Trudeau was not afraid of criticism when he thought he was right about something. At the end of one editorial he wrote without hesitation: "Anyway, that is what I think. And I think I am right: that is why I had this published."

One day Trudeau decided to switch to international French. "I must have been about fourteen or fifteen years old," he remembered. "From that time on I was beginning to read Racine, Corneille, Molière, and God knows that the words I was speaking weren't really the words that were written. And I said, 'Either I start reading something else, or I start speaking a bit more the way it's supposed to be done.'" In vain his family and friends accused him of putting on airs; he was undeterred.

Shortly after the death of his father, Trudeau took his mother's name, and began speaking like a native of France. Could it be that he did so to reject his father's French-Canadian roots and tie himself more closely to the Anglo-Saxon heritage of his mother, Grace Elliott?

At the very least it resulted in a few colourful articles from the young student with a penchant for rhetoric (and puns). Under the pseudonym "Chevalier True de la Roche-Ondine," he playfully nicknamed his friends "Monsieur Hilfet de Lafrase" (he who uses flowery language), "Jean Féïtou" (I do everything), "Sassonne

Lecreux" (it rings hollow), "A. Lhume Lalumière" (light the light), and "cher Shé Taclé" (find your key).

In the April 1939 issue of *Brébeuf*, on the same page where Charles Lussier, later a senior federal mandarin, wrote a serious piece about the election of the French novelist Georges Duhamel to the Académie française, Trudeau indulged in a mixture of poetry and humour to describe how he broke his leg skiing.

. . . Climbing in skiing is always a reality. At the beginning you can entertain yourself by calculating the angle of elevation and the value of its sine; a little higher, you estimate the weight of your backpack and the distance covered; and, if the hillside is particularly long, you can take courage from the imperturbability of your shadow on the snow.

Once the summit has been reached, the thought of the descent brightens the spirit and reality becomes less arduous. Scrutinizing the forest that barred the way to the promised land, I spied an opening. We pushed off.

Silence and shadow.

Our first steps were tentative; then I was struck by the strength of my skis flattening the virgin snow.

Meanwhile, the corridor widened, and soon we pulled up in an immense and luminous crypt, vaulted in azure and carpeted with ermine. Near the summit a squirrel scurried; with a broad gesture, a pine branch snowed a cloud of silver powder that shimmered in a sunbeam. A bird sang . . .

Out of curiosity I explored a path between two conifers draped in white. I saw that it led to a clearing where fairies had been dancing. Seeing their footprints on the snow, I hastily withdrew.

When we arrived at the edge of the woods, we felt as if we were lost in some imaginary land. It was almost twilight. The sky was shedding its azure veil, which was falling delicately to earth. But the great tapering pines had poked star holes in the firmament here and there; a heavy, dark fluid was already filling the bottom of the valley. We had to hurry.

. . . A bump was enough to throw me into the sky where you see neither mountain, nor valley, only the lights

of the village, glowing like a handful of pearls at the bottom
of a lake, and the Big Dipper, suspended like a sign in the
sky, and the innumerable stars like snowflakes.

Blessed is he who ends his celestial flight by tumbling
into the snow, coldly real, but soft.

Others are destined to come to earth differently. Your leg
lovingly encircles a maple, and winds up in a pine for 40
days. Skis of ash and crutches of pine. So much for Utopia.

Sometimes Trudeau's sense of humour took a more scabrous
turn, but as vice-president of the student council and editor-in-
chief of the college paper, he managed to escape censure. In this
vein he penned a satirical account of the adventures of a new
boarder whose neighbour in the college dormitory snored like a
locomotive.

One night, when a head cold was "doing nothing to improve the
sound" the schoolboy got up and "seized the delinquent's facial
protrusion between his thumb and forefinger and . . . 'Dirty pig!'"
Trudeau continued. "My fingers encountered a soft, gluey substance
that left a revolting impression. The nose, the cold . . . Oh, my God,
what an awful feeling. How could I have guessed that the snorer,
tired of having his nose pulled, had coated it with Vaseline?"

The students at Brébeuf must have enjoyed this kind of literature,
because of the dozen pieces Trudeau wrote for the paper over eight
years, none makes any reference to the great debates of the day, let
alone to the storm brewing in Europe. Yet, here and there, certain
allusions could be found that suggested a political interest.

In 1939, for instance, Liberal leader Adélard Godbout had seized
power from Maurice Duplessis, and Trudeau observed: "Quebeckers go clinging blindly to the opinions of their forefathers, and it
would be most unsound to found a party that is neither '*bleu*' nor
'*rouge*,' Tory nor Grit. Old habits die hard . . . "

Twenty years before thinking of founding his own leftist movement, Trudeau did not make a great deal of his province switching
from the Conservatives to the Liberals. To him, they were all the
same old parties.

In the same November 1939 issue — Canada had just declared
war on Germany — Trudeau wrote: "War can only be explained as
absurd behaviour, because very few people prefer war to peace.
War is still considered a small affair between friends where you get

together for a few days to wave the flags and beat the drum, then call the whole thing off after taking a few shots and killing three or four men—a small formality. But real wars, where soldiers clash and the bombs kill, nobody likes that. Meanwhile the soldiers daren't say they would rather stop after a few years, because it's hard for them to get shot at. And the generals daren't ask for peace for fear they will look bad in the eyes of the soldiers."

Pierre Trudeau, antimilitarist? John Diefenbaker's Conservatives insinuated that he was a draft dodger to discredit him in the eyes of veterans. But can this term have any meaning when nearly all French Canadians voted against conscription?

At the time, Hitler didn't bother Trudeau. On the contrary, he made use of him to scold his compatriots who were badmouthing the English. "If the monster of Berlin emerges victorious, life will no longer be easy for us," announced Trudeau in the April 1941 issue of *Quartier latin*, the University of Montreal student paper, imitating the political rhetoric of the era. "As colonials of perfidious Germany," he continued (as though he were talking about England —perfidious Albion), "we will find her an implacable mistress who will attempt to assimilate us any way she can. She will destroy our faith, impose the German language, and belittle our culture, aims which will earn us only her most deadly attentions. She will dominate our economy and reduce us to subaltern status in industry. Our countryside will be emptied and our natural resources seized. And then we will know the demoralizing mockery of a traitorous press, a crushing oligarchy, and a government that exploits the people it is supposed to protect."

It is not the least surprising, given such opinions, that Pierre Trudeau was invited to leave the Canadian Officers' Training Corps, "for lack of discipline," as he admits himself, nor that he finished the war with a reserve unit, the Mont-Royal Fusiliers. In any case, it was far quieter than the beaches of Bernières in Normandy where "the boys from the famous Régiment de la Chaudière" found themselves at the time.

One can just imagine the reaction of the right-thinking burghers of Ste. Agathe, a Laurentian village north of Montreal, when, at the height of the war, Trudeau, accompanied by his friend Roger Rolland, roared down the street on his Harley-Davidson, wearing a pointed Prussian army helmet.

"They were playing practical jokes like the bourgeois they were," commented Gérard Pelletier. "I could laugh at them sometimes, but such things didn't interest me. I found it quite pointless; at a time when there were more pressing matters at stake."

When Trudeau graduated from Brébeuf in 1940, the best thing he took with him was friendship — friendship for people he liked to party with, like Roger Rolland in Paris, and for others with whom he would eventually break, like Pierre Vadeboncoeur. As for comrades in arms, like Gérard Pelletier; intimates during his years in power, like Marc Lalonde; and those who would follow other roads to success, like Jean de Grandpré, all of them were at the time actively occupied elsewhere.

The best passages Trudeau ever wrote are about friendship. Like these, after returning from a canoe trip: "It is a school of friendship, where you learn that your best friend is not the rifle, but the one who shares your rest each night, after ten hours of paddling at the other end of the canoe.

"Suppose you have to get up a set of rapids, and it is your turn to stay in the canoe and guide it: you see your friend tripping on logs, sliding on rocks, sinking in the muck, scraping his legs, and swallowing water for which he has no thirst, but never letting go of the rope, while you, safe in the midst of the rapid, make fun of him. When this same man has also fed you exactly half of his catch of fish, and done a double portage because you've hurt yourself, you can boast of having a friend for life, and one who knows much about you."

All Trudeau had acquired by the age of twenty-one was a network of acquaintances with whom he had travelled up the Harricana, or with whom he had traded punches in the schoolyard and *bons mots* in the oratorical contests.

His sense of his country was more in his body than in his spirit. The only definition of nationalism he had expressed thus far was impressed upon him during his trips to the wilderness, where he challenged the forces of nature: "I knew a man whose schooling could never teach him nationalism," he wrote, as though speaking of himself, "but who developed this virtue when he felt the immensity of his land in his flesh, when his skin tingled with the grandeur of those who created his country."

In fact, apart from being possessed of "a clean mind in a clean body" (something that greatly satisfied the ambitions of the Jesuit fathers at Brébeuf), Pierre Elliott Trudeau, who had been Pierre-Philippe, and Piotr, then Elliott, then Pierre, had little idea of where he was headed when he entered university.

"If you're a doctor, people think you're a killer. If you're a monk they say you're lazy. If you go into politics, they say you're a crook. If you're enthusiastic, you'll be called scatter-brained; seek wisdom and you're 'a young old man.' If you're an artist or a thinker, you're considered unapproachable. I don't know which direction to take any more."

Since he had just reached adulthood and only the American continent had been spared from the war, Pierre Trudeau registered at the University of Montreal, his way of putting off the moment of choice. The only thing he was sure of was that he didn't want to get involved. No more with political movements than with the Canadian army.

In 1939, Gérard Pelletier, already active with the student Catholic Action movement, challenged his fellow students from other colleges to get involved. "I ask under the patronage of the JEC [Jeunesses Etudiantes Catholiques] which joins them all, that each student newspaper define its attitude, in the words of its student editor, in its next issue."

That year, the editor of *Le Brébeuf* happened to be Pierre Elliott Trudeau himself. He responded with a text somewhat pompously entitled: "This is the editorial."

"The paper has a well-defined attitude," Trudeau wrote in an intransigent tone. "It consists of having no definite attitude."

"He took the mickey out of me," Pelletier admitted later, after a long friendship had rendered him indulgent.

Nonetheless, the day would come when Trudeau would feel the need to be in on things, and he would remember the old militants from the Catholic Action movement, just as he would remember the labour movement and the leftists. But it was not yet time.

2

The Wrong University

"Pierre hated studying law," his sister Suzette confided. "I think the only reason he finished law school was that he had committed himself to it. He didn't enjoy the classes." Trudeau at first denied this mildly, then admitted he didn't really take to his law studies until after two years at university.

When he left Brébeuf with his Bachelor of Arts degree in 1940, Trudeau was independently wealthy. The $2 million that Charles Trudeau had bequeathed to his widow and his three children gave him entrée to the best (or at least the most expensive) universities.

Grace Elliott was not one to impose her opinions on her eldest son. She was often away, travelling with friends on long trips to far-flung corners of the world, and in any case, she knew better than to dictate to Pierre, whose spirit of independence would have made him do just the opposite of what she suggested.

Pierre Trudeau chose to go to the University of Montreal when he could have afforded to go to Harvard, for reasons that remain a mystery. Perhaps it was because in the United States he would have been too far removed from the great French masters, who were just about all his Jesuit teachers had talked about. As for Europe, it was cut off by the war.

For sentimental reasons—he was engaged to a psychology student at the time—and also out of personal preference, no doubt, Trudeau would probably rather have entered the more cerebral disciplines, psychology in particular. But in 1940, psychology was not yet taught at the University of Montreal.

Finally, before he died, Charles Trudeau had advised his son, as did all French-Canadian fathers of the time, to go into law. "Study law," he had said. "That will give you a solid base, and then you can do other things, as I have."

Despite their fathers' wishes, the law had a profoundly soporific effect on promising young French Canadians. "Law studies are a source of mortal boredom," declared René Lévesque, then suffering through law studies at Laval University. "A judge repeats a lecture on Roman law in a monotone, the same lecture he concocted a quarter of a century ago and which hasn't changed one whit since — no more than Roman law itself."

Thus, at the age of twenty-one, Pierre Trudeau more or less fell into what was then, as Gérard Filion, former publisher of *Le Devoir*, recalled, "a poor excuse for a university" where the business school — the Ecole des Hautes Etudes Commerciales — was the only one among all the faculties and affiliated schools to have full-time professors.

Other graduates from Trudeau's class at Brébeuf, like Jean de Grandpré, later president of Bell Canada Enterprises, opted for the more prestigious McGill University, which was far better endowed financially and academically. In choosing his university, the "bicultural" Pierre Trudeau took a path that led him toward the French-Canadian bourgeoisie, rather than the Anglo-Canadian élite, just as he had done when he entered Brébeuf.

Given his independent means, Trudeau could have enrolled in the only Quebec university faculty which found favour in his eyes, the social sciences school at Laval University, founded in 1932, which had recently come under the directorship of the educator Father Georges-Henri Lévesque, whose fights against the Duplessis regime would make him a legend in Quebec.

"This Dominican," explained Trudeau, "was one of the rare examples among us of a man who, in his mature years, permits reflection and scientific research to overthrow the idols of his youth. Father Lévesque, now a liberal, organized the teaching on a rational basis, fostered the intellectual development of professors by giving them the opportunity to study abroad, accepted the fact that science eliminates prejudice, and recognized that the teaching of Catholic social morality cannot dispense with intellectual integrity."

It is therefore surprising that Pierre Trudeau stranded himself in a university he held in such deep contempt. That much was obvious in his writing — his essay "The Province of Quebec at the Time of the Asbestos Strike," for instance, in which he dealt harshly with some of the university's reigning academic icons like Edouard Montpetit, Brother Marie-Victorin, and many others.

During the time Trudeau was enrolled at the University of Montreal, it was setting up its sociology institute. "Misrepresentation," commented Trudeau. "The so-called institute conducts the study of sociology as if they were compiling telephone directories.

"Our French-Canadian faculties of law need not detain us. Busy lawyers came there to teach students how to find their way among the different law codes of the Province of Quebec. Any notions of the sociology of law were scrupulously avoided; the major currents in the philosophy of law were ignored by our law faculties; the infrequent courses in constitutional law were completely worthless, and the very names of Jean Bodin and Jeremy Bentham were unknown."

If Trudeau could make such acid comments about his alma mater in 1956, it was because by then he had studied at three other more prestigious and more ancient faculties: Harvard, the Sorbonne, and the London School of Economics, where he had come in contact with works like *Six Books of the Republic* (Bodin) and *Treatise on Civil and Penal Legislation* (Bentham).

Trudeau pointed out that the proportion of French Canadians in the liberal professions and in the management ranks of industry and commerce was distinctly lower than their numbers warranted in the overall demographic scheme. "In short, French Canadians have always been the hewers of wood and the drawers of water in the industrial revolution. Over a period of twenty years, our educational institutions have not caused our percentage of technicians to increase more rapidly than our percentage of workers."

The university rectors had no more interest in seeing the universities become instruments of social change than did the tenured professors. "The role of the university is to conserve and transmit knowledge, much more than to increase it," stated the University of Montreal's brief to the Royal Commission of Inquiry on Constitutional Problems, even as recently as 1954.

Nevertheless, in 1940 Pierre Trudeau seemed to reconcile himself to this situation without difficulty. Certainly he wrote nothing at the time denouncing it.

Much later, when he was introducing his longtime friend at the launching of his Liberal leadership campaign, Gérard Pelletier recalled: "From these years of our youth, the clearest memory is of articles in *Quartier latin*: incisive, polemic, leavened with ferocious and ironic humour, which addressed the political problems of the time with rare passion."

All of this no doubt looked good in Trudeau's official biography. However, a systematic search of the University of Montreal's microfilm library reveals that it is more the stuff of legend than reality. In all, during the three years that Trudeau spent at the university, he had barely half a dozen articles printed in the student paper, including one letter to the editor and a critique of a scientific treatise, *The Origins of the American Man* — which he panned in some detail, saying that "there are those who read all the reviews and none of the books: thus the prestige of my name might help to popularize a few phrases by the obscure Professor Paul Rivet." There was also an ode to motorcycling that has become famous over the years.

Pierre Trudeau has always liked to call attention to himself with his vehicles as much as with his clothes: the Harley, the Jaguar, the Mercedes. Although Michel Chartrand groaned, "It was a rattle-trap that machine, it was like sitting on the ground," it didn't matter. Trudeau spoke of his motorcycle the way Richard III spoke of his horse.

In the March 30, 1944, issue of *Quartier latin*, Trudeau rose to the defence of his poor motorbike, heaping scorn on the old-fashioned "anachronists" who failed to understand that the motorcycle could be more than a commonplace means of locomotion. *"Pritt, zoum, bing,"* read the headline on page 8.

> The perfect escape mechanism. Look at the profile of the motorcycle against the light of day and you cannot help but admire its light, compact structure. Two wheels, because one would be unstable and slow, and three would be too many. There's the motor, because muscles have better things to do than turn pedals. There's the tank, which is for gas and not, as you might think, because the rider should have a saddle to fill the space between the wheels harmoniously. And then there are the two bags at the side, which are the

only possible baggage. They preclude calculated and long-drawn-out departures because they fill up quickly.

This machine, ready to leap forward with the flick of a finger, is put together with such simple ingenuity that an excess of logic sometimes makes me think that man was created with motorcycling in mind: nostrils flared downward and ears flattened to the side of the head, permitting maximum acceleration without scooping up the wind and the dust. The motorcycle is controlled by two handles; we have two hands . . .

You who praise team sports, observe the motorcyclist and his passenger . . . Is there a mountain to climb? A difficult stretch of sandy beach to cross? Both grip their mount with their knees, feeling the same heat against their calves. Both see the plain surging toward them beyond the crest of the summit, or the road straightening itself out after coming through a curve. One grips the handlebars, the other shifts his weight to avoid treacherous bumps; one sees a field of buckwheat, the other notices the sweet scent; one feels like going swimming, but it is the other who stops the motorcycle at the edge of the beach . . .

Trudeau the bohemian was no doubt talking about himself in that article. It certainly isn't hard to imagine him roaring over manicured hotel lawns and around city squares, through thickets, along beaches and docks, and even on the Plains of Abraham. Pierre Trudeau, the biker ancestor; a portrait of the poet as Hell's Angel.

The whole time Trudeau was at university, there was a war on — "that conflict which was our generation's great adventure," as René Lévesque described it. But Pierre Trudeau never intended to get involved.

At the beginning of the 1940s, when a ration coupon was worth a pound of sugar, two ounces of tea, or half a pound of coffee or butter, Pierre Trudeau entertained friends and lived the life of an aristocrat.

It was, among other things, those evenings in the basement of the Trudeau family home, in which lively discussions of books and ideas were interspersed with sessions of listening to classical recordings, that brought Gérard Pelletier in contact with the "Brébeuf gang." François Hertel, an exceptional Jesuit and a superb philosophy teacher, often joined the group and refereed the debates. Some evenings, Trudeau himself would read to the assembly from *L'Equipée*, a posthumous work by the Breton poet Victor Segalen.

Trudeau felt somewhat uneasy as a rich kid. He was well aware that 48 percent of the undergraduates at the University of Montreal came from the professional milieu, though professionals represented only 10 percent of the work force. "These figures suggest," he wrote, "that financial and social status are of prime importance in determining access to university studies. The great majority of children born into poor families, then, must be satisfied with a few years of primary school, where their readers and their arithmetic problems extol the bourgeois virtues and illustrate the glories of the free enterprise system."

But Trudeau only wrote these lines in 1956, after he had become active in the left-wing movements and the labour unions. In 1941, in the pages of *Quartier latin*, he preferred to view his situation with humour: "My venerable profession and my great personal value assure my access to the most distinguished milieus of our Dominion. To the envy of those who have escaped luxury, I mix with statesmen, businessmen, and people from other countries. I am no stranger to the university nor to the highest ranks of the clergy. And I will surprise no one by saying that great numbers of my acquaintances will be immortalized in bronze statues when they die."

Behind the irony, there appears an acute awareness of belonging to a privileged class. But Pierre Trudeau never showed off his privileges. After all, had his Brébeuf schoolmates not spoken of "a good and devoted friend"?

The airy tone of Trudeau's early writing and of his few public sorties contrasted sharply with the inflamed tirades of André Laurendeau and with the position of Gérard Pelletier, Maurice Sauvé, and others, who were deeply involved in the Catholic Action movement. In a special issue of *Quartier latin* on federalism and French-Canadian nationalism, there is no trace of Trudeau.

His sole appearance in the political domain came briefly, during the conscription debate. Since 1941 the large English-Canadian newspapers, like the *Winnipeg Free Press*, the *Globe and Mail*, and the *Ottawa Citizen*, had been demanding that Quebec be brought into line. They accused French Canadians of being slackers, traitors, even racists, because they refused to fight beside the English in defence of the motherland. In response, the publisher of *Le Devoir* at the time, Georges Pelletier, along with André Laurendeau, Gérard Filion, Jean Drapeau, and others, had formed the League for the Defence of Canada.

The ranks of the Canadian army in Europe consisted of 125,000 men, all volunteers. Although compulsory military service did exist, it was only for the defence of Canada itself. But once the United States entered the war and it expanded across the globe, Canada had to beef up its contingent in Europe. Notwithstanding the federal government's promises, there would be conscription, and Ottawa called a referendum to approve its decision.

When Canada voted on conscription in April 1942, Quebec voted one way and English Canada another. Trudeau was on the Quebec side. Quebec voted 71 percent against conscription, while the anglophone provinces voted 80 percent in favour.

"It is the most amazing phenomenon," remarked André Laurendeau. "Even without having been reached by the League's propaganda, French minorities in Canada, wherever they form a significant group, have mostly voted no. It seems to be an instinctive reflex."

One evening in November 1942, Trudeau's own instinctive reflexes carried him to the stage of a rally at the Ecole Lajoie in Outremont, where he stood with people like Jean Drapeau, Michel Chartrand, and D'Iberville Fortier. "In Ottawa, the policy is *après moi le déluge*," he declared. "It would be merely idiotic if it weren't so infuriating. The government declared war at a time when America was not threatened by invasion, even before Hitler had won his crushing victories."

A quarter of a century later, Trudeau confided: "I fear my motives were not the most noble. I think I was hoping sort of to bug the government." But it is true that by then Trudeau had already taken an interest in the leadership of the Liberal Party of Canada . . .

Trudeau always had a contradictory streak. "There is no other constant in my thinking than to oppose accepted opinions: from the time I was in college I had already made up my mind to swim against the tide."

During the 1940s, "the rational content of our electoral and parliamentary debates was so minuscule that there was no need for politicians to educate Quebec voters. In our political arenas, elections were alternately won with nationalistic coups or cases of 'white lightning.' Passions were rampant and some of the least edifying of these infiltrated the public administration."

So when English Canada and its political parties sought to draft the province, Trudeau preached insurrection.

It was a bitter and frustrated Pierre Trudeau, full of scorn for his own people, who was admitted to the Quebec Bar in 1943.

Neil Morrisson, who was active in the McGill chapter of the Canadian Youth Congress, remembers Pelletier and Claude Ryan at the national student conferences.

"Trudeau? We never saw him in those days," he said.

A few years later André Laurendeau took a swipe at Trudeau for his virulent attacks on Quebec's universities. "[Trudeau] makes judgements, he demands that heads roll, and we have already seen that his guillotine functions a little too arbitrarily. I sense in Trudeau the signs of a bitter deception."

Gérard Filion agreed. "It's possible," he said, "that Trudeau felt he had gone to the wrong university."

Unlike Jean de Grandpré, for example, who, upon graduating from McGill at the same time, had the doors of the most prestigious law firms in town swing open before him, Trudeau was even more bored by the practice of law than he had been by its study. "I practised for a year," he said later, "and found it simply intolerable."

The big question facing him in 1943 was how a young twenty-four-year-old, single and rich to boot, was going to deal with his free time. "It was becoming unbearable," wrote René Lévesque in his memoirs. "Unless you were in uniform, you couldn't get any girls."

Not Trudeau . . .

3

Avoiding Marriage

One of the most enduring elements of Pierre Trudeau's legend concerns his relations with a succession of beautiful women and his reputed talents as a ladies' man. Yet at the same time, as his bachelorhood dragged on, there were those who circulated the rumour that he was a homosexual.

Trudeau's escapades provided the gossip columnists with such grist for their mills that on his foreign tours greater attention would be paid to his social exploits and his female company than to his discussions with the heads of state he was scheduled to meet. In Washington, for instance, Trudeau was far more likely to find himself in the prestigious *Washington Post*'s Style section, pictured with someone like Margot Kidder on his arm, than in the paper's political pages.

For a long time, Trudeau was like a hummingbird in his liaisons, according to a woman who knew him, hovering here and there for an instant before flying off, never quite alighting on a single flower, never settling down.

"He's searching out his way of life," said friends. "He has resisted all attachments," said Gérard Pelletier, "including marriage."

"I've been a bachelor so long that I don't remember why I decided to become one," Trudeau confided to Norman DePoe in 1965. "I guess I'm basically a shifty guy; I can't see me settled down. There are so many beautiful women around Montreal . . . Pardon me, I should have said beautiful and interesting."

Even so, two women came close to changing the course of history. They did so at opposite ends of his adulthood. They were Thérèse Gouin in 1941, and Margaret Sinclair in 1976.

In the Quebec of the 1930s, the moral climate was considerably stricter than it is today. Nice women didn't let their necklines plunge or their hemlines creep over their knees, nor did they dance the Charleston. During his college years, in both his school work and his recreational pursuits, Pierre Trudeau lived in a man's world. His greatest pleasure was to throw himself into some adventurous expedition, to match himself against the hostile forces of nature, and to feel in his scrapes and his fatigue "the joys of the hard life."

When he wasn't out shooting the rapids on some raging northern stream, Trudeau liked to read. He preferred fairly weighty stuff most of the time, like the religious books, some of them in Latin, recommended by Father Robert Bernier, his young philosophy mentor, just arrived from Manitoba. Women who knew him during his twenties remember him as "unkempt, with a sallow complexion and a serious case of acne. Moreover, he lived with his mother." Not someone to turn the heads of Outremont's eligible young ladies.

Still, while attending the University of Montreal, Trudeau became officially engaged to Thérèse Gouin. Though people who knew them then will now discuss it only in veiled terms, Trudeau was obviously seriously involved in this relationship and was contemplating marriage.

Thérèse was a frequent visitor to the house on McCulloch Street, suffering through the strained afternoon teas where people spoke in low voices and fixed you with frigid stares if you drew attention to yourself by rattling your spoon in your fine porcelain cup.

It was during one of these tedious afternoon exercises that Thérèse Gouin began to detach herself from Pierre Trudeau. "My dear," he told her at one point in front of the other guests, "don't have any more of these *petits fours* or you'll find yourself rounding out too much."

The incident might have seemed trivial, but their relationship went downhill from there. Trudeau remained a bachelor; Thérèse Gouin finally married Vianney Décarie. She pursued a career as a psychology professor at the University of Montreal, and in 1968 it was she and her husband who organized a petition, signed by numerous prominent Quebeckers, asking Trudeau to run for the Liberal leadership after Lester Pearson announced his retirement.

What if Trudeau had been somewhat more gallant toward his fiancée? What if he had married then? He would probably have settled down to become a learned professor or a lawyer or maybe a businessman like his father.

In April 1968, on the floor of the Ottawa Civic Centre where
Pierre Trudeau was being consecrated as Canada's new prime minister, Alec Pelletier, Gérard's wife, confided to a *Toronto Star*
reporter: "Thérèse said no, and maybe it changed Pierre's life.
French Canadians have undergone a great liberation. Women went
through a phase of being their own bosses, almost overnight, without telling anyone. It has always been a mystery why he didn't
marry. Many will interpret it many ways."

Quebec women had just won the right to vote, and Quebec
society was just beginning to shed its traditional matriarchal trap-
pings. The rural, arcadian side of Trudeau's makeup would have
gladly accepted the ordered life of Outremont's "petite bourgeoisie." But by throwing him over, Thérèse Gouin had shown she had
character.

Hence, in 1941, Trudeau had, in spite of himself, preserved his
"freedom of movement," as he so often told friends who tried to
interest him in various political adventures. He was rich and single,
with a brilliant mind and he found it fairly easy to console himself
after Thérèse dumped him. Some say all the women were after him
by then.

A few years later Michèle Juneau saw the raffish side of Pierre
Trudeau that was so prominent during the 1950s. She had met him
through her brother Pierre, a friend of Trudeau's at the time he
was approached by the Jeunesses Etudiantes Catholiques (Catholic
Youth Movement). Trudeau would later install him as a senior
federal mandarin and president of the CBC. Michèle Juneau was
pursuing a career as a television actress at the time.

In those days the bohemian element in Montreal would often
gather at a funky bar called l'Echouerie, where you could run into
people like the sculptor Armand Vaillancourt or the poet Leonard
Cohen. One evening Trudeau swept in accompanied by one of the
blondes he was forever turning up with. "Each one blonder than
the last one," said Pelletier.

"Michèle, you've brought me into a dive," he whispered in
Michèle Juneau's ear. "I feel like slumming."

Another popular place, though not quite as fashionable, was the
Plaza Hotel on Place Jacques-Cartier. "It was a hole, but the beer
was cheap," recalls Michèle Juneau. And since Trudeau wanted to

slum, she told herself, she might as well show him some real slumming.

So one day their group went to Old Montreal and installed themselves at a table in the Plaza Hotel bar behind some huge pitchers of beer. Trudeau spied a party of sailors at a neighbouring table, their arms covered with tattoos.

"Invite them to our table," Trudeau told her suddenly.

"But Pierre," she protested, "I don't know those guys . . . "

"I mean it," Trudeau insisted. "I'll pay for the beer, you invite them over."

With some apprehension, Michèle Juneau approached the table of sailors.

"The guy over there wants to invite you over for a beer," she told them. The sailors must have noted some hesitation in her voice, because they turned slowly and looked at Trudeau without saying a word.

As though he wanted to descend to their level, but with such awkwardness that it made his two female companions laugh out loud, Trudeau called to the sailors in that nasal voice that he uses when he's looking for a scrap: "Hey guys. What'cha doin' here?"

His tone was so patronizing, Michèle remembers, that Trudeau barely escaped having his face rearranged by four sailors.

Though there was never anything between them, she remembers that all the women her age dreamed of being asked out by Pierre Trudeau, this fascinating conversationalist who drove around in a Jaguar. "When Pierre Elliott would ask us out for a beer, we'd feel proud," she said.

When Trudeau wasn't in a mood for slumming, he usually hung out in bars on the English side of Montreal, on Mountain, Stanley, or Bishop streets. Places like the Casa Espagnol or El Cortijo. "He was pretty quiet, he kept apart a lot, not saying a word," said Marie Choquet, who knew him both in Montreal and in Ottawa. "He had a kind of mysterious aura about him, and it fascinated all the women."

He could also be jealous on occasion.

Marie Choquet remembers walking home with a male friend one night. After a while they noticed they were being followed by Trudeau, who stayed behind them until they reached the building where she lived at the corner of Guy and Sherbrooke. When her friend left early the next morning, he was surprised to find Trudeau still haunting the street corner by her door. When he halted at the bus stop, Trudeau approached him, said in a threatening tone, "She's mine!" and seized him by his necktie.

Whenever Trudeau found a woman who caught his eye, he would make his move, and before long they would be off in a corner, engaged in deep discussion. During a conference at the Maison Montmorency near Quebec City, Trudeau spied a leggy blonde in the translation booth who looked as if she was getting weary of the proceedings. Trudeau gallantly offered to sit in for her so she could take a rest. The young lady appreciated the gesture, but the anglophones attending the conference, who relied on the simultaneous translation to follow the debate, were less grateful. After a few minutes Trudeau relinquished the microphone in frustration. "*Merde*," he declared, "English is such a wretched language!"

Though most of the young women who were in his circle at the time are quite proud of having been seen at his side, Trudeau's behaviour today would be considered insufferably chauvinistic and egotistical.

When he decided to marry Margaret Sinclair, Madeleine Gobeil, his companion at the time, asked to be warned in advance so she could leave the federal capital to avoid embarrassing questions from the horde of reporters that was sure to descend on her. In the end the task fell to Gérard Pelletier, who informed her at the last minute, when Trudeau was already on the plane to Vancouver to tie the knot.

Even in politics, Trudeau's relations with women were ambiguous. Many of them who sat in his cabinets felt uneasy, because they were never treated quite the same as their male colleagues. Monique Bégin told a colleague one time that she never really felt accepted by Trudeau until the day he tore a strip off her during a cabinet meeting. Being Trudeau's equal meant being spoken to as a man.

All of Trudeau's assistants from past years, as well as his ministers, have some anecdotes about his private life. Some of them involve rather delicate situations. Jean Marchand himself once complained to a friend: "Trudeau brings his girls here, gives them all sorts of ideas, and then we're stuck with them."

On occasion he even took chances with women journalists that could have cost him dearly. For Trudeau, a pretty woman was a pretty woman. She might be a journalist, but he couldn't resist any opportunity to flirt.

During the 1980 campaign, while travelling in the Northwest Territories, Trudeau hopped on a snowmobile and invited a young woman reporter from the *Toronto Star* to ride on the back with him. A few weeks later, to her great surprise, she was invited for an intimate dinner at the prime minister's residence.

Her colleagues in the National Press Gallery eagerly anticipated a juicy report from the encounter, but they were cruelly disappointed. The prime minister conducted himself irreproachably at all times. He was a lively conversationalist throughout, and even ventured a few dance steps on the disco floor that Maureen McTeer had had installed at 24 Sussex Drive during Joe Clark's brief tenure as prime minister. At the end of the evening, Trudeau accompanied her to the door, left her with a supremely chaste kiss, and ordered his chauffeur to drive her home.

Trudeau's evident penchant for young and comely women has, on occasion, inspired a few newspaper editors to attempt to take advantage of the situation. For example, after Trudeau had retreated into retirement, the *Ottawa Citizen* dispatched one of its prettiest female reporters to see if she could entice him into giving an interview.

The young lady arranged to run into him "accidentally" in the elevator at the law firm where he now works as a special adviser, and it didn't take much for her to get invited to lunch. But when Trudeau's suspicions became aroused, she had to confess her real motives for the encounter. In the end the *Citizen* had to settle for an innocuous little column instead of the banner headline it had anticipated.

A young cub reporter from the *Sherbrooke Record* had better luck during the 1980 campaign. Pierre Trudeau and his campaign entourage of aides and journalists had stopped over at a midtown Holiday Inn. As is his custom, Trudeau commandeered the hotel pool for a few solitary lengths under the watchful scrutiny of his RCMP bodyguards.

Meanwhile, young Carole Treiser, no doubt in cahoots with the hotel manager, slipped into the pool, which was closed to other hotel guests. After a few lengths, Trudeau, in a joking tone, invited her to join him in the sauna.

"But I don't have a towel," she protested.

"That shouldn't be a problem," Trudeau replied in a tone that left little room for refusal.

It was a bright, though fleeting, moment of glory for the young reporter as the hundred-odd senior national reporters covering Trudeau fought for copies of the small-town *Sherbrooke Record* the next day. Actually, nothing improper transpired between the young lady and the prime minister. She recounted that she was drawn to him despite herself. "He is the elusive jester who dared us to catch him, and laughed as we tried," she wrote the next day.

Trudeau's so-called adventures with women often ended in this inconclusive manner. "Trudeau is a guy who can't make up his mind," Simone Monet-Chartrand, the wife of union leader Michel Chartrand, and her friends whispered to each other.

Jealous husbands often worried needlessly. One evening, while visiting friends in Aylmer, who lived in a splendid house designed by Arthur Erickson, Trudeau kept apart, sitting on the balcony steps with one of the other guests, a woman.

The prime minister had recently obtained his divorce. The husband of the lady with whom he was engrossed in conversation was, at the very least, curious to know what their conversation was about. They talked for forty-five minutes, and she was the only person with whom Trudeau spoke at the party. But rather than amusing her with his usual gallantries, Trudeau had been earnestly discussing the problems of raising three children as a single parent.

Fans of boudoir indiscretions have always come up empty with Pierre Trudeau. Even Margaret Trudeau's "confessions," published in her memoir, *Beyond Reason*, and her gushing interviews with the likes of journalists from *People* magazine, only served to enlist the sympathy of the public for Trudeau, particularly in Quebec, where the media have been significantly more restrained in the coverage of his social life than in English Canada.

Finally, much of Trudeau's legend is also the result of his irrepressible exhibitionism. "He has always been a show-off, even with women," recalls Michèle Juneau, who has contributed her part to the legend. He likes the company of good-looking women the way he likes fast cars, eccentric outfits, or the distinctive art deco house, designed by Ernest Cormier, that he bought for his retirement on Pine Avenue in Montreal.

Trudeau has always been a devout Catholic. Given the education he received from the Jesuits, he is hardly debauched by any stretch of the imagination. "What's more," suggested a friend, "the Jesuit in Pierre is what led him to marry a woman thirty years his junior, who had something of a colourful past. He hoped to reform her, and in return she would give him healthy children."

Still, Trudeau's closest friendships have always been with men. Gérard Pelletier even went so far as to suggest in 1968 that Trudeau's interest in women had more to do with his sense of curiosity than a penchant for vice.

To those who suggested that Trudeau was a mass of contradictions, Gérard Pelletier responded: "What can I say, now that this man, who became a minister while still single, has presented an omnibus bill dealing with laws on divorce, homosexuality, and abortion? Personally I don't find anything contradictory or ridiculous in that. St. Francis of Assisi knew more about sin than Roger Vadim [the director who with God created Brigitte Bardot]; and François de Sales knew more about women than Don Juan. At best there may be an inherent paradox, but paradox is a healthy sign . . . "

In good health then, and free as the air, the hummingbird was not content to look for nectar in his own backyard. In 1944, the twenty-five-year-old Pierre Trudeau, still somewhat timid and still with a bit of a skin problem, left to conquer the universe.

The young and slightly awkward Quebecker, whom the Jesuits had inspired with the pursuit of excellence but who somehow felt he had failed in his studies, hung a new sign on his bedroom door: "Pierre Trudeau, Citizen of the World."

4

Citizen of the World

The official biography issued by the Liberal Party of Canada says that "a licence to practise law and admission to the Quebec Bar in 1944 completed P.E. Trudeau's education in Quebec, and from then until the beginning of the 1950s he was almost constantly away from home."

In 1944 Trudeau was essentially a francophone in search of an identity, even "a provincial without a metropolis" (the words of his close friend Jean LeMoyne, who would later write his speeches).

At the time, people didn't think to question the nature of Quebec, much less its destiny. A province existed to be administered in goodwill and with competence and people worried much more about a government's particular qualities than the scope of its powers. It is unlikely that Trudeau thought of himself as a "Québécois." No one, and certainly not he, used the word at the time, except perhaps in relation to residents of Quebec City.

A few months of legal practice were enough to persuade Trudeau that his studies had prepared him to be something more than a simple clerk in a law firm, but not enough to float in the middle of the great currents of ideas to which the Jesuits had introduced him.

"I've probably read more works of Dostoyevski, of Stendhal, and Tolstoy than the average statesman," said Trudeau of himself, "but less of Keynes, Mill, and Marx," he added. He said that until he went to Harvard and the London School of Economics, he read "mostly in French and Latin."

The Jesuits had made a classicist of him, and as such the great intellectual currents of the day had not yet reached him. As for his law studies, they had shown him the distance between the horizons opened up to him by the likes of François Hertel and Robert Bernier, and the limited perspectives of a practising provincial lawyer. At this point, however, Trudeau was still — with all the disdain he would inject into the word when he threw it at his political adversaries — merely "a provincial."

Even more important, Trudeau was unsure whether he wanted to be *un Canadien* or a Canadian. Not long after his father's death, one of his teachers at Brébeuf, Father Vigneault, told him, "Pierre, one of these days you will have a big decision to make: you will have to decide if you want to be a French Canadian or an English Canadian."

By then the Quebec nationalist writers like Lionel Groulx, Monseigneur Paquet, François-Xavier Garneau, Edouard Montpetit, Esdras Minville, and Maximilien Caron, had begun to be published. But these were not the sort of authors one would find on the Brébeuf reading lists. Pierre Trudeau looked with a jaundiced eye on his schoolmates, who rushed out for every issue of *Action*. Founded in Quebec City, the paper vigorously defended religious values, and leaned too heavily, Trudeau thought, on the nationalist chord.

What history was taught in Quebec's classical colleges in the 1930s safely ended before the unpleasantries of 1837. If Canada didn't really exist for Pierre Trudeau, why should he bother trying to find out if there was one Canada or two Canadas, and if one was better than the other?

Years later, Trudeau himself admitted that he wasn't terribly interested in what was going on in the world during his college years. "I was bored by the present," he said. "I applied myself to reading all that was written on the great political currents, from ancient times onward. I finished up with Hitler, Mussolini, Lenin, etc., but it all seemed too abstract. I didn't make any connection with the situation at the time."

In this frame of mind, Pierre Trudeau "fled" Montreal and the practice of law. When he talked about it later, to journalists or to English-Canadian audiences, he gave the impression of a man suddenly throwing back his head and filling his chest with a great gulp of fresh air. As though to rid himself of the influence of Abbé Groulx, Pierre Trudeau was about to prove, from Harvard to the London School of Economics by way of the Sorbonne, that he was the inheritor of the ideas of de Tocqueville, Montesquieu, and John Locke.

Like all French Canadians of his generation, Trudeau ought normally to have gone to Paris. But during this summer of 1944, the Allies were still bogged down in Europe, and Paris was not yet liberated. In a way he was a prisoner of the North American continent.

"The majors in political science at Harvard had read more about Roman law and Montesquieu than I had as a lawyer," he said later. "I realized then that we were taught law as a trade in Quebec and not as a discipline."

Though Trudeau was not particularly in need of a profession, he was possessed of an eternally inquiring mind. "I went to Harvard," he explained in an interview reported in his official biography, "to learn more about the organization of society. I wanted to know the laws that governed the economy, the banks, and monetary systems. I wanted to study political science. I wanted to know how governments work."

Trudeau studied under Joseph Schumpeter and Wassily Leontiev. And, as if embarrassed by his American friends who knew their Montesquieu better than he did, Trudeau put aside his birth certificate for the time being and hung the now-famous sign on his door: "Pierre Trudeau: Citizen of the World."

For two years he had almost no contact with Quebec.

Gérard Pelletier, who had known him in 1941, says he lost sight of him completely. Trudeau would make occasional visits to Outremont during the summers, but at the time Pelletier was busy crisscrossing the province, organizing and recruiting for Catholic Action.

It was in Paris, when the war was over, that old acquaintances from Quebec, like Pelletier and Roger Rolland, got back together with Pierre Trudeau. And with good reason.

Pierre Trudeau's opinion of the Sorbonne was only slightly more flattering than his attitude toward the University of Montreal: "Barely out of Harvard, I can say, with all modesty, that I knew more about my subjects than most of my professors."

During the year he spent at the Sorbonne's law faculty and school of political science, Trudeau was less than a diligent student. At the end of his year he left without obtaining a degree.

Having rediscovered his former partner in crime, Roger Rolland, the two would occasionally get together for freewheeling escapades that recalled their days in the Laurentians, at Brébeuf, and at the University of Montreal. He even made first-hand acquaintance with the Black Marias, those rattletrap vans into which the not-so-gentle Paris gendarmes would herd students when their festivities disturbed the peace of the Champs-Elysées bourgeoisie.

When Trudeau arrived in Europe during the summer of 1946, Gérard Pelletier was already in Geneva as secretary of the World Student Relief Fund. He had been there since January, "distributing money to people in the process of decolonization to help them become communist," as Trudeau put it.

The two saw each other only four or five times during that year. But Pelletier, already something of an activist, would come with fresh news from Quebec, while Trudeau, flushed with his new-found liberation, began pronouncing his first judgements on the French-Canadian people.

"From Paris," recalled Gérard Pelletier, "Pierre saw a great dis-equilibrium in the Canadian federation. Quebec wasn't playing its full role, largely because it hadn't yet entered the modern era."

It was in Paris that he first evolved the thesis he would develop in years to come in *Cité libre*: "With the exception of Laurier, I fail to see a single French Canadian in more than three-quarters of a century whose presence in the federal cabinet might be considered indispensable to the history of Canada — except at election time, of course, when the tribe always invokes the aid of its witch doctors."

The next year, in London, he found that the archives in the Public Records Office contained more about Canadian history than the library of the University of Montreal. There Trudeau rounded out his reflections on Canada and concluded that ever since the railway era, "French Canadians have let themselves be screwed."

At the London School of Economics, Trudeau was deeply influenced by the book *Leviathan* by Thomas Hobbes and by the *Essays* of Lord Acton. He became a disciple of Harold Laski, "a communist to be sure, but above all an exceptional teacher and a very well-ordered mind." Laski turned Trudeau into a leftist, into the Pierre Trudeau who would turn up a few years later at the head of the Rassemblement démocratique (Democratic Movement), shoulder-to-shoulder with ecologist Pierre Dansereau. The Pierre Trudeau who promised Michel Chartrand one day shortly after his return from Europe: "We're going to build socialism [here]. For a country with such a small population there is no alternative." The Pierre Trudeau whom the province's socialists, for a brief season, envisaged as their leader.

It was most likely the time he spent in the United States and in London, more than the Scots blood in his veins, that made Pierre Trudeau think like an Anglo-Saxon. His great admiration for British philosophers and American economists reinforced (as if reinforcement was necessary) his disdain for the French-Canadian élites of the day.

It is therefore probably no coincidence that he wrote his famous essay, "The Province of Quebec at the Time of the Asbestos Strike," during an extended stay in London seven years later. In it he puts the Quebec of the 1940s on trial.

Trudeau did not return directly to Canada. He took another fifteen months to travel around the world. He must have attached great importance to this trip because in his official biography he wrote: "His studies and his travels reinforced his growing suspicion of nationalism."

During his youth, Trudeau had often described how he regarded his travels.

Before tackling the Harricana by canoe in 1943, he explained: "The canoe, the paddle, the blanket, the knife, the salt pork, the fishing line, and the rifle: these are the sum of all riches. By stripping the human heritage of all its useless baggage in this manner, the spirit is freed from calculation, from memory, and from trivial preoccupations."

The theme was the same as in his ode to his motorcycle, in which he had underlined the presence of those two saddlebags, so quickly packed, which discouraged elaborate departures and long goodbyes.

The Pierre Trudeau who left London at the end of the summer of 1947 was dressed in sandals and old jeans, "grubby as a beggar," according to those who crossed his path at the time. He took only the clothes he could carry in his backpack. He said he circled the globe with $800 in his pocket, crossing many frontiers without a visa.

"I had gone through the schools and universities, and I had proved myself to the extent that I could do well there," he told his biographer. "But what about the real world? Could I do well there? How would I handle myself in China, for example, not knowing the language and being absolutely alone and having nobody to rely on but myself?"

Not only did he put himself to the test in pursuit "of strong emotions," as he put it, he also proved to himself that he hadn't passed up the war out of cowardice. "Having missed a world war more through inadvertence than effort, I looked for other battles."

And he found them.

From occupied Germany he travelled to Austria, then through Eastern Europe. He reached Turkey after a frightful journey in a truck filled with Arab irregulars. He found himself in Palestine just after Bernadotte was assassinated. He had grown a beard by then. He was barefoot, wearing a burnoose, and since he was more at ease in English than in Arabic he was suspected of being an agent for the Haganah, the Israeli secret service.

From the Middle East he moved on to Pakistan, which he entered illegally. He was in Shanghai when Mao's troops breached the city's defences and he escaped with the Americans. He crossed Burma while civil war raged across the countryside and he had to seek protection from the French when he arrived in Vietnam.

With the exception of what was then still called Indochina, Trudeau had, in effect, made a tour of the British Empire, which was in the full throes of decolonization that year. From Europe, ravaged by Hitler and Mussolini and divided into two blocs; from Asia and the Middle East, where peoples or tribes massacred each other in the name of religion or race, Trudeau returned with a veritable obsession. He would speak of it twenty years later when he declared war on "separatism."

"I am opposed to any political system based on race and religion. All such politics are reactionary, and for the past 150 years, nationalism has been an anachronistic notion. Through an accident of history, Canada has an advance of almost seventy-five years on the rest of the world in the formation of a multinational state, and I believe that humanity's hope resides in multinationalism."

Pierre Trudeau has, in fact, said relatively little about his travels. Only a few close friends have heard him talk about his experiences abroad during casual conversations in various Outremont homes. Without realizing it, in 1949 Canada could count on at least one young intellectual, erudite and schooled in systems of government, with a storehouse of memories from wide-ranging travels.

At his cabinet meetings and during his future travels abroad as prime minister, Trudeau would unfailingly impress people with the range of his knowledge.

The timid young man who left Montreal in 1944 returned close to six years later self-assured and keenly aware, to the point of arrogance, even disdain, of his own superiority.

Trudeau wrote about his travels on two occasions only. In 1961 he co-authored an account of a trip to China with Jacques Hébert, whom he later made a senator. But given the speed with which *Two Innocents in Red China* was written after their return, it seems likely that Hébert, a professional writer more familiar with the travelogue style, did most of the writing.

On the other hand, Trudeau himself wrote a piece for *Le Devoir* in 1952 about a visit to Moscow for an international economic conference. The conference had been organized out of Copenhagen by an international committee composed of people with widely divergent opinions. The Soviet Union was the only country that offered to admit all participants without exception, and as a result the meeting was scheduled for Moscow.

There were those who tried to dissuade Trudeau from going, suggesting he would be making a pact with the devil. But he wasn't about to refuse, as he explained, "an opportunity to discuss world affairs with the most prominent economists, to applaud Lepechins-kaya and Ulanova at the Bolshoi, or to devour caviar by the spoonful."

All of which he would do, but in his own way.

Instead of taking the plane to Moscow via Paris and Prague like everyone else, Trudeau took a train which passed through occupied Germany, and left him stranded at the border. He threw himself on the mercy of the Soviets and arrived in Moscow four days ahead of the other conference participants. The Soviets, he concluded, were not quite as backward as one was led to believe in McCarthyist America.

He was offered a driver and a Ziss, but he asked for a map of the city instead. Discouraged, the Soviets let him venture forth on the metro and bus lines, and were only slightly surprised when he thumbed his nose at the KGB agent who was following him too closely.

When he announced his intention to go to mass on Sunday, his hosts did their best to respect his wishes. But when he stepped up his special requests, asking to attend trials, to speak to priests, to study the economic basis of the Gosplan, and to meet academics, their patience snapped. "They began to find me tiresome," he recalled, "even insolent."

One day, weary of seeing the portrait of "the little father of the revolution" everywhere he went, Trudeau, affectionately, he claims, threw a snowball at a statue of Stalin. "I explained to them" he said, "that in Ottawa I threw snowballs at the statues of Canadian prime ministers, which was absolutely true, and they released me after a reprimand."

Ever the nonconformist, "the Canadian delegate" remained in Moscow after the conference, installing himself in a more central and modest hotel and eating in neighbourhood restaurants. "In the trains and the theatres and the cafés I found a people who are loquacious and energetic in their youth, serious and strained when they've had nothing to drink; stoic when they are unhappy; quiet when they are not carried away by slogans; and always generous, though sickeningly conventional."

In a series of seven articles Trudeau demolished a number of myths about Bolshevism, and hailed the achievements of the Soviet regime. He wrote that he felt no compunction about courting the disapproval of his compatriots, "for French Canadians, anti-Bolshevik as they may be, still harbour a healthy disdain for their good neighbours over the border. I think that at worst I will be seen as a loiterer, who, after having followed his bohemian instinct across the world, has succumbed to the temptation of a fresh unknown."

In the Russia of the mid-1950s, at the very height of the Cold War, Trudeau noted that the best cars were exact replicas of American models, that they were building skyscrapers in the Lenin Hills, and that Tarzan was on the marquee of half a dozen Moscow movie houses. "Before long," he said, "it will be Coca-Cola."

Finally, after insisting a little too forcefully to be allowed to visit Leningrad, Trudeau was expelled from the Soviet Union. Still, he had managed to spend four weeks in the country. One wonders which is more unfortunate: that Trudeau didn't become a reporter, or that Stalin never uttered the word *glasnost*.

When Trudeau returned from his first trip around the world, he found that Quebec had adopted its fleur-de-lys flag in January of 1948. Louis St. Laurent ("Uncle Louis" as he was familiarly known in Quebec) governed in Ottawa, and Duplessis was more firmly entrenched than ever in Quebec.

Members of the provinces's élite, who had graduated from the very colleges and universities Pierre Trudeau held in such contempt, had taken the activist route. Jean Marchand was becoming a relentless adversary of the Duplessis regime. René Lévesque, back from the battlefields of Europe, where he had been a war correspondent for the U.S. Army, was preparing to go to Korea. Gérard Pelletier was shaking up the province with his articles about labour conflicts in *Le Devoir*.

As for Trudeau, his long absences had made him "an academic somewhat removed from the Canadian reality," as Pelletier said upon Trudeau's return to Montreal.

The day after he arrived back in the country, Trudeau phoned Pelletier and told him, in a tone both anxious and eager: "You have to take me to see that."

"That" was the seemingly interminable miners' strike at the Canadian Johns-Manville mine in the town of Asbestos in the Eastern Townships.

Part Two

The "True" Revolutionary (1950-1965)

*"Nationalism, autonomy, bilingualism,
clericalism, socialism, centralization: so many
words that make us jump with enthusiasm or
indignation, and for no reason."*

5

The Duplessis Years

"There were other big strikes in French Canada before the asbestos strike, and there will be others afterwards," wrote Trudeau in his account of Quebec's historic labour confrontation. "But this one was of particular significance because it occurred at a time when we were seeing the end of a world we had known; at the very moment that our social framework — already decrepit because it was built for another era — was ready to explode."

As it happened, the fire in the asbestos industry broke out in 1949. And Trudeau almost didn't make it back in time to fan the flames. Or to extinguish them.

When Trudeau returned to Quebec after a six-year absence, the miners employed by the Canadian Johns-Manville Company Ltd. had already been on strike for nine weeks. On the night of February 13, they rejected the arbitration proposal that the American-owned company was determined to make them swallow.

"Illegal strike," concluded the government. The miners threw up picket lines and resolved to hold them at all costs. One week later, 150 provincial policemen invaded the streets of the town of Asbestos.

On the first day of the conflict, Gérard Filion, then the publisher of *Le Devoir*, assigned one of his brightest young reporters to cover the strike full time. His name was Gérard Pelletier; his news editor was one Pierre Laporte.

The Asbestos town council, largely sympathetic toward the strikers, complained about police thuggery. One day they had stopped a miner who had left home without his driver's licence. They gave him a choice: cross the picket line and go back to work, or pay a $30 fine, a crushing penalty for a miner with a family to feed.

Since April 19, the company had been operating the mine with imported non-union labour. On the eve of Trudeau's visit, Johns-Manville threatened to evict striking miners from company houses so they could be used to lodge the company's scabs. Even the Duplessis administration felt compelled to say that they "deplored this decision."

"Trudeau, oddly enough, knew enough about the conflict to be seriously intrigued," recalled Gérard Pelletier. Odd, because he had spent the last six years travelling in parts of the world where there were no Canadian newspapers to be found. Of course, even if he had come across some, perhaps in London or Hong Kong, he wouldn't have learned much more about what was happening in Asbestos. Quebec's English-language newspapers, *The Gazette* in particular, either ignored the conflict or referred to it only in denouncing the savagery of Quebec's unions.

Nevertheless, Trudeau was impatient to go and see for himself. The day after he arrived back home he begged Pelletier to take him with him on his assignment.

There was a demonstration in Asbestos the day they arrived. The company had begun bringing in strike breakers, and the tension was mounting. Author and journalist Gilles Beausoleil gave this account in *The Asbestos Strike*:

> Early in the morning of April 22, as the scabs were going to work, a long procession of strikers marched through the streets of Asbestos in an attempt to shame them. Gérard Pelletier, a reporter for the newspaper *Le Devoir*, and two friends, G. Charpentier and P.E. Trudeau, who were watching the demonstration, were arrested by the provincial police and given half an hour to get out of town. When they refused to leave, they were taken to the Iroquois Club where they were interrogated by a high-ranking officer by the name of Gagné. When he realized that he was dealing with a press reporter and citizens who were not about to be browbeaten, his arrogance gave way to politeness.

"Not about to be browbeaten." That description fitted Trudeau to a T at the time. During his peregrinations he had faced Arab police in Palestine, Mao's People's Army, and the jungle fighters of Indochina. He'd been in tighter squeezes before.

In a characteristic display of bravado, Trudeau showed up in Asbestos dressed in sandals and rumpled clothes. A long scraggly blond beard emphasized his emaciated features. The bemused miners immediately nicknamed him "Saint Joseph."

It was Pelletier who introduced Trudeau to Jean Marchand. For Marchand, then general secretary to the Confederation of Catholic Workers, this young lawyer who had studied at Harvard, the Sorbonne, and the London School of Economics, and had travelled around the world, was something of a bonus.

The miners had been off the job for an extended period by then. The government, the police, and even a major portion of public opinion were lined up against them. The conflict was entering an increasingly violent phase. Day after day the miners' morale had to be boosted, and anyone capable of giving a speech long enough to keep their spirits from flagging was more than welcome.

Marchand was hoping Trudeau would give them some practical advice about their rights and what legal recourse remained open to them. But Trudeau, who had been greatly inspired by the numerous revolutions he had encountered abroad, instead urged the miners to resist their oppressors.

"The company is like a sick cow with an infected wound," declared Trudeau. "You have to apply ointment to the wound, but don't touch it. Throw the ointment instead."

That same evening, all the windows at the Johns-Manville office were shattered by rock-throwing strikers. "All the same," muttered Marchand, disturbed by the outburst, "the miners aren't schoolchildren."

By this time policemen were pouring into town by the truckload. They were preparing for a round of mass arrests, and the government was poised to proclaim the riot act. This was no time to pour oil on the flames.

"Pierre," recounted Gérard Pelletier after the event, "felt a little like an intellectual in an ivory tower, and there he saw us, up to our necks in the thick of the action. He wanted to work with any group that was trying to modernize Quebec. When he found that this was what we were doing, he made a great effort to participate."

Three months later, the asbestos miners went back to their dust-choked pits with a ten-cent raise in their pockets.

The Archbishop of Montreal, who had sided with the strikers in the bloody street battles that were part of the conflict, was transferred to Vancouver "for health reasons."

And Trudeau was blackballed by the University of Montreal.

This didn't prevent that same Trudeau, with his ragged beard and shiny Jaguar, from showing up, often unannounced, on picket lines around the province during the fifties. Michel Chartrand still remembers the day Trudeau cropped up at Murdochville in the Gaspé peninsula at another miners' strike, this one against the Gaspé Copper Mine Inc. The policemen on hand had been lobbing tear gas grenades and were standing by, ominously cocking their firearms.

Trudeau arrived in shorts and sandals, with a camera slung around his neck. He stuck out like a wino at a temperance meeting, but the workers found him amusing. All things considered, they appreciated that this odd intellectual would come all this way to stand by them, if only for half a day, against the impending police onslaught.

Trudeau defended a few of the strikers in court, but his contribution in this regard was less memorable than that of others, most notably Jean Drapeau. If his name has since become associated with that landmark in Quebec's modern history, the asbestos strike, it was mainly because of what he wrote about it. But that was seven years after the fact.

Back then, Trudeau was still out of the country for much of the time, according to his friends. Near the end of 1951 he left to spend almost six months in Africa. In 1952 he was in the Soviet Union. In 1955 he attended another international conference in Lahore, Pakistan. On his way back from there he stopped over in Europe for another six months, most of which he spent in London. It was there that he wrote the famous introductory chapter to *The Asbestos Strike*, a volume of essays published by *Cité libre*. In 1957 he took advantage of another World University Service conference, this time in Nigeria, to undertake a tour of Africa. So it is not surprising that it took him two years to respond to a critique of the book published in the Jesuit review *Relations*, by one Father Cousineau.

Trudeau came close to admitting to his official biographer that he had become somewhat rootless at that stage of his life. "I guess I was like Herman Melville's hero: after being back for a while, I felt that I had to take to the sea again, otherwise I'd get down in the streets and knock people's hats off. I suppose you could get some psychologist to analyze that."

If Trudeau wrote so little, and so long after the events themselves, it is perhaps because he took writing very seriously. "I never saw Trudeau write a text off the top of his head," explained Gérard Pelletier. "To begin with, it was hard for him to write, and he put a lot of effort into his writing. That's why his preface to the book on the asbestos strike was something of an event."

If Trudeau's writing had such an impact, it was also because he wrote so rarely. In June 1950 Trudeau started work on an essay, "*Politique fonctionnelle*" (functional politics), yet the second part of it didn't appear until eight months later, in February 1951.

In 1958, Jacques Hébert founded a small weekly called *Vrai*. In its columns, Trudeau's name appears beside the likes of Gérard Pelletier, Victor Barbeau, and Roland Parenteau. His copy would often arrive at the last minute, and just as often, in the middle of the night, when the pages of his columns on "The March of Politics" were ready to go to press, the author himself would show up, full of anguish over a misplaced word or a badly constructed sentence, asking for last-minute changes.

In 1956 Trudeau published his first lengthy work, ninety pages of tightly scripted text, "The Province of Quebec at the Time of the Asbestos Strike." It was the only time that this brilliant intellectual produced a book or a major political treatise. It was as though he were incapable of writing anything of substantial length.

This prompted Trudeau's enemies to brand him a dilettante, a label that infuriated his friends.

Among the eight members of Quebec's rising young intellectual guard who contributed to the book on the asbestos industry strike were sociologists Abbé Gérard Dion and Fernand Dumont, union leader Jean Gérin-Lajoie, lawyers Charles Lussier and Maurice Sauvé, and Gérard Pelletier. But it created such a stir largely because of the critical backlash it provoked among the province's intelligentsia, who zeroed in on Trudeau's analysis of Quebec's social and political culture. Among the critics was André Laurendeau.

No one took issue with his essential premise—that Quebec's institutions were ill-adapted to the changes caused by the industrial revolution, which had been rocking the foundations of the province's rural-based society since the turn of the century. Quebec was like a pressure cooker; one way or another the lid was bound to blow off.

Laurendeau also agreed with Trudeau's conclusion: "The phenomenon of the industrial revolution has confronted Quebec with problems which have to be resolved." He was gratified to note that Trudeau had recognized in passing that "alternative approaches had been tried in certain areas," and that "the Second World War, this breaker of traditions, had engendered a state of awakening."

But nothing and no one found any great favour in Trudeau's eyes in what amounted to a summary prosecution of Quebec society and its élites. Laurendeau found his remarks so overblown that he unleashed a terrible judgement on Trudeau that was to dog his footsteps for the rest of his political career. "He is a French Canadian deceived by his own kind. His research brings him face to face with a monolithic presence which intellectually he rejects, but which wounds him in his innermost being. I think he is ashamed to have had such ancestors." Incidentally, Trudeau never responded directly to this scathing verdict.

Thirty years later, Quebec's nationalist élite would echo Laurendeau's words in their attacks on Trudeau. Still bearing the scars from the times she had sided with René Lévesque in late-night political encounter sessions with Trudeau, Michèle Juneau would contend, "Pure chance made Trudeau a Quebecker. And how he must curse his luck!"

Whether or not "the dice were loaded," as Laurendeau put it, Trudeau's analysis was nevertheless a master stroke. "A *pièce de résistance*, a work of great value, though it didn't have quite the effrontery of his letter on Meech Lake [in May 1987]," recalled Senator Arthur Tremblay.

The trouble with "Trudeau's book" was not so much its content, but that it came on the scene too late. New élites had already emerged after the asbestos struggle. They had been locked in opposition to the Duplessis juggernaut for some time now. Hardened by the struggle and confirmed in their activism, they were not quite so ready to reject their ancestors.

After all, despite the prevailing gloom which had enveloped Quebec, despite this "conservatism which impregnates the social ideologies" of the era and its universities that Trudeau held in such contempt, the province produced a generation of intellectuals who would become the mandarins of his years in power.

The asbestos strike, which mobilized a new élite against Duplessis, and which, in Trudeau's words, was "like a speck of crystallization in a saturated solution, and from which the province of Quebec [would] emerge in an altered form," was not enough, however, to make Trudeau park his political allegiances in any one garage. He preferred a hit-and-run approach to politics at the time. On his own, he didn't make much of a difference, and his comrades in arms, like Michel Chartrand, found themselves alone in jail or shunned by a society still in the grip of the "tyrant."

A few months after the strike ended, Trudeau accepted a job with the Privy Council Office in Ottawa. His position in the prestigious PCO, the inner sanctum where federal strategy was conceived for Louis St. Laurent's skirmishes with Duplessis, would greatly impress the prime minister's future biographers.

But his boss at the time, Gordon Robertson, one of the legendary figures of the Ottawa mandarinate, has little more than vague recollections of Trudeau at the time. He was merely another of the "junior officers" whose duties were more closely related to making notes than to determining government policies and the course of national events.

"He was thirty-one years old at the time and he was just back from an extended period abroad," recalled the former cabinet secretary for federal-provincial relations. "He was a young man who had studied political science and the law, and who had a good theoretical knowledge of political systems. We gave him small research jobs."

Robertson recalls that in 1949 the office was conducting a study of constitutional patriation and amending formulas. "But at the time we were just getting off the ground. The great questions that dominated the 1970s and the 1980s, particularly the issue of the Quebec veto, weren't even raised."

These were the days when Trudeau would, by his own admission, stroll the streets of Ottawa in winter, throwing snowballs at the statues of Canadian prime ministers. Others remember seeing him doing handstands in the austere corridors of the prime minister's office.

The life of a junior civil servant did not seem to excite Pierre Trudeau any more than the prospect of a life in a bourgeois law firm. He would take every opportunity to jump on his Harley and roar back to Montreal. Jean Marchand offered him a full-time job with the union after being impressed by the younger man's intellectual acumen. "We regarded him as a valuable intellectual asset," he said. "But not as leadership material. I don't recall anyone ever asking him to lead a group," he told Radwanski. "We were happy to have him with us, but not up front."

Marchand offered him a job as an adviser to the union in 1951, but Trudeau turned him down. "He wanted to maintain his freedom of movement," said Pelletier. The fact remained; at this point in his life Trudeau was still refusing to work for anyone else.

For the time being, he chose instead to join a group of friends in the publication of *Cité libre*. The birth of this storied periodical was a long-drawn-out and difficult process. The founders were scattered throughout the province or, as in the case of Guy Cormier in New Brunswick, outside Quebec. The big guns of Quebec journalism regarded the project with a jaundiced eye. "It's the kind of self-indulgent writing which one should avoid," Claude Ryan sourly advised Gérard Pelletier.

The widely dispersed editorial team had trouble getting its act together. One of the founders, (was it Pierre Vadeboncoeur or Maurice Sauvé?) wanted nothing to do with Pierre Trudeau. The core of the *Cité libre* group was formed of former Catholic Action militants, and one of them said, "I don't want to see Trudeau around here. He's not one of us. He'll never be one of us."

The founders celebrated the first issue, dated June 1950, with a party at the Pelletier home on Ile Perrot, west of Montreal. Pierre Trudeau showed his colours by proposing a toast: "We wish to bear witness to the French fact and the Christian fact in North America."

He added that the group would work from a clean slate. "All the political categories passed down to us by the intermediate generation must be subjected to methodical scrutiny."

A Quebec academic, who was on sabbatical in France, recalls receiving the first issue of *Cité libre* from a French professor who had been in Quebec. "It looked a little sophomoric to us," he said. "But we also told ourselves that something was going to come of it."

If the paper's birth was laborious, it was also because the founders didn't have enough money to get it printed, much less arrange for distribution of the several hundred copies that eventually rolled off the presses. The official history of *Cité libre* holds that each member of the cooperative came up with three hundred dollars of his own to put out the first issue.

But not all of them had three hundred dollars readily available for such a purpose. According to sources close to the participants, the episode highlighted another aspect of Trudeau's character — his reluctance to part with his money.

In the spring of 1950, when the editorial board was contemplating its accounts for the first issue, it was determined that two thousand dollars would be required to bring it out. Some members looked to Trudeau, who, everyone knew, had the means. But in the end it was Alec Pelletier, wife of Gérard, who offered to guarantee a loan at the Caisse Populaire.

All sorts of tall tales have been invented about Trudeau's legendary parsimony, even though he often gave generously of his time: to friends like Jacques Hébert, whom he defended when his book, *J'accuse les assassins de Coffin*, threatened to get him jailed; to Quebeckers who found themselves penniless in Paris; to the Johns-Manville strikers and others whom he defended in court without charging a fee.

Yet it is true that he has an instinctive horror of digging into his own pockets, which more often than not are empty anyway. If, as was the case when he was prime minister, he could be justly reproached for not knowing the price of a pound of butter, it wasn't only because he wasn't in the habit of doing his own grocery shopping. Had he taken it into his head to do so, he would probably have found himself in an embarrassing situation at the cash register. He would often borrow money from aides or secretaries to settle some small personal account. And most of the time the donor would not be reimbursed.

Whatever the circumstances of *Cité libre*'s birth, it gave Trudeau a way of being involved without having to make a political commitment. A personal letter published by Gérard Pelletier in his memoirs tells of Trudeau's reluctance to ally himself with one group or another, and of his conflicting desires to go globetrotting and at the same time be in on the action.

At that time the union movement, in the wake of the asbestos struggle, was thinking of running labour candidates in highly unionized ridings like Asbestos, Shawinigan, and Thetford Mines. Marchand, who hadn't been able to lure Trudeau into the union fold, thought of him as a possible candidate for the 1952 election.

"The idea of being a candidate in the provincial election was seductive," Trudeau wrote in March 1952, "probably in the asbestos region, with the full support of the union forces and, of course, my friends. I found it seductive because never in my life had I been so completely available, physically and morally, because I was ready for the worst follies, and because, all things considered, I felt quite wretched just then."

At the time Trudeau was en route to the Soviet Union for the international economics conference, so he signed his letter "Trudienko." His plan, he had already decided, was to head to Sicily afterwards, to "vegetate and write in the sunshine." His history of the strike, no doubt.

Marchand's project fell flat, but Trudeau's letter to his friend Pelletier showed to what extent he felt marginal and useless. He even went so far as to wonder whether Marchand's political plan would cancel out his offer of a post as "technical adviser" with the Catholic Trades Council.

It must be remembered that by this time, Trudeau had been rejected for several teaching posts at the University of Montreal, "because I was, it seemed, anticlerical and communist," he explained. This rejection weighed heavily on him. To the point, as he said, that he had to go abroad so as not to go picking fights on the streets back home.

Over the years Trudeau trailed his ennui from one group to another, never quite integrating himself with any one. As he entered his thirties, he was, Pelletier observed, "in a state of perpetual temptation to accept any offer that would come to him."

But Trudeau also cultivated the art of paradox. The only constant of his thinking, as he often repeated, was to oppose accepted opinions.

Hence, at a time when Quebec, on the whole, regarded socialism as "treason and apostasy," Trudeau became a socialist.

6

Flirting with the Left

"We are going to build socialism," Pierre Trudeau promised labour activist Michel Chartrand. And he tried, for quite a long time. But in his own way. And with his own party!

When Trudeau took an interest — finally, said some — in Canadian politics, he was thirty years old with little choice but to become "marginal." But at the time, a whole generation of Quebeckers found itself in the margins.

Of the two great traditional parties, the Liberals and the Conservatives, one was as unpalatable as the other. Elections were won with goon squads who would silence the slightest protest with a punch in the mouth and break legs if necessary. Candidates generally preferred not to know who was contributing to their political war chests and slush funds, certain that if they did, they would find several supporters with mob connections, more likely candidates for the slammer than for the Senate or the Order of Canada.

Former journalists like Gérard Pelletier, René Lévesque, and Pierre Laporte have bitterly recalled the days when every member of the legislative press gallery would be slipped an envelope containing fifty or sixty dollars at election time — in days when reporters were paid barely forty dollars a week.

When they and others like them succumbed to the temptations of politics during the 1950s, it was the result of a democratic reflex against Maurice Duplessis's abuse of power. The collusion between the big bosses — absentee owners like the Americans who owned Johns-Manville — and the provincial police literally pushed Pierre Trudeau into the arms of those who stood in opposition to both: the militant trade unionists.

In keeping with his habit of mixing with all sorts of people and all kinds of causes, Trudeau took up with both Jean Marchand's independent Quebec Catholic union movement and the "international" unions, made up of various American trade unions and affiliated with the Canadian Labour Congress. There he encountered people like Louis Laberge and Fernand Daoust, today the president and general secretary of the Quebec Federation of Labour, respectively.

He often worked for them, preparing briefs to be presented to the provincial government committee on constitutional reform, which righteously championed the cause of provincial autonomy. He also helped organize resistance against anti-labour legislation, and on occasion he would chair arbitration board meetings, such as the one at which Michel Chartrand was readmitted to the inner council of the Confederation of National Trade Unions. Chartrand was considered somewhat too close to the "anarchist" fringe by some, like Marchand, who wanted him kicked out. Then, it was Pierre Elliott Trudeau who wanted him kicked out!

All of those people moved in a circle that would occasionally congregate in the comfortable salon of Thérèse Casgrain's gracious home on Mount Pleasant Avenue on Mount Royal's Westmount slope. Thérèse Casgrain also counted Trudeau's mother, Grace Elliott, among her friends. Grace Elliott accompanied her on a tour of Asia about then, at the time that her son was back home working to lay the foundations of a truly Québécois socialist government.

With her reputation as a leader in the suffragette struggles in the late 1930s, Thérèse Casgrain was something of a sainted figure in the eyes of these young activist intellectuals, who were smitten by the cause of social justice. If this small, stubborn woman had succeeded in getting women admitted to the sanctity of the voting booth in 1940, the standard bearers of the coming generation of Quebeckers who congregated in her living room took as their mission nothing less than the democratization of Quebec. What mattered most to them was to get the government out of the relentless grip of the old parties and to make it serve the people.

Not only did the group have a fighting godmother, it had a forum in the Canadian Institute of Public Affairs which brought together all those who counted as progressives in Quebec at a hotel in the Laurentians in 1954.

It was during this period of democratic ferment in Quebec that Trudeau began his well-known flirtation with the "left." What has gone unnoticed till now, however, is that this liaison was based on a misunderstanding.

What brought together the nationalists and the socialists was their mutual desire to see the emergence of a modern state in Quebec that would devote more of its attention to the needs of the people than perpetuating the privileges of a dominant minority. Trudeau sent up this pampered minority when he said sarcastically, "Isn't it true that the bagmen always have to have their rights preserved?"

The ambiguity of Trudeau's relations with the Quebec left stems not from the fact that he and they envisaged a larger and better role for the government, but from the fact that they weren't talking about the same level of government.

From 1953 onward, Trudeau was already turning up his nose at the Quebec left.

Spurred by the demands of the war effort, the federal state began to flex its muscles once the conflict was over. In 1940 Ottawa brought in unemployment insurance. Family allowances were established before the end of the war. The government opened vocational schools, launched campaigns against illiteracy, set up job-creation programs, built housing, let unionism proceed, controlled prices, and moved timidly towards universal old age pensions by recognizing the right of veterans to retirement benefits. Ottawa was on the move.

Canadian socialism, born of the Depression in Saskatchewan, inspired the creation of new parties. The socialists took power in Regina, and formed the opposition in Manitoba, Nova Scotia, British Columbia, and even in Ontario, where they would eventually come to within four seats of forming the government.

But in Quebec, the socialist wave broke on the jagged rock of nationalism. In the 1944 provincial election, the Bloc populaire, the left-leaning Quebec nationalist party, captured 15 percent of the popular vote, while the Cooperative Commonwealth Federation (the forerunner of the New Democratic Party) picked up a comparatively pitiful 2.8 percent.

In 1953, against all expectations, "Oncle Louis" St. Laurent beat George Drew's Conservatives in the federal election. In that election the Liberals ran as the most conservative of the three parties. Where the Conservatives spoke of health insurance, and the CCF talked about social security, the Liberals promised nothing. Yet they won, thanks largely to their Quebec vote: sixty-six seats to a mere four for the Conservatives.

Trudeau exploded: "Can the CCF build any hopes on Quebec? After taking 2.8 percent of the vote in 1944, the CCF fell to 0.5 percent in 1948, moved up marginally to 1.1 percent in 1949 and 1952, and to 1.6 percent in 1953. These negligible tallies don't even amount to a groundswell. But, then, French Canadians are being true to their history. They would never have supported the Conservatives had it not been for [George-Etienne] Cartier, as they would not have been Liberal had it not been for Laurier, Lapointe, and St. Laurent. They have never really adhered to a Canadian political party; they have allied themselves instead (for reasons of their own) to parties in which they form a semi-detachable wing."

As a result, there never could be a Quebec left.

When he entered politics in 1965, Trudeau explained his flirtation with the left. He said the feeling of "repugnance" against injustice that he felt "perhaps stems from the fact that I had a privileged life, and that I never had to deprive myself to complete my studies. I saw classmates at university prepare for their exams on the corner of a kitchen table while a dozen brothers and sisters milled around, while I could work quietly in my own room of the house."

Those who are disinclined to forgive him anything point out that the workers at Belmont Park, of which the Trudeau family was a major shareholder, were never paid any better than workers else-where. And, rich as he was, Trudeau never paid his membership dues in the Socialist Democratic Party, headed by Madame Casgrain. "We found him sincere," said one of the secretaries for the young socialists at the time. "He flirted with just about everybody, but his leftism was more pink than red." He was seen to be comfortable with the labour movement, and everybody was content with that.

Madame Casgrain, who had been single-handedly running the Socialist Democratic Party for some time, offered it to Trudeau on a silver platter.

"Take it. You're the only one who can do it. Take it, Pierre," she begged him.

But in the end he demurred, and it was Michel Chartrand who applied himself to the task.

As Marchand often said, many groups regarded Trudeau as a valuable intellectual asset, even though they were aware that his butterfly nature made him ill-suited for assuming responsibility for a movement.

In 1954, with its *Manifesto for the Quebec People*, the old Quebec Federation of Labour heralded its entry into active politics. Pierre Trudeau, who wasn't far away, jumped on the idea and sought to expand it. He wanted to assemble all "democratic" forces in Quebec, not just the League for Socialist Action.

In September 1956, as Duplessis once again humiliated the Liberals and Quebec intellectuals despaired of ever emerging from the prevailing gloom, Trudeau participated in the founding of the Rassemblement démocratique (Democratic Assembly). It was a group of thinkers more than a political movement. Its name said it all: it was an assembly in favour of democratizing the state apparatus, rather than a movement to prepare for sweeping social change.

The ambiguities of this group were evident from the founding convention on. Appointing Pierre Dansereau president was easy. As dean of the Faculty of Social Sciences of the University of Montreal, he had the good manners of fine Outremont families, he was a well-travelled professor with an international reputation, and had no discernible political attachments.

But there was a showdown over the vice-presidency between Arthur Tremblay, backed by Jean Marchand and the Catholic unions, and Pierre Trudeau, behind whom were ranged the "true socialists" from the CCF, and the unions affiliated with the Canadian Labour Congress and the Quebec Federation of Labour.

Two trains of thought collided within the Rassemblement. There was Trudeau's—he was nicknamed "the dreamer" who thought in terms of European socialism—and that of Arthur Tremblay, who tended to place greater emphasis on practical solutions to the problems posed by the Duplessis regime.

Pelletier insists that it was the founding convention of the Rassemblement in 1956, rather than his election to Parliament in 1965,

that marked Pierre Trudeau's real entry into politics. This may be
true, but if it is, he came in the wrong door.

In May 1958, Trudeau embarked on a lengthy analysis of the 1958
federal election that had taken place two months earlier, in which
John Diefenbaker's Conservatives had swept the country. Election
campaigns, it seems, have always provoked strong reactions from
Trudeau, and spurred him to write some of his more notable commentaries—at least until his own political career became an issue.

Dismayed by the sight of the two big parties fighting over which
was the more nationalist without putting forward any concrete
economic plans of their own, Trudeau turned his attention to the
question of how Canada could be saved from domination by foreign powers.

His program, directly inspired by the British Labour movement,
would surely not be disowned by Canadian socialists. Foreign capital, Trudeau proposed, must submit to two great priorities. First,
social benefit must take precedence over economic returns. Houses,
schools, and hospitals must come before factories and mills. Second, renewable resources should be exploited before we turn to
those which could wait until Canadians needed them. For instance,
waterfalls and forests would be exploited before mines and petroleum deposits.

Trudeau also laid out certain requirements that would later turn
up in his own government's policies: hiring preference for Canadian
technicians and specialized workers; allocation of mining claims
on a checkerboard grid; domestic processing of natural resources;
allocation of exploitation rights in such a way as to maximize
Canada's competitive advantage.

In 1958, then, a full quarter-century before the fact, Trudeau
had already traced the outline of the National Energy Program that
his energy minister, Marc Lalonde, introduced at the beginning of
the 1980s and of the mining policy that followed it. Had the mag-
nates of Bay Street and Wall Street read French, and *Cité libre* in
particular, they would not have been caught quite so badly off
guard as they were twenty-five years later.

But then they can be excused, because even in Quebec no one
paid much attention to Trudeau's thesis. Among the few who took
note was Gilberte Côté-Mercier, the high priestess of the right-wing

Créditistes, who saw the devil's work in Trudeau's writing. "Brace yourself for an eternity in the company of Pierre Trudeau," she intoned.

At the time there was more talk about a *Cité libre* piece Trudeau had published five months after his tract on how to save Canada from foreign economic domination. This was his "Democratic Manifesto," which he drew up himself and on which he never achieved consensus.

In May 1958, Trudeau had already let drop, as though in passing, that Quebeckers tended too often to believe that they were victims of the phenomenon of economic domination solely because of their status as an ethnic minority. Subtly, without anyone noticing, Trudeau had brought the word "Québécois" into his vocabulary. But it was to illustrate that his socioeconomic perspectives were broader, and that those of his nationalist friends were comparably narrower.

For the time being, Trudeau had one main preoccupation: to rid the province of the Duplessis regime. And who could have known then that the ogre would die suddenly in Schefferville, eleven months later?

"We have to revive and give new meaning to the provincial state," said Trudeau, convinced that his people had "inherited authoritarian traditions from the outset (the church, absolute monarchy, the feudal system) and developed a siege mentality under the English regime: as such it is not surprising that democracy does not seem to stick to us."

Pierre Trudeau would have liked to build a sort of "Democratic Union" starting with a base of socialists, provided that they had as "pink" an outlook as he. But, on the basis of that year's elections, he concluded that "social democratic thought has barely penetrated our province."

At thirty-nine, Trudeau was in a hurry. Every election brought new names to the list of socialist candidates, "but these were not new forces come to add themselves to the old, as much as forces come to replace those that are burned out, one after the other." He was thinking, no doubt, about close friends like Pierre Vadeboncoeur, for whom he had worked in Beloeil during another unsuccessful campaign in 1956.

Finally, Trudeau had so little faith in the provincial administration, even one run by the Liberals, that he "did not feel particularly pressed to demand nationalizations and controls: incompetence, fraud, and oppression are already so characteristic of the administration of public affairs in every respect that the population feels incapable of taking corrective measures."

Hence Trudeau's insistence on "Democracy first" in his manifesto. Having flitted around so much during his interminable political adolescence, Trudeau was familiar with the Catholic Action groups, the arts, journalism, unionism, and the cooperative movement. He envisaged something resembling a "revolution" suddenly surging from this ferment of ideas and personalities. But, he added, "the political reform forces in this province are too weak to carry out two revolutions simultaneously: the liberal and the socialist, not to mention the nationalist . . . Free men should regroup around a common objective—democracy." And he had an answer prepared for the critics that were sure to follow.

The Bloc populaire may have lost every election since it was founded, but its objective was nationalism, not socialism.

A number of liberal democracies, like England and Sweden, had evolved towards socialism: why couldn't it happen in Quebec? In Quebec it was at least as possible to try to complete the democratic revolution begun by Louis Papineau in 1837 and carried on by Laurier, without letting it get bogged down in nationalist quarrels and bourgeois partisan interests.

Trudeau had an answer for everything. To one objection in particular, which came from his friends in the Rassemblement démocratique: they felt betrayed. And they had every right to feel that way.

When Trudeau took over the presidency of the group's convention in 1959, his first act was to scuttle the movement. "Like a tyrant," charged his former allies in the Socialist Action League. Instead of sending out the agenda of the conference he was supposed to organize to the Rassemblement membership, he announced that the movement should take a year's sabbatical. Then he disappeared to Scandinavia for several months.

People who had been active with Trudeau in the Rassemblement noted that within the framework of a political movement, "he was no longer the oracle who had held crowds of workers spellbound. We were finding out that he was an uncomfortable bedfellow."

Was this simply bitterness on the part of people who felt betrayed? Or was it a realistic judgement on a man who had never liked party discipline, except when he himself applied it? The remarks strangely foreshadow the dispirited reaction of many Liberals to Trudeau's departure thirty years later, when they realized that their longtime leader was leaving the party with little more than its name, a mounting debt, and a disenchanted rank-and-file membership.

In Trudeau's defence, it must be said that the Rassemblement was little more than a marriage of convenience between the Liberals and the "Socio-Democrats," both of whom were primarily interested in making the movement serve their own partisan interests. The only thing that held this loose coalition together was their hatred of Duplessis.

"Is there no way we can unite against this insidious Union nationale dictatorship?" Trudeau asked almost pathetically in his Manifesto in October 1958. He was beginning to think that a short-term objective—defeating Duplessis—would hold people together better than a long-term initiative, the establishment of true democracy.

It wasn't a bad idea, and for several months at least, it excited a good portion of the province's intelligentsia. Meetings were organized and there were extensive negotiations among groups to present one single bona fide opponent against Duplessis in every riding.

Because, concluded Trudeau, quoting Kahlil Gibran in English, "If you wish to dethrone a despot, first make sure that his throne is destroyed within you."

In the end it was destiny that freed Quebec from its "despot" not long thereafter — and Trudeau showed bitterness when he discovered that Quebec had no more need of his party of the left.

As for the active political forces in the province, the major preoccupation was to hurl themselves into battle over the vacant throne. Had he read further in Kahlil Gibran, Trudeau could have quoted, in reference to himself: "As such your freedom, when it loses its chains, becomes the shackles of a greater freedom."

As it turned out, the "little people" on whose behalf he and Michel Chartrand had dreamed of socialism, displayed greater vigour than he had imagined they possessed. Quebec threw itself into two revolutions at once: the liberal revolution first, and then, before that one was finished, the nationalist revolution.

Trudeau's heart was still on the left, and he said so. He greeted the June 22, 1960, election that brought Jean Lesage's Liberals to power by stating that it had "delivered us from the plague of the Union nationale." He advised the left to rally to the Liberals rather than be shut out of power by remaining divided.

On the eve of the 1962 election Trudeau wrote that "the only man of the left who has exercised power in this province in a generation has done so as a minister in a purely liberal government." He was referring, of course, to René Lévesque.

In 1963, during the federal election campaign this time, Trudeau solemnly announced that he intended to vote for the New Democratic Party.

Trudeau identified himself so closely with the leftist cause that for many years he was forbidden from entering the United States, though he did visit it semi-clandestinely on occasion with a carload of laughing friends who would be waved across the border by an indulgent small-town customs inspector.

Given his past, it is not surprising that when he came to power, western Conservatives would regard him as a dangerous hard-core socialist, if not worse. His cry of "Viva Castro" during a state visit to Cuba only confirmed their worst suspicions.

As it was, Trudeau believed in a central-planning approach to his dreams of social justice and of freeing the country from foreign economic domination. But at the end of the 1950s he was cornered. He needed a state to enact his program, but here the provincial state had just emancipated itself. And it had done so without him.

As he said himself in 1967: "I let myself be catapulted [into federal politics] because the federal government was too weak." This makes sense. At the time the Quiet Revolution in Quebec was starting to scare him.

But we are getting ahead of our story. For the time being, during the 1950s and the *Cité libre* years, Trudeau had to put up with belonging to a "people who have yet to learn to govern themselves, people among whom democracy cannot be taken for granted."

Perhaps he simply wanted to provoke them, or perhaps he wanted to break with them completely, without remorse. Whatever the reason, Trudeau devoted his first political tracts to French Canadians.

And "the tribe" would feel his sting.

7

A Half-Civilized Tribe

"S ometimes," wrote Gérard Pelletier, "one feels appallingly ignorant while reading some of Trudeau's writings."

Ignorant? Surely not Pelletier. Perhaps it was more a case of his
failing memory, for in the first volume of his memoirs, aptly entitled
The Years of Impatience, he wrote not a word about the tone of
Trudeau's first declarations about the French-Canadian people.

If he had, he might have noticed that Trudeau seemed to view
his compatriots as savages. He liked to use the image of the "tribe"
when referring to French Canadians. In his eyes their political élites
acted like so many country bumpkins.

Maintained by their British occupiers and blessed by the church
authorities, French Canadians were, in the eyes of Grace Elliott's
son, little more than "a disgusting race of blackmailers."

Pierre Trudeau didn't learn his nationalism at school. Instead,
his nationalist fervour was aroused when he felt the immensity of
the land in his flesh, "when he felt the greatness of the land's
creators through his skin."

Trudeau spoke of a country he had discovered as a traveller in
the wilds, like a "*coureur de bois*," skinning his knees on jagged
rocks, having his skin seared by the Arctic winds, straining his
muscles against a boiling current. As for Quebec's political élites,
he had observed them from afar, from Brébeuf College, which was
a "little world of our own, a joyful place where everything was
beautiful," as his literature professor once said.

When Trudeau left Quebec in the summer of 1944, the least one
could say of him was that he wasn't especially politicized. He roared
off to Cambridge, as it were, with one last blast from his Harley-
Davidson.

When he came back after five years and some months, he tore around in a Jaguar, catching the closing weeks of the strike in the streets of Asbestos before exiling himself to the Privy Council Office in Ottawa.

He felt isolated in the Anglo-Saxon confines of the federal bureaucracy, and he warned his compatriots to beware of the federal civil service, "where our ethnic group is likely to be underrepresented." He felt the first stirrings of "French power" while working with Gordon Robertson. But despite Louis St. Laurent's presence at the head of government, Ottawa would be conquered only through sheer perseverance.

The morning of July 15, 1950, the small *Cité libre* group celebrated the publication of its first issue at the Pelletier home on Ile Perrot, as Pelletier recalled, "in good spirits, with a glass of red wine in hand." Trudeau had arrived the night before, on holiday from his job in Ottawa. "The strategy of resistance will no longer contribute to the success of *Cité libre*," Trudeau proclaimed. He called on his people to redouble their efforts, and to rid themselves of the last taboos that stood between themselves and the light at the end of the tunnel.

Had he already decided then that the tunnel would end up in Ottawa rather than Quebec?

Trudeau's first two pieces for *Cité libre* were published eight months apart, though this time the delay was not because of another trip abroad, but because of the disorganization that reigned at the paper. Under the heading *"Politique fonctionnelle"* (functional politics), the articles set forth the basic ideas for an extensive program of constitutional and administrative reform that would be taken up and further elaborated by one Marc Lalonde fourteen years later. Lalonde's elaboration would subsequently be translated for *Canadian Forum* by one Michael Pitfield and resurrected from the parliamentary archives in 1982.

Trudeau was nothing if not consistent in his ideas over the years.

Wary of emotion, Trudeau promised to exorcise all those ideas which, in his vocabulary, could "make them jump with enthusiasm or indignation, for no reason." He would confront the "isms" that bedevilled French Canadians: nationalism, self-determinism, bilingualism, clericalism, socialism, centralism.

＊   ＊   ＊

At thirty-one, Trudeau's only direct contacts with the political world had been through his father, who had backed Duplessis, though he detested him personally, and who had been a bagman for the mayor of Montreal. He must have remembered Camillien Houde's visits, and his way of filling up the campaign kitty during his run for the leadership of the provincial Conservative party.

"I need oxygen," Houde would say.

And Charles Trudeau would send his accountant to get $100 from the till.

Trudeau was therefore speaking of himself when he wrote in December 1952: "Stories of electoral dishonesty are so much a part of our collective childhood memory that they scandalize practically no one."

It didn't take long for Trudeau's ideas to elicit retaliation from Duplessis's ministers and the minions of Cardinal Paul-Emile Léger, then Archbishop of Montreal. But they also stirred up considerable enthusiasm among the younger generation.

Exported to English Canada by McGill professors, Trudeau's writings were published in the *Canadian Journal of Economics and Political Science* and *Canadian Forum*, thereby planting the seeds of numerous prejudices against French Canadians. Since there was no French version of "Some Obstacles to Democracy in Quebec," it was translated by Pierre Vadeboncoeur, who hadn't yet been turned off by Trudeau's ideas.

Trudeau's thesis was simple. Neither French Canadians nor English Canadians believe in democracy; the former abuse it incorrigibly, while the latter pay the price to keep the peace. Meanwhile, between stops of the gravy train, French Canadians huddle within their own society: Catholic, feudal, and immoral.

With such statements, Trudeau "succeeded in displeasing all Canadians, francophones and anglophones," as he himself recognized. But that did not stop him propagating his ideas: first in *Cité libre*, then at the Canadian Institute of Public Affairs in 1954, and in English Canada after 1956.

By then a number of his most avid readers had begun referring to themselves as "Québécois," only to discover that Pierre Trudeau was talking about them. For them he became a "traitor," and out of spite, he declared he would henceforth refuse to "let himself be pigeonholed as a Québécois."

"History [which he must have learned in London, since it wasn't taught in Quebec's classic colleges] has shown us that French Canadians do not really believe in democracy for themselves; and English Canadians do not really want it for others," he wrote. Appropriating one of Lord Durham's conclusions for his own ends, Trudeau noted that French Canada, which had never had to fight for freedom, had been initiated to responsible government at the wrong end: "a people who had not been entrusted with the governing of a parish were suddenly enabled through their votes to influence the destiny of the state." A dangerous situation, particularly for a minority threatened with assimilation. "Our entire policy consisted of saying no, and we hailed as our leaders those who put up an effective resistance." This is how Trudeau tipped his hat, in passing, to the "Patriots" of 1837 who had fought to the death for democratic principles.

Convinced that they had been had by the English, French Canadians more or less backed into the federation, and henceforth "guile, compromise and a subtle kind of blackmail decided their course and determined their allegiances."

In words that still awaken an echo in English Canada, particularly in the west, Trudeau noted that "the words Tory and Grit, Conservative and Liberal, refer neither to political ideals nor to administrative techniques. They are meaningless labels affixed to alternatives which permit the auctioneering of one's support; they have no more meaning than *bleu* or *rouge*, which eventually replaced them in popular speech."

In one fine stroke of the pen, Trudeau obliterated Duplessis's battles to finance "his" universities, a fight he was to take up four years later, and concluded that "survival was above all a parasitic affair."

Trudeau wrapped up his thesis with a harsh judgement on the Quebec élites, of which he was so ashamed to be a member. "In our relations with the state we are quite immoral; we corrupt our civil servants, we blackmail our legislators, we pressure the courts, we cheat the taxman, and we turn a blind eye to anything, as long as it works to our profit. In electoral matters, our immorality is shocking. A farmer who would never dream of entering a brothel thinks nothing of selling his vote for a bottle of whiskey at election time. A lawyer who will argue forcefully for the maximum punishment for a robber who has emptied the church's poorbox doesn't hesitate to add two thousand fictitious names to the electoral lists."

Some might wonder how a society that was so profoundly Catholic and so completely dominated by the church could regard the corruption of its political morals with such complacency. But Trudeau had an answer for that as well.

For French Canadians, authority stemmed from God. Elections were, to them, "Anglo-Saxon, Protestant forms of amusement, of which the deeper significance [was] obscure, but which yield an immediate material return in bottles of whiskey, parish halls, and contracts for building roads."

Trudeau recounted one incident that explained the extent to which the press, as well as the whole of Quebec society, still lived a fragile existence in the shadow of the authoritarian power of the church. He was listening to CBF — the Radio-Canada station in Montreal — on June 20, 1956, the morning of the 1956 provincial election, when he heard something that almost made him choke on his scrambled eggs.

"Sovereign authority," the radio intoned, "by whatever government it is exercised, is derived solely from God, the supreme and eternal source of all power. It is therefore an absolute error to believe that authority comes from the multitudes, from the masses, from the people, to pretend that authority does not properly belong to those who exercise it, but that they have only a simple mandate revocable at any time by the people. This error, which dates from the Reformation, rests on the false notion that a man has no other master than his own individual reason."

This was broadcast by the Interdiocesan Radio Action Committee, and its spokesman warned listeners against this kind of democracy, which, if allowed to survive, would, "in consequence weaken authority, make it a myth, give it an unstable and changeable basis, stimulate popular passions, and encourage sedition."

The French-Canadian people were lagging far behind the twentieth century. Meanwhile, the French in Europe had established their fourth republic, after having gone through two empires and restored a monarchy, and John Kennedy was already a member of the U.S. Senate.

Trudeau has a way of slipping certain phrases into his speeches, such as: "I was in Ghana during the months after its independence." But this was not just an affectation. What he was doing was using his travel experiences to counter the thesis of the nation-state. Quoting whole paragraphs out of the *Statesman's Yearbook* and the *Encyclopaedia Britannica* as well as entries from his own travel journals, he pointed out that India was a sovereign republic that recognized four official languages; that Ceylon (now Sri Lanka) comprised three principle ethnic groups and four religions; that Vietnam, "in addition to the Tonkinese, the Annamese, and the Cochin Chinese, includes nine major tribes." As for Algeria, "along with inhabitants of French, Spanish, Italian, Jewish, Greek, and Levantine origin, there are also Berbers, Kabyles, Arabs, Moroccans, Tuaregs, Mzabites, and a number of raccoons."

So why shouldn't two societies, English and French, Catholic and Protestant (not to mention the raccoons), form a single state?

To avoid being accused of one-sidedness, Trudeau was equally critical of English-Canadian nationalism. "It was the constant threat of American domination which, for better or for worse, forced British Canada to recognize the nationality of French Canadians: the poor English-Canadian nationalist has never been able to hold his head very high."

In effect, he was suggesting that the strength of English Canada depended greatly on French Canada's weakness. "But beware," he cautioned, "there is nothing meaner than a coward who has overcome his fear."

With a fervour that bordered on the obsessive, Trudeau refused to recognize any frontier, even a dotted line, separating Canada's two nations — perhaps because he belonged to both of them.

French Canadian by birth and mother tongue, English with a touch of Scots in his upbringing, "citizen of the world" on top of that, Trudeau refused to be identified, not just with the "Québécois," but with any group. Deep down, Trudeau wasn't too sure who he was, for fear, perhaps, of being ashamed.

All he knew is that he wanted to fight. At Maurice Duplessis's side if necessary.

8

The Autonomist

"Something, somewhere, isn't working," Pierre Trudeau told himself in 1957.

For a brief period of his life, at about the same time he was denouncing the flabbiness of the French-Canadian "tribe" to the English-Canadian majority, he became the prophet of the progressive movement in Quebec.

At the time, "Pierre Elliott," as his fellow union militants called him, spent most of his time writing briefs for the Federation of Quebec Industrial Unions, the forerunner of today's Quebec Federation of Labour. The briefs were presented before a Legislative Assembly committee of inquiry into constitutional affairs.

It is ironic that, at the beginning of the 1950s, Trudeau found himself in the ranks of those who were promoting the concept of provincial "autonomy," the foremost champion of the cause at the time being Maurice Duplessis. His method may have been to "negotiate like a thug," Trudeau thought, but he had the right idea.

Here was yet another instance where Trudeau allowed his reason to overpower his emotion, in particular his visceral antipathy toward Duplessis. At the same time, he was going against some of his best friends, like Pierre Dansereau. He had little choice but to go along with the likes of François-Albert Angers, the right-wing nationalist firebrand, whom he quoted: "In general, the Canadian state is not the central government so much as the sum of the central and provincial governments."

What drove Trudeau into the provincial rights camp at the time, at least into the Quebec provincial rights camp, was the famous battle over university funding.

In September 1951, the Royal Commission on National Development in the Arts, Letters, and Sciences in Canada, headed by Governor-General-to-be Vincent Massey, recommended that the federal government provide direct financial assistance to Canadian universities without going through the provincial governments, which normally had constitutional jurisdiction over education in their respective territories. The idea was generally well received. The universities, as always, were hard up for money, and since the war, Ottawa had been fairly bursting with initiatives in the social sphere.

A few months later, the federal government voted sixteen million dollars in university funding credits for all of Canada — "a plate of scraps," in Trudeau's estimation. Maurice Duplessis was preoccupied by an election campaign at the time and agreed to accept his share of seven million for one year. The next year, re-elected as usual, he took advantage of the negotiations for a new set of federal-provincial fiscal accords to demand his "booty."

And, as usual, he negotiated like a thug.

Quebec universities, he decreed, would not accept Ottawa's cheques. If they did, he would cut them off. Even the very English McGill University had to think twice about defying Duplessis's edict. At the time the cheque for the provincial government's subsidy to the school, amounting to several million dollars, was not sent directly to the university's chancellor, nor to the Board of Governors, but by way of a Union nationale bagman.

On January 15, 1954, the crisis reached a head. Duplessis had been working since 1945 to repatriate part of Quebec's direct taxation which had been "lent" to Ottawa during the war. That day he introduced a bill in the legislature whereby he would appropriate 15 percent of the tax revenue paid by the province to the federal government.

In effect, he challenged Ottawa to try and collect that 15 percent. This left Quebec taxpayers in a tight squeeze between two hard-fisted collectors. "It's a circus," Trudeau immediately decided.

In English Canada, public opinion mounted against this "secessionist" gesture by Quebec. There were calls that the International Civil Aviation Organization (ICAO) headquarters be moved from Montreal, preferably to Toronto.

The battle over university funding was at the heart of the hearings of the legislature's Committee on Constitutional Affairs. Tru-

deau went to work on behalf of the Confederation of National
Trade Unions.

In a brief full of remarkable logic that Jacques Parizeau — who
also negotiated like a thug — would use more than twenty years
later in negotiations with Trudeau's ministers, most notably Jean
Chrétien, Trudeau demolished St. Laurent's arguments one by one.

His theory was simple: everyone for himself, and God help the
taxpayers. "The Canadian treasury's assets should be divided
between the federal government and the provincial governments in
such a way that each can deal *as it sees fit* [he underlined] with the
part of the common weal under its jurisdiction."

He dismissed the equalization argument as poppycock, since
Ottawa was proposing to finance universities in all provinces, both
rich and poor.

He also dismissed the "macroeconomic stabilization" argument,
saying that it didn't hold water, since the economy was growing
steadily. The Korean war was on, and the factories were humming.
He suggested Ottawa should reduce its social expenditures instead
of charging ahead with a new tax program.

On the topic of joint Ottawa-Quebec jurisdiction, Trudeau pro-
fessed to be frankly embarrassed. Had not Léon Dion, a respected
university professor, said that "the university should not fall under
any sphere of influence wherever it may be"? Yet here was St.
Laurent himself turning sixteen million dollars over to the Canadian Universities Foundation, rather than to the institutions themselves, thereby proving the weakness of his position.

In the argument over spending powers, Trudeau stood four-
square behind Duplessis, who, he observed, "may not read much,
but he seems to remember everything." Each government, he urged,
should avoid collecting too much tax, particularly taxes to finance
programs not in its jurisdiction. "The fact that the province of
Quebec does not raise enough taxes to finance its education needs
has nothing to do with it," he said. "The victim's folly cannot be
invoked as an extenuating circumstance by a thief."

It certainly galled him at times to find himself coming almost uncon-
ditionally to the defence of Duplessis. "He negotiates without manners, without dignity," he complained, "through press conferences
and in ways barely worthy of the U.N. Security Council."

But at least he was negotiating. Duplessis was even asking for less revenue in the form of tax points than Ottawa was offering by way of fiscal accords.

But Trudeau was already swimming against the tide by then, though it was not his penchant for opposing accepted wisdom that guided him at the time. During the course of the debate — in fact, from 1953 to 1957 — he was distinctly out of step with many of his Québécois friends and contemporaries.

To begin with, he was not a university professor. The university authorities wanted no part of him, and even if he had been offered a teaching position, he might well have refused it, just as he had turned down every other job offer that would have tied him to Montreal.

Trudeau was therefore ill at ease with what he called "the argument of hunger." To put the debate in the context of the time, it is useful to remember that the Duplessis government's budget for 1960 allocated $74 million for health services, $82 million for social welfare programs, $110 million for public instruction—that is for the entire education sector — and $112 million for "road repairs."

"We cannot afford to wait," said university professor Pierre Dansereau, "the need is too urgent."

"Does a starving man consider the colour of the hand offering him bread?" protested the academic groups. Even Vianney Décarie, a close friend of Trudeau's, declared, "The desperate needs of the universities are staring us in the face."

Trudeau sympathized with the few professors who had the courage to oppose the federal grants, such as François-Albert Angers, Esdras Minville, and Michel Brunet, who, he said, were fighting for "a society that has constantly shown them contempt."

Trudeau launched another attack on French-Canadian intellectuals, accusing them of revealing their servile mentality once more by jumping into the arms of whoever brandished the fattest chequebook.

It seemed he couldn't avoid getting into fights — in Ottawa and in Quebec.

"Come now, gentlemen," he hectored the federal government, "a paltry sixteen million [in 1957 dollars] for the universities you claim to consider so important—surely you are joking? That's just a plate of scraps. Since you have unlimited power to give, why not give a few grants to poorly paid provincial civil servants? In return, the provincial government could offer a bonus to federal civil servants who could demonstrate that they are bilingual. That way, everyone could meddle in the affairs of everyone else. Citizens who are discontented with their provincial government could go to Ottawa to find solutions, and vice versa."

But behind the sarcasm can be seen the two faces of Pierre Trudeau, whose cold logic drove him to prefer the advantages of centralization, but whose native French-Canadian atavism, bolstered by a superior intellect, allowed him to understand that his people had always been cheated when they allowed themselves to be "bought" by Ottawa.

"Suicide," he told his friends who demanded that Duplessis give in. All the provinces had tried, in effect, to blackmail Ottawa from time to time for sums of money. Duplessis was hardly unique in this respect. But because of his stubbornness, and because of the federal government's eagerness to profit from it since 1947, "Ottawa has exclusively occupied the personal income tax field in all provinces, including Quebec, and in return has paid various sums to all provinces, with the exception of Quebec," said Trudeau.

Though Duplessis had managed to establish a meagre provincial income tax, the federal government was making no move to reduce its taxation proportionately. As a result, Quebeckers were doubly taxed. Yet, since the premier blocked all federal intrusions into provincial jurisdictions—such as the construction of the Trans-Canada highway—the province was also doubly deprived. Quebeckers paid taxes to Ottawa for services that the federal government was not allowed to provide. And they paid money to the provincial government which the federal government refused to take into account.

Trudeau went even further, saying that he could not condemn Duplessis's strong-arm tactics. He recognized that Ottawa had never taken the lead in redressing injustices suffered by French Canadians because it never really believed in Canada's bi-ethnic character: "Our small victories have been won only through displays that made Ottawa's guts quake with the fear of our electoral strength."

In fact, Trudeau was convinced (and he had no hesitation in writing this in *Cité libre*) that since Sir Wilfrid Laurier, the Liberal Party of Canada had always been dominated by the English, and that the few French Canadians who rose to high-level posts in the party, including a prime minister like Louis St. Laurent, were mere tokens or pawns.

Trudeau's position in the debate over university financing stemmed from his Québécois heritage and his ferocious instinct for democracy. He was angry with the intellectuals for letting themselves be tempted by Ottawa's fat wallet, rather than bending themselves to the true task — electing a better government in Quebec.

"There is a kind of unconscious but specious paternalism in the attitude of our intelligentsia," he wrote. "It wants to save French-Canadian culture — and yet it does not see that the necessity for this operation must be convincingly demonstrated to the people, whose culture it is and on whom provincial elections depend."

And all this time, Trudeau maintained, Ottawa and Quebec have been playing political football with the Constitution.

A lot of people who were around at the time have suggested that the impact of Trudeau's ideas then was not nearly as profound as it seems in retrospect. They insist that his writing was largely reserved for a fairly small circle of initiates.

"Who reads briefs to parliamentary committees anyway?" he himself once asked.

But some historians, like Michel Brunet, insist that "the Tremblay Commission of Inquiry into Constitutional Problems [1953-1956] gave Quebec the opportunity to search its conscience. Never before had French Canadians made such an effort and analyzed their own collective problems with such lucidity."

The effort was especially important since the federal government, after a series of commissions of its own — Rowell-Sirois on federal-provincial relations, and Massey-Lévesque on the advancement of the arts in Canada — was beginning to play its cards.

Without his realizing it, the rigour of Trudeau's arguments had influenced a provincial commission which was preparing to denounce Ottawa's centralizing role, and which was to unleash a whole wave of claims from the Quiet Revolution, each one more self-determinist than the one before.

During the 1950s Trudeau appeared to be swimming against the intellectual current of the day. But he did so with implacable logic. His arguments were so tightly knit that they allowed not the slightest compromise to pass through. At times he fell into the trap of his own logic — in fact, that is what happened to him at the height of the battle over university funding.

Trudeau was still a legal adviser for the union movement, but this time he was on the other side of the fence. Maurice Duplessis had introduced two pieces of legislation so notorious that they are still remembered by their numbers, Bill 19 and Bill 20. The former allowed the government to decertify any union whose leadership included individuals with "communist" ideas. The second intended nothing less than to eliminate the Montreal Teachers' Alliance.

The anti-union thrust of the two bills caused some to demand that Ottawa use its power of disallowance to force Duplessis to withdraw his legislation. But Trudeau opposed that option with the same fervour he showed in arguing that Ottawa should not get mixed up in funding Quebec universities.

"It would only shift the problem," he said. And the workers applauded when he declared, "The remedy is in your hands. Elect a government that is less anti-union."

Was Trudeau a self-determinist, then? Or was he a centralist? He applied the same intelligence to one position or the other. And since he didn't yet know what to do with his intelligence, he took to the road again.

9

"Where's Trudeau?"

In 1950 the life of a low-level civil servant, even within the prestigious confines of the Privy Council Office, was not enough to keep Pierre Trudeau in Ottawa.

In 1951 Trudeau turned down Jean Marchand's offer of a job as special adviser to the Catholic trades council (CTCC).

In 1952 the prospect of running as a labour candidate in the provincial election raised more doubts in his mind than enthusiasm.

Until 1965, Trudeau's only steady activity was working on *Cité libre*. He seemed to be everywhere and nowhere at the same time. Even Gérard Pelletier asked him one day, "Pierre, isn't it a catastrophe to be rich?"

Trudeau's lack of purpose in life, which, out of shame, he hid under a veneer of devil-may-care bravado, began to weigh heavily on him.

It wasn't that he needed money: his father's investments brought in a healthy return, he lived at home most of the time with his mother, and he travelled light and inexpensively.

Nor was he worried about becoming slothful. He was passionately involved in intellectual debates and even let himself be dragged into working as a stringer for Jacques Hébert's weekly, *Vrai*. And on occasion he would go slumming with his friends' sisters.

It's not that he didn't keep busy. But he was approaching forty. His ideas aroused considerable interest but there was a certain sameness to them after a while. Cracks were appearing in his intellectual armour.

René Lévesque found him pedantic and laughed openly at his mania for using quotations. His columns in *Vrai* were looking more and more like showcases of erudition. He was forever dressing them up with quotations from Plato, Pascal, Thoreau, John Locke, and the inevitable Lord Acton.

One of his articles, which incidentally led off with a quote from Manegold de Lautenbach—"theologian-monk of the eleventh century," he felt obliged to specify — quoted a series of texts which Trudeau used to reflect "in simple terms" on authority and obedience. His "political travels," he said, followed paths as ancient as political philosophy itself, in the footsteps of thinkers from all countries.

"For educated Quebeckers, all these people have apparently never existed," he wrote, reproaching them for their limited thinking. Trudeau didn't merely display his knowledge, he laid it on with a trowel.

In two small columns of close-set type he managed to cite the names of no fewer than thirty-two authors. It was a veritable litany, straight out of a literary encyclopedia, in which he happened to include — oh sweet irony — one "Duplessis-Mornay, probable author of *Vindiciae contra tyrannos*.

But pedantry didn't sell papers, and it didn't make his publisher, Jacques Hébert, a rich man. Nor did it ensure the success of *Cité libre*.

So what was Trudeau's influence at the end of the 1950s? "Marginal," said Gérard Filion without hesitation. "Had Pelletier, Trudeau, and Marchand not gone into politics, no one would be talking about *Cité libre* anymore. It was a small revue, badly laid out and badly put together. It appeared intermittently, and it contained ideas that were, at best, interesting for the time."

André Laurendeau, editor-in-chief of *Le Devoir*, noted that without his paper's investigation into administrative corruption in Montreal, Jean Drapeau would not have been elected to city hall. And without the natural gas scandal — unearthed by Pierre Laporte — the Duplessis government would not have caved in so quickly. *Le Devoir* was as much of a crusading paper as *Cité libre*, but far more widely read than the sheet in which Trudeau expounded his ideas. During its running battle with Duplessis, *Le Devoir*'s circulation climbed from 17,000 to 40,000. *Cité libre* never sold more than a few hundred copies per issue.

Trudeau was part of a circle of up-and-coming intellectuals who often met in his basement or in Gérard Pelletier's living room "to remake the world," a glass of red wine in hand. Laurendeau was there, and Lévesque, and Marchand when he had the time, among others.

"All these guys were nighthawks," said Filion grumpily. "They'd get up at eleven in the morning, if not one in the afternoon. And by then they would have forgotten most of what they were talking about the night before."

Still, these meetings where "the disorder of the night followed the order of the day" would often produce an idea for an editorial by the editor of *Le Devoir* or a noteworthy passage in a speech by the general secretary of the Catholic trades council. Not all was lost.

To say that the *Cité libre* crowd fathered the Quiet Revolution is to understate the influence of the union movement or the School of Social Sciences at Laval University. The tidal wave that surged across Quebec in 1960 had been fed by all manner of channels, and some of them were exceedingly tortuous.

Trudeau, who so often spoke of the "cybernetic revolution," missed the most important revolution of all. While he was off in Moscow throwing snowballs at statues of Stalin, hundreds of thousands of small screens across Quebec lit up with the blurry grey images.

It was the fall of 1952 and Radio-Canada was broadcasting its first television programs. Some feared that the new medium would become a bottomless pit for public funds and that its productions would be amateurish. In short, that it would be an expensive waste of time. Instead it was a triumph.

"I was worried that television would become a millstone around my neck, but instead it became a halo around my head," marvelled Prime Minister Louis St. Laurent.

Suddenly Quebeckers were able to speak to each other and see each other throughout the province. They were listening to each other and discovering themselves.

In the fall of 1956, while Trudeau was ruminating over the defeat of the "democratic forces" in the last provincial election, the legendary news magazine show *Point de mire* came on the air. Its host, René Lévesque, had beginner's luck. On his first show he predicted the Suez crisis, and it happened the next day. Overnight he was propelled to the forefront of current events, his map of the world tucked under his arm.

Like Trudeau, Lévesque travelled around the world, but he did so to produce his popular reports. Ordinary people in the streets and in the taverns would speak of "Monsieur Lévesque" while only in the salons reserved for university professors did they speak of "Trudeau." It was a nuance that escaped no one, particularly party leaders in need of star candidates.

If Pierre Trudeau was interested by the new phenomenon of television, he didn't let on, nor did he make any attempt to use the new medium to lend weight to his avant-garde ideas. On the contrary, the only times Trudeau was on TV back then, as far as anyone can remember, was as a participant in a pseudo-literary game show called *Le Nez de Cléopâtre* (Cleopatra's Nose). And even then, the stars of the show were Paul Berval and Jacques Normand, who were well-known actors.

In this way René Lévesque passed for an intellectual (which he wasn't) who knew how to use television. Trudeau, with his shyness, passed as an intellectual who disliked television, when, in fact, he simply didn't have the nerve to use it.

Radio-Canada and television became Lévesque's road to Damascus. For Trudeau it was a dead end. In 1949 Trudeau was late for the asbestos strike. In 1959 he was in bed when Radio-Canada flickered out.

The English management of the Canadian Broadcasting Corporation, which had jurisdiction over the French-language branch, had decided that since Radio-Canada's producers directed production crews, they were management personnel and thus ineligible for union membership. On the night of December 28, 1958, they went on strike.

Much as the asbestos strike had done a decade before, the Radio-Canada strike captured the province's imagination. Jean Marchand, who directed the strike, had a lot to do with that. But it also gave French Canadians a chance to vent their feelings against another oppressor, the "damned English." All the more damned because they were depriving Quebeckers of their favourite TV programs by not settling with the producers.

René Lévesque had to have his arm twisted a bit before he would show up on the picket line. He was a freelancer who wanted to respect his contract, or, more likely, who was afraid of losing his job. But he eventually made his way to the front lines along with Jean Duceppe and all of Radio-Canada's stars and, more important, with the hundreds of people who turned out to provide coffee for the strikers on the picket line and food baskets for their families.

As for Trudeau, no one recalls seeing him around. But he had a good reason. Gérard Pelletier recounts in his memoirs that he had unfortunately broken a foot on some Laurentian ski slope. Thus it was from his room in the family home on McCulloch Street that Trudeau followed the agitation outside Radio-Canada headquarters on Dorchester Boulevard (now renamed after René Lévesque), "with a right foot encased in an enormous plaster cast suspended from the ceiling."

The 1950s were drawing to a close. Pelletier would call them *The Years of Impatience*. Others saw the end coming before he did, and called them "the years of long patience." Notable among these was Arthur Tremblay, who took Paul Sauvé's historic "Henceforth" at face value, because during his short "One Hundred Days" in office before he died, he introduced a series of progressive education bills.

Whatever they were, some people came out of the 1950s with the measured strides of a long-distance runner; Pierre Trudeau entered the sixties on crutches.

For once Pierre Trudeau, the great political analyst — his commentaries on election campaigns are still fascinating — was wrong. He had not registered the full effect of the turbulence that had swept Quebec during the past four years. He later admitted, "After the 1956 election, I never thought that the electoral equation in 1960 would be so simple."

The Rassemblement démocratique had been a rallying point for a whole generation of progressives. After being defeated as mayor of Montreal in 1957, Jean Drapeau launched his Civic Action group on the provincial scene. In July 1958 the Social Democratic Party allied itself with — or, as Trudeau has claimed, it infiltrated — the labour movement. The Social Credit grew into the Ralliement créditiste. None of these upstart parties was able to assemble a sufficiently credible list of candidates to stand in the next election, but together they generated a groundswell of organizers, militants, and voters who had had enough of the Union nationale.

Trudeau was actually quite peeved with the socialists, "Drapeauists," and other Catholics who failed to follow up on his proposal for a democratic union of opposition forces, for fear of being associated with the corrupt Liberals. Was it perhaps because he wanted to become its leader?

In any case, Trudeau's plan came too late. Death claimed Duplessis and his successor, Paul Sauvé. And no one took Antonio Barrette seriously when he tried to take their place. Whatever Trudeau's plans, he was overtaken by destiny.

Moreover, at about the time when Trudeau was hoping to organize his holy alliance against the Union nationale, the provincial Liberal party, under the somewhat erratic leadership of Jean-Louis Gagnon, was cleaning up its act and gaining renewed vigour in the process. What was suddenly happening — which Trudeau was forced to recognize in 1960 — was that the Liberals were making every effort to attract all those who had been alienated from the Union nationale and inspired to political involvement by Trudeau.

Trudeau realized that he had been trapped in his own game of "democracy first." Whether the revolution was to be liberal or socialist — he didn't go so far as to say nationalist, though he may have thought it — didn't matter so much, as long as there was an appropriate vehicle for it: a democratic party.

And as a good team player, he offered his services to the Liberal party, though he felt little admiration for Jean Lesage. "The net result," he wrote in the issue of *Cité libre* that appeared on the eve of the June 22, 1960, election, "is that the Liberals have, without much effort and at little cost, gained a monopoly of the opposition vote. The corollary is that a certain René Lévesque, gripped by a sudden desire to take political action, has no other practical choice than to do it within the Liberal party. So much the better for them; I won't hold their good fortune against them."

Though Trudeau rallied to the cause, he did so without much enthusiasm. His participation in that historic election campaign was largely limited to helping out his friend Pierre Vadeboncoeur once again. As the Socialist candidate in Verchères this time he wound up with a grand total of twenty-eight votes.

Gérard Pelletier, who was "more refined and more subtle" according to one of Trudeau's friends, could not involve himself in partisan activities, since he was a working journalist. Still, he attended a few rallies in support of "that man." That man being René Lévesque.

It was a notable example of what has often separated Trudeau and Pelletier: one keeps talking while the other is already moving on the right track.

Men in public life have a tendency to rewrite history after they have made it. So there are now two versions of this historic election.

The discrepancy between the two raises the question: did Lesage want four musketeers or three wise men?

The Lévesque version: The Liberal party was thinking of recruiting not only himself, but also Jean Marchand, Pierre Trudeau, and Gérard Pelletier. They had even met to discuss it in Jean Marchand's room at the Mount Royal Hotel while Jean Lesage waited impatiently in a suite at the Windsor Hotel two blocks down the street. Trudeau's emphatic "no" to the proposition—he was already troubled by the Quebec Liberals' flirtation with nationalism — made both Marchand and Pelletier hesitate. Otherwise Marchand would have been eager to get involved. Nationalism wasn't a word that scared him.

The Pelletier version: The Liberals did indeed put a big rush on Marchand, but never, ever (and here he puts his hand on his heart and says he has checked this with Trudeau), did they make an offer to Trudeau or himself. Yes, Marchand had made some speeches, but both he and Trudeau had written things that were not altogether favourable to the Liberals.

Pelletier calls Lévesque's account "unpardonable," and says that at best there was a vague proposal for him to run in Joliette in a by-election after Antonio Barrette's resignation, but he never took it seriously.

And the Trudeau version? Asking him the question has never guaranteed a response. Whatever his version, the fact is that when the starter's gun sounded for the official beginning of the Quiet Revolution, Trudeau was on the sidelines. Taking notes.

He was even voicing doubts in the *Cité libre* edition that preceded the election.

"What will happen after the election?" he wrote.

"If, by luck, the Liberals win the next election, it is likely that the democratic elements of the party will still be too weak to avoid being crushed by the starving in the rush to the trough."

Trudeau, of course, couldn't have known that the wily Jean Lesage would appoint René Lévesque as his minister of public works and that Lévesque would take malicious pleasure in turning away the party-hack gravel contractors and patronage brokers who queued up at his door seeking government contracts. The post-Quiet-Revolution government was to be a modern administration that did public works on a grand scale. It would build highways, not just do road repairs, and it would support large enterprises, and practise "good patronage."

"If, on the other hand, the Liberals are beaten in the next election . . . " continued Trudeau in his *Cité libre* editorial. But history never gave him a chance to find out.

After the Liberal victory, Jean Marchand and Gérard Pelletier continued to submit briefs to cabinet ministers in Quebec City. But now they were on a first-name basis with the new ministers.

And what about Trudeau?

Well, Trudeau was in China, with Jacques Hébert and a group of friends. This was Mao's China, and information offered by the tourist guides of the day were lifted directly from the pages of the *Little Red Book*. Trudeau was bored to death and, as usual, pirouetted off.

The Liberal party's official biography of Trudeau suggests that he was quite busy at the time. "He found time to perfect his skiing technique (he was at one time an intercollegial champion at the University of Montreal), he learned to fly a plane, he practised deep-sea diving, and went on a number of lengthy canoe trips. These trips were his favourite pastime, and as an expert canoeist and nature lover, he acquired a substantial knowledge of Canada's flora and fauna over the years." So much for the 1980 official biography.

Where was Trudeau?

In Quebec in 1960, fewer and fewer people were asking. They had more important things to do.

10

The State of Quebec

Pierre Trudeau was in a bad mood. He was looking to pick a fight again.

"Since June 22, 1960, since it has become possible to show courage without running any risks, it is amazing to see how many brave souls have come out of the woodwork. The province is now at a full rhetorical boil, in full rhetorical development, and in full rhetorical progress."

But Trudeau wasn't only put out by the verbosity that had overtaken Quebec. He also suspected that the new Quebec government was letting itself be carried to nationalist extremes.

One month after his election, Jean Lesage took advantage of a federal-provincial conference to claim 25 percent of federal tax revenues from individuals and corporations, and 100 percent of succession duties.

"It suggests to me that this conversion of the provincial Liberals (who were the most committed of centralists not so long ago) should be watched closely," grumbled Trudeau. "I am moved to wonder if history will not interpret this as the posthumous triumph of Monsieur Duplessis."

The revolutionary that still lurked within him felt that things were not moving fast enough. "Imagine how much more rapidly this revolution — because it is a revolution — would have been accomplished had there been more people like Lévesque in power."

Despite appearances, Jean Lesage's election victory was fairly slim. Only 5 percent of the voters changed sides on June 22, 1960, and most of the Liberal victories, as well as the defeats, had been decided by narrow margins.

Trudeau noted in passing that the Union nationale had boosted its vote in Westmount, Notre Dame de Grâce, Verdun, and Jacques Cartier, ridings with a high percentage of anglophone voters. "The propensity of Anglo-Quebeckers to row against the current is not something new," he sneered. (But then he should know, one is tempted to add.)

Despite the fact that the Liberal victory hung by a thread, that the cabinet was entirely made up of neophytes, and that the bureaucracy was short on professionals, the new government faced little opposition. "The paradox," concluded Trudeau, "is that the government will have to count on the very people who can be its only effective opposition."

He would thus remain in opposition. Soon he would find it a lonely place.

That fall, Trudeau was finally accepted for an assistant professorship at the University of Montreal's legal research institute. "What better job could I find?" he confided to his friends. "I'm working in a field I know well, and for a few years I'd like to have a chance to read and re-evaluate my opinions."

"I miss chewing the fat with Laurendeau, Marchand, Trudeau, and you," René Lévesque told Gérard Pelletier, who by then was editor-in-chief of *La Presse*. At the suggestion of the minister of public works and water resources, the "four musketeers" began to meet every two weeks, preferably on Friday nights, at Pelletier's home on Elm Street in Westmount.

Lévesque was generally late, whereas Trudeau, who was not a night-owl and needed his nine hours of sleep a night, often left early. Therefore they crossed paths more often than they actually crossed verbal swords. During these get-togethers, Trudeau tended to listen more than talk. Lévesque, voluble as always and often foul-mouthed, would compensate for Trudeau's silences.

It was during one of these evenings at Pelletier's house that they heard the first FLQ bomb going off in a Westmount mailbox. They were there the night of November 22, 1963, the day the president of the United States was assassinated. The violence exploding on their doorstep would soon separate them forever.

When the minister arrived at these bi-weekly meetings, he would always be brimming over with projects, his own and the government's, which he was anxious to put before these intellectuals whom he respected. Pelletier and Laurendeau, editors of *La Presse* and *Le Devoir*, respectively, were on an extended honeymoon with the Liberal government they had helped to elect. Trudeau distanced himself more and more from the other members of the group.

On one of these Friday evenings, this time at Jean Marchand's place on St. Hubert Street, the inevitable flare-up occurred. Lévesque arrived, on time for once, even more excited than usual, talking about "his" plan to nationalize electrical production in Quebec.

It was a sound business proposition, he insisted. Jacques Parizeau had said so and Roland Giroux had run it past his colleagues on the Montreal Stock Exchange. It would be profitable in all respects. Hydro construction sites would contribute to regional development far better than the old "colonization" programs. It would be a hothouse for Quebec entrepreneurs, engineers, and administrators. Besides, it had been done everywhere else in Canada. Why not *"chez nous"*?

Trudeau was unmoved. "We're so far behind in education," he said. "Why invest three hundred million dollars in companies that are already working well?"

The economist in him was speaking that night. But on the eve of the November 14, 1962, election, Jean Lesage's *"Maîtres chez nous"* slogan (masters in our own house) provoked such a reaction in Trudeau that he finally said what really bothered him about this "nationalization" business.

"I can see the technological advantages," he said. "But I fear greatly that the nationalist passions that all this will arouse will ultimately prevent us from making any profit."

Despite this swipe at the nationalists, Trudeau eventually came around. For the past thirty years, he said, nationalization of electricity has become "the symbol of our political virility. If Quebec draws back now, it will appear impotent in the eyes of the big Canadian trusts."

But this government, which he was watching so closely, would give him ample opportunity for knitting his brows. The Quebec Liberals were throwing themselves in all directions.

On the international level, Jean Lesage was received like a head of state in Paris, and the French government upgraded the status of the Quebec delegation and its "diplomats." The province also established delegations in London and New York.

Lesage initiated a series of "interprovincial" conferences, where, for the first time, the provinces could meet to discuss their common interests without the intrusive presence of "big brother" from Ottawa. And the Quebec government created a department of intergovernmental affairs.

There was also more and more talk of independence. Pierre Trudeau even attended the opening of the offices of the Rassemblement pour l'Indépendance Nationale (RIN) on Mackay Street, but it was only as a courtesy to Pierre Bourgault, whom he had known for years.

At the university, young professors infuriated Trudeau with their claims that without independence Quebec could not fulfil the promise of the Quiet Revolution. Nothing angered Trudeau more than these unrealistic and improvised plans. The idea that independence would settle everything simply insulted his intelligence.

"You fools, everything remains to be done," he said. "It is an illusion to think that Quebec has reached such a point."

His young colleagues might laugh at him, but Trudeau was convinced he was right. And the federal election on June 18, 1962, allowed him to demonstrate his point.

John Diefenbaker suffered a serious setback, particularly in Quebec. The number of Conservative MPs in the province plummeted from fifty to fourteen. But the switch wasn't all to the advantage of Pearson's Liberals, whose Quebec caucus increased from twenty-five to thirty-five.

What seized Trudeau's imagination was the election of twenty-six Social Credit MPs in Quebec. "Democracy has just been born in Quebec," he said, "and has spoken its first halting words."

In 1958 French Canadians had, for the first time in their history, voted massively for a party (the Conservatives) whose principal figures were not French Canadians. Not so much out of ideological conviction as because St. Laurent's Liberals were starting to take the province for granted.

In 1962, said Pierre Trudeau, "Quebec completed its democratic primer: by giving a quarter of its votes and a third of its seats to the Social Credit, it proved that the rise of a third party, opposed to the traditional parties, is possible."

Still, he could not refrain from sounding a final warning. A democratic Quebec had been born, said Trudeau, but could the infant survive? "The Weimar republic was in its infancy when it brought Hitler to power through the democratic process," he noted. "This doubt is particularly pertinent when a nationalist wind is blowing."

It was the first time, though certainly not the last, that Trudeau invoked the spectre of fascism, even anti-Semitism, in reference to the emerging independence movement.

In any case, he did not have long to savour the Social Credit break-through. The Lesage government was building up steam with its hydro nationalization project and the provincial election it had called to endorse it. This time Pierre Trudeau found himself almost completely alone. As it turned out, it was the strength of the Socred movement that saved him.

During the federal election in June, Jean Marchand noticed with dismay that many of his own troops were falling for Réal Caouette's populist charms. He conducted a vigorous campaign against the Créditistes, particularly among the Lac St. Jean region's aluminum workers.

René Lévesque was also feeling somewhat isolated in the Liberal party. The fight he had had to put up at the decisive cabinet meeting at Lac à l'Epaule, where the hydro nationalization plan was confirmed, had taught him that it was dangerous for a progressive to go too far out on a limb in one of the old, established parties.

Trudeau fully agreed with him, and expressed the hope that Lesage would bolster his "left wing." He encouraged both Pelletier and Marchand to enlist as candidates for the National Assembly. As for himself, it was out of the question. He felt he had too many enemies in the party, not to mention his distinctly chilly relationship with Jean Lesage.

By the fall of 1962, negotiations had progressed to the point at which Marchand had advised the executive of his labour union, which by this time had become the Confederation of National Trade Unions (CNTU), that he would take the plunge in the coming election. He had even been assured that he would become labour minister.

But Lesage broke off negotiations abruptly, without explanation. There are those who suggest that René Lévesque had a hand in the breakdown.

As it was, the Liberals were not inclined to lean too heavily on their nationalization proposal. They were already being accused of playing into the hands of the communists. And since the Créditistes had a score to settle with Marchand from the summer's federal election, Lesage decided it simply wasn't worth the trouble to give the right more ammunition by having a militant unionist like Marchand in his front ranks. Besides, he might scare away Créditistes who could otherwise be persuaded to vote Liberal.

What made it worse is that Lesage did not explain why he had dropped Marchand, who had always dreamed of a career in provincial politics. Marchand was devastated. Something snapped in him; his relations with René Lévesque were never the same again.

Between politicians of the same political stripe, there is a constant flow of information, particularly on the eve of election campaigns. The federal Liberals, on the lookout for any advantage that would help them trip up Diefenbaker, soon got wind that Marchand was available.

For some time now Maurice Lamontagne and Louis de Gonzague Giguère, both talent scouts for the federal Liberal party, had had their eye on Jean Marchand. Lamontagne, an economist and the MP for Outremont, knew the *Cité libre* crowd well. Giguère, who had been one of the founders of the Canadian Institute of Public Affairs, was always looking for young Turks who were keen to thump Tories.

But the list of available candidates became shorter and shorter as the Quiet Revolution funnelled off the best talent of the generation toward Quebec City. Marchand interested the Liberals because of his immense popularity throughout the province, and because he was "clean, clean, clean" at a time when the Liberals felt a need to upgrade their image in keeping with the times.

Trudeau also interested the federal Liberals, who saw him as a confirmed Canadian, although he was unpredictable. But with his abrasive character, Jean Chrétien predicted, "We won't be able to get him elected anywhere."

The party was also taking a long, careful look at publisher Jean-Louis Gagnon. The bankruptcy of the *Nouveau Journal*, after only ten months of existence, had also made him available. In short, the Liberals were already looking for three wise men at the time: Marchand, Trudeau, and Gagnon.

But Trudeau's independent nature frightened the Liberals. And with good reason. As it turned out, Trudeau would turn on them so viciously that all of Giguère and Lamontagne's plans would fall through.

Pierre Trudeau has never been fond of the military. Nor does he particularly like Americans. Whenever one or the other started to meddle in Canadian politics, it sent Trudeau off like a rocket.

In 1961 he had vigorously denounced the decision by the two "Ks" — Khrushchev and Kennedy — to resume nuclear testing, which had been suspended since 1958 "by all but puny France."

Trudeau's analysis was interesting not only because it illustrated his deep pacifist convictions, but also because it gave him the chance to pick another fight with his compatriots.

He was familiar with the English-Canadian pacifist movements, with which he maintained occasional contacts. "But what are the French Canadians doing?" he asked. "Most of these movements have their token members in Quebec. But the leadership is lacking. Leaders in sufficient numbers who would give a certain priority to the survival of the human race."

"In my time," said Trudeau, who was getting on in his forties, "young people would shake up their elders and challenge their consciences. Today young people speak of separatism, they resolutely turn their faces to the past and attack problems for which solutions were found a century ago."

Once again French-Canadian society felt the sting of his lash: the businessmen in their forties, gathered in their clubs, the women in their literary clubs or sewing circles, the clergy in their presbyteries and teaching institutions, the professors, the directors of the press, and the radio stations . . .

"What are all these adults talking about? What are they inquiring into? What are they considering so seriously?" asked Trudeau. "Separatism, independence, 'Laurentia' [a reference to the Mouvement Laurentien, the earliest of the independence movements]."

Happily, this kind of prose did not go much further than the *Cité libre* circle. But when Lester Pearson, head of the Liberal party and recipient of a Nobel peace prize, chose to support the American decision to deploy nuclear warheads on Bomarc missiles stationed in Canada, Trudeau replied with a dynamite blast.

His friends may well have explained later to Pearson that it wasn't Trudeau but Pierre Vadeboncoeur who came up with the stinging nickname, "the unfrocked prince of peace." But Trudeau made no bones about how he felt. He spoke of Pearson's "apostasy," of the "decadence of Canadian political thought," and of "intellectual corruption."

Even worse, and the U.S. State Department would remember this in the years to come, he suspected Pearson of being manipulated by the CIA.

"It has been clear for some time that the U.S.A. does not like Diefenbaker," Trudeau explained after the 1963 election which returned the Liberals to power in Ottawa.

There were reasons for this. The "Old Lion" from Prince Albert in Saskatchewan wanted to decrease Canada's economic dependence on the U.S. by encouraging greater economic ties with the United Kingdom. He had created a commission of inquiry into the dominance of American publications in Canada. He sold Canadian wheat to communist China. He refused to boycott Cuba. Worse yet, it took him three days to come out in support of Kennedy during the Cuban missile crisis.

"'Diefenbaker must go,' the Americans said." At least that was Trudeau's opinion. "You think I'm dramatizing the situation? Do you think the U.S. would treat Canada any differently from Guatemala, should reasons of state demand it?"

These verbal excesses, translated into English in the diplomatic notes put out by the Canadian External Affairs Department and the U.S. Embassy, nearly sabotaged Trudeau's political career. It was worse even than voting for an NDP candidate, which is what Trudeau effectively did that election!

The efforts of the Liberal recruiters in the province were not completely wasted, however. During this election, which Trudeau and Marchand sat out, one Jean Chrétien, then a twenty-nine-year-old lawyer, was elected in the riding of St. Maurice-La Flèche. He won his seat by ousting a Créditiste; Trudeau's theory of the emergence of third parties in Quebec didn't hold water for long.

Chrétien soon caught Pearson's eye. Less than a year after being elected to the House of Commons, the rookie MP managed to manoeuvre John Diefenbaker's Conservatives into voting in favour of changing the name of Trans-Canada Airlines to Air Canada. Young Chrétien almost made it into the federal cabinet before Trudeau.

Jean Marchand, meanwhile, had embarked on the path that would eventually lead him to Ottawa. He had accepted an offer to become a member of the newly formed Royal Commission on Bilingualism and Biculturalism. Moreover, he had begun secret discussions with the federal Liberals, which said a lot about his regard for Pierre Trudeau.

Ottawa and Quebec were playing constitutional ping-pong at this time, pitting one royal commission against another. The Royal Commission of Inquiry on Constitutional Problems (the Tremblay commission), created by Duplessis in 1956, had proclaimed, "Quebec is at a crossroads." It wanted neither separatism nor greater centralization. Denouncing the excesses of Ottawa's centralizing tendencies, the commission called for "the sincere practice of federalism."

On July 19, 1963, Pearson replied with his own commission on biculturalism. André Laurendeau had already called for it in January 1962, but Diefenbaker had rejected the idea. Finally, it was Jean Marchand who, after a long evening at his home in Cap Rouge on the outskirts of Quebec City, convinced Laurendeau to accept the co-chairmanship of the commission along with Davidson Dunton.

But why not Trudeau? Who other than Trudeau was best qualified to head such a commission, given his background and intellectual gifts? And Trudeau was available at the time. But Marchand was profoundly Québécois, and he felt uncomfortable in the anglophone milieu of federal politics. In the end he turned to a fervent nationalist to accompany him to Ottawa, rather than to an anti-nationalist.

A close friend of Marchand's, who was at the meeting at Cap Rouge, later explained: "Marchand was Québécois through and through. I never felt that Trudeau was Québécois to the same extent." Had he been so, he would no doubt have cured himself. A matter of "reason over passion" . . .

In Quebec City, Jean Lesage continued to pursue his course. When the federal government wanted to set up a universal pension system, Quebec refused to participate. Instead it asked for tax points and created its own system. It was the first time that the term "opting out" had been heard in Canada. It was a term that would obsess Trudeau throughout the whole of his political career. He called it "a bonus for separation."

Quebec's last great constitutional victory came in 1964, though English Canada was not immediately aware of its scope.

At the same time as it set up its own pension system, Quebec created its own pension fund, the Caisse de dépôt et placement. The fund accumulated rapidly, since the population was young and there were relatively few beneficiaries. Eighteen years later, one of Trudeau's last political initiatives would be an attempt to clip the wings of the Quebec fund, which had since grown into the largest pool of capital in the country.

All that was still in the future. But the reality of the new situation did not escape an observer as astute as Trudeau: Quebec now had a modern state, and high-calibre professionals to serve it, people like Arthur Tremblay, Michel Bélanger, Roch Bolduc, Jacques Parizeau, Roland Giroux, and Claude Morin.

In Ottawa things were coming unstuck. French Canadian heads were rolling one after the other as a series of scandals rocked the administration. Their demise was hastened by an opposition that appeared to take particular delight in zeroing in on the Quebec ministers in Pearson's cabinet.

This caused Trudeau considerable pain, no doubt. He never allowed outsiders to mock his compatriots in his presence, not even René Lévesque. When Patrick Watson came to see him at the University of Montreal to offer him a position as co-host of a new CBC public affairs program to be called *Inquiry*, Trudeau turned him down.

He told Watson, "I've been thinking it's time to get back into the mêlée."

Part Three

"The Quebecker We Need"
(1965-1969)

The price people pay for taking no interest in public affairs is to be governed by people who are worse than themselves.

Plato, as quoted by Pierre Trudeau in 1965

11

The Myth of the Three Wise Men or *A Gathering of Hawks**

In 1965, Canada became infatuated with the phrase "The Three Wise Men" — a term coined by the *Toronto Star*'s Quebec correspondent, Robert McKenzie. Or, as Jean V. Dufresne freely translated it for the Quebec audience, "*les trois colombes*," (the three doves).

"Wise men" they were not, surely. Their past even made Pearson distinctly nervous. But Ontario liked to believe that the party it was preparing to bring to power had disinfected its Quebec wing of the gangrene that was gnawing at its extremities. The Quebec contingent of federal Liberals had been decimated by scandals, and the new faces of Marchand, Pelletier, and Trudeau were welcomed to give the party a new look.

As for "doves," that remained to be seen. Trudeau's political baggage included his pacifist crusades. Marchand brought with him a reputation as a "union boss" that had withstood Michel Chartrand's barbed comments over the years. Gérard Pelletier, who was available, having been dismissed by *La Presse*, had the least distinct image, as he was the editor-in-chief of a newspaper whose readers paid scant attention to the editorial page.

---

* For his help in the preparation of this and later chapters on Trudeau's entry into politics, I am indebted to my colleague Pierre Godin, who has provided me with information for as-yet-unpublished interviews with Jean Marchand before his death and with Maurice Sauvé before his position as "prince consort" prevented him from speaking on these issues.

Of the three, Marchand was the best known, even in English Canada. Newspapers across the country had been speculating for some months now about the Liberals' star recruit. Pelletier's annual appearances at conventions of the Canadian Institute of Public Affairs had extended his reputation beyond Quebec, though largely within the restricted circles of the Toronto intelligentsia.

July 1965, however, found Marchand and Pelletier on the shores of Lake Couchiching in Ontario. Maurice Sauvé, the junior forestry minister, was also in attendance, and he wasn't terribly impressed. Maurice Lamontagne and Louis de Gonzague Giguère had over-stepped themselves in their recruiting efforts. Quite a few of the Liberal warhorses were miffed at seeing the "three wise men" being portrayed as the saviours of the Liberal party. They remembered how, not very long ago in *Cité libre*, Trudeau had portrayed them as "jackasses" and inconsequential second fiddles.

The three had reached a decision two months earlier in Gérard Pelletier's living room. Originally they were to have been four musketeers, as in Quebec in 1960. But even before Jean-Paul Lefebvre, who was to have been the fourth in the group, could inform Marchand that he would have to pass on the opportunity for personal reasons, Trudeau betrayed his impatience by throwing his own hat into the ring.

As for Gérard Pelletier, his function was the same as it had been since April 22, 1949: to act as a bridge between Trudeau and Marchand, who were so different that they had difficulty understanding each other. "I knew that those two didn't communicate very well," he explained later.

During the long Labour Day weekend of 1965, while René Lévesque was at a federal-provincial energy ministers' conference in Newfoundland, the news finally made the papers. Lévesque called Pelletier at his cottage at Lac Ouareau in the Laurentians where Marchand and Trudeau were spending the weekend. He felt that he had played a role in the three wise men's decision to become federal galley slaves. But the die was not yet cast. Far from it.

The "leak" to *Le Devoir*, which had been about the trio's plunge into federal politics and was published in the paper's September 2 edition, had been engineered by a clutch of Quebec cabinet ministers who were hostile toward Pelletier, and even more so toward Trudeau.

At the time things were going badly all around for Lester Pearson's French Canadians. Yvon Dupuis, a minister without portfolio, had been toppled by a scandal surrounding some questionable dealings with a race-track owner. A few months later it was Guy Favreau's turn to find himself in hot water. Members of his staff at the justice department had talked him into a dubious protection scheme for a notorious hood named Lucien Rivard, who was pulling all the strings at his disposal to avoid being extradited to the U.S. Then Maurice Lamontagne and René Tremblay got tangled up in the bankruptcy of a furniture dealership in the Gaspé. The Diefenbaker Conservatives, led on the floor of the Commons by the up-and-coming member from the Yukon, Erik Nielsen (later to become deputy prime minister under Brian Mulroney), were like a pack of hounds in full cry.

(Nielsen recounted in his 1989 memoir how he was alerted to the case by a young Conservative political aide named Lowell Murray, who would go on to play a prominent role in the Brian Mulroney administration. With the collaboration of a Toronto radio reporter, the Quebec ministers were ensnared, one after the other. The Conservatives had even found a way to listen in on the room where the Liberals held their caucus meetings. According to Nielsen, a number of ministers in the present Conservative government took advantage of this opportunity.)

The advent of the three wise men was not exactly greeted with hosannas in the Liberal caucus. Some of the younger Quebec members were happy to see Marchand, but only Marchand. As the leader of the group, he would be the natural heir to the position of Quebec lieutenant, then held by Guy Favreau. But there were others, like Lucien Cardin, who aspired to the job. Others still, like Jean Chrétien, worried that the new arrivals would usurp cabinet jobs that might otherwise have been theirs.

During the summer of 1965 Maurice Sauvé had taken it upon himself to plead with Pearson that he should accept Trudeau and Pelletier along with Marchand. Sauvé had been agitating for a housecleaning in the Quebec caucus for some time, and the flood of recent resignations lent weight to his arguments.

Pearson didn't know the trio personally, but Sauvé assured him that they were respected intellectuals in Quebec. "And good Canadians as well," he added.

"I have no objection, but clear it with Favreau first," Pearson told him.

At the next regular meeting of the Quebec ministers following Pearson's decision, the reaction was unanimous: nobody wanted Trudeau. In an effort to sabotage the operation, the leak to *Le Devoir* was organized. Pearson finally had to issue a direct order to his Quebec lieutenant to "work at bringing Marchand, Pelletier, and Trudeau into the party."

Favreau, Lamontagne, and Giguère arranged a secret meeting at the Windsor Hotel. Marchand was so confident of the outcome that he arranged for a press conference the next day, September 10, and tipped off several reporters. Maurice Sauvé also managed to invite himself to the meeting, which began at 8:00 p.m. (At least Sauvé *says* he was there; Pelletier says he doesn't remember him being there and Marchand categorically denied it.)

Gérard Pelletier, who had been called back from Winnipeg on short notice, arrived late. And though Marchand was greeted by Pearson's ministers with open arms, Trudeau was treated to a warning. "You don't have a future in politics," Maurice Lamontagne told him. "Some of the things you've written about Pearson were too brutal."

Trudeau knew enough about politics to realize that it was in his best interests to neutralize the resistance of Pearson's emissaries. In any case, he knew from his conversations with Marc Lalonde and Michael Pitfield that once elected he would no longer need them. But for the time being he didn't even have a riding in which to run, and neither did Pelletier.

At one point the three retired to an adjoining room. Trudeau was all for calling their bluff. "Why don't we just say we want to join the Liberal Party of Canada?" he said. "Let's see if they have the nerve to refuse."

Trudeau initially hoped to run in a francophone riding. At one point he even entertained a fantasy about becoming the MP for St. Michel de Napierville, the village of his paternal ancestors. This generated a wave of laughter through the newsrooms of Montreal: Trudeau, the bourgeois Outremont intellectual campaigning in the south shore farming country?

Trudeau finally had to make do with Mount-Royal, a riding with a strong anglophone majority, because the Liberal backroom pros didn't think he could get himself elected in a "difficult" riding.

It was the same with Gérard Pelletier, who was at first slotted to run in the west-end Montreal riding of Dollard until it was learned that Jean-Pierre Goyer, one of Giguère's young protégés, wanted it for himself. He was finally assigned Hochelaga, a riding that had voted Liberal since 1925.

Even then Trudeau's and Pelletier's move to federal politics was regarded as "treason" by their former colleagues in the *Cité libre* group. One last time, they felt obliged to explain.

Why active politics? "After having told others for fifteen years what to do and how to do it, why is it so surprising that we should be tempted to try politics ourselves?"

Why federal politics? "Quebec has become strong and the central government has weakened. Quebeckers continue to be governed by Ottawa, and they still pay more than half their taxes to Ottawa. But they are becoming less and less a presence there, intellectually, psychologically, and even physically."

It was just as well that Guy Favreau and Trudeau's other future colleagues did not see the liberal interpretation of Plato's quote with which Trudeau intended to cap his missive to *Cité libre*: "The punishment of intelligent citizens who ignore public affairs is to be governed by imbeciles." (In the end it was Pelletier who made the more faithful, and more diplomatic, translation quoted at the beginning of this chapter.)

And why the Liberal party? Charles Taylor, a member of the *Cité libre* group, reproached them for having turned their backs on Trudeau's previous third-party crusades. He announced he would run against Trudeau in Mount-Royal on the NDP ticket.

Trudeau and Pelletier replied: "Without being alarmist, we believe that a certain state of emergency exists in Canada. The course of federal affairs, if it continues in its present atmosphere, threatens to produce results that in the short term will be damaging to the Canadian political union."

This was indeed the situation at the time, and it is why Pitfield and Lalonde hastened to ally themselves with Trudeau.

In the late spring of 1967, before anyone was talking about a Liberal leadership race, two visitors from Ottawa came to spend the weekend at Marchand's place in Cap Rouge along with Pelletier and Trudeau.

For the sake of posterity, Marchand's wife, Georgette, took a photo to commemorate the historic moment. Beside the "three wise men" stood Marc Lalonde and Michael Pitfield. At the time Lalonde was a special assistant to the prime minister, and Pitfield was deputy clerk of the Privy Council.

Fifteen years later, on April 17, 1982, as Queen Elizabeth II was about to proclaim the new Canadian Constitution, Trudeau observed: "When the Quiet Revolution began drifting toward the politics of grandeur, and institutions began to attach so much importance to what turned into the red carpet wars, I told myself this was getting to be a bit much. I felt it was the wrong direction for Quebec.

"I entered federal politics precisely to say No."

No to the provinces, of course. And if there were only one holdout — Quebec — the answer would still be no!

Pierre Trudeau had already written about this in *Cité libre* in May 1964, in his manifesto on "functional politics." His plan was to make a clean sweep and build up a new country the same way an architect using a "functional" approach would knock down every old building to design "*la nouvelle cité*" — a new city.

His plan was hatched. And he already had two architects in place in Ottawa: Lalonde and Pitfield.

Lalonde and Pitfield had met in 1959 in the office of Davie Fulton, Diefenbaker's minister of justice. At the time, they were both working on proposals for a new constitutional amending formula.

In 1962, Pitfield was secretary for the royal commission assigned to examine Canada's fiscal structures. One of the commission members, Carl Goldenberg (who would later become Trudeau's constitutional adviser), organized a reception at his house in Montreal, and Pitfield invited Lalonde, who in turn invited Pierre Trudeau.

Captivated by Trudeau's brilliant mind, Pitfield tried to lure him to Ottawa to join the commission staff. Trudeau declined, but Lalonde accepted a post as an adviser. The three kept in touch.

Michael Pitfield and Marc Lalonde were very much like Trudeau. Together they represented his English-French ancestry. Intellectually they were so close to him that one wonders whether it is not Pitfield and Lalonde who invented him. One thing was certain, however: Trudeau's first piece in *Cité libre* in 1950 had already drawn a rough outline of his concept of federalism. In 1964 Pitfield and Lalonde asked him to refine his theory.

Pitfield was a millionaire and a Montreal intellectual. But the comparison with Trudeau stopped there.

He was the scion of two of Montreal's richest families. His father, Ward Pitfield, had founded the blue-chip brokerage house of Pitfield, Mackay & Ross. His mother, Grace (like Mrs. Elliott) MacDougall, came from Montreal's most prominent shipping family, the Redfords. The Pitfield family home in Saraguay, sold for $1 million in 1965, was large enough to be converted into a convent.

Grace Elliott had gone to school with Pitfield's mother for a time. Had she followed her lead and married one of the prominent sons of the Square Mile (the area in central Montreal with the country's greatest density of millionaires at the time) rather than Charles Emile Trudeau, her son would have grown up into a rich Westmount bourgeois, attended McGill University, and probably never become prime minister.

Marc Lalonde was the kind of French Canadian in whom Trudeau always took pride. Like Charles Trudeau, Lalonde was the son of an Ile Perrot farmer. He managed to get his law degree at the University of Montreal and a master's in political science from Oxford by working hard and winning top scholarships with his considerable intelligence. Unlike Charles Trudeau, however, who was an inveterate poker player and hail-fellow-well-met type, Lalonde was a serious-minded and tireless worker, so deeply attached to family values that he never moved his wife and four children to Ottawa, despite the inconvenience of commuting to Montreal.

In short, Trudeau found in Pitfield and Lalonde the rich son that he could have been, and the father he would like to have had.

The legend of the "three wise men" would endure long enough to obscure the profound change in Pierre Trudeau's circle of friends after his arrival in Ottawa.

At all the important moments of Pierre Elliott Trudeau's political career, Pitfield and Lalonde were close at hand.

When Trudeau decided to run for the Liberal leadership, it was Marc Lalonde who convinced Lester Pearson to send him on a tour of the provincial capitals. The objective was to get Trudeau's name into the headlines from one end of English Canada to the other.

On the evening of the day he was elected leader of the Liberal party, Trudeau disappeared, telling his organizers, "See you tomorrow." Everyone thought he'd gone off with a woman. In fact, he dined with Michael Pitfield.

When Trudeau became prime minister, Pitfield was director of planning at the Privy Council Office. He immediately gave control over the federal bureaucracy to the prime minister's office. Meanwhile, as Trudeau's principal secretary, Marc Lalonde took over control of the party.

When the Quebec MPs were wavering in the face of the crises that swept the province, it was Lalonde who braced the troops and got them all marching in the same direction. He quickly earned the nickname *"Le Père Fouettard"* after the brother in some of the stricter monastic orders assigned to administer corporal punishment. The "wet hens," as he called dissidents of any stripe, had no choice but to stand aside, like Jean Marchand, or get out.

At the time Trudeau was mounting his constitutional *coup de force* in 1980, Gordon Robertson, secretary to the cabinet for federal-provincial relations, had just resigned. Michael Pitfield replaced this highly respected gentleman with the hard-nosed, abrasive Michael Kirby, whose specialty was military strategy.

In 1969, Marc Lalonde promised to "apply reason to Canada's social and economic problems." He kept his word with a firmness that even Trudeau found hard to take at times.

According to Michael Pitfield, "During the Pearson era, the federal government had the naive idea that it would always get cooperation from the provinces." From then on, and for the next fifteen years, the federal government went head to head with the provinces. And it invariably won, because Pitfield had built one of the most aggressive bureaucracies in the country's history.

It didn't take Trudeau long to learn the lesson: "The provinces take and don't even say thank you. That kind of federalism is finished."

All of that was implied in the 1964 article on functional politics. "The primacy accorded to regional interests and the absence of leadership at the central government level threatens a dislocation of the central state," wrote Trudeau and Lalonde. Eighteen years later, flushed with the sweet taste of triumph on the day after the patriation of the Constitution in 1982, Pitfield pulled out a yellowed copy of the original *Cité libre* article.

"We weren't sure how we were going to get there," he said, "but we knew where we were going."

Although they weren't aware of it, Jean Marchand and Gérard Pelletier were effectively isolated from Trudeau soon after their election to the House of Commons. Marchand was too busy reorganizing the Quebec wing of the party; Pelletier suffered from culture shock in Ottawa. Marginalized by the anglophone power élite, he seriously considered resigning before his first term was up.

A few months after his election to Parliament, Trudeau was appointed Pearson's parliamentary secretary. Everyone thought it a sinecure. But around Pearson there was also Marc Lalonde and Michael Pitfield. Gérard Pelletier's conscience and Jean Marchand's "Québécois soul" were already relics of the past.

By now Trudeau was relying on Marc Lalonde's cold reason and the strategies Michael Pitfield had learned during his sojourn at West Point military academy. It was the kind of thing he liked: his brawler's instinct was coming to the fore again.

"All of a sudden Pierre became a cowboy," recalled one of the mandarins of the time.

But in Quebec they were still talking about "the three doves," little realizing that three hawks had taken over the perches of power in Ottawa.

12

Lost in the Translation

"My father taught me how to box and how to shoot a rifle," Pierre Elliott Trudeau explained one day.

But installed in Ottawa, Trudeau did not take up arms. "At least not right away," say those who remember the War Measures Act of October 1970 with bitterness. But he would put up his fists. And the finger on occasion.

The most remarkable thing about his first election campaign in Mount-Royal in 1965 is that it occurred without the slightest remarkable incident. This was no doubt due to the fact that Trudeau was far from the best known among the star candidates of the day, and the media paid scant attention to what everyone regarded as just another shoo-in Liberal riding race.

Before he entered politics, Trudeau had shown himself to be a noteworthy wordsmith. He had a gift for coining striking phrases, and his finely honed pen could inflict painful wounds. Though his writing was remarked on from time to time, his words were not exactly trumpeted across the country.

At the time he entered public life, television was establishing itself irrevocably as the medium that would dominate election campaigns, and Pierre Trudeau initially had trouble adjusting. He was incautious at first, and was surprised when some of his off-the-cuff ruminations popped up as newspaper headlines.

When he first arrived in Ottawa, the new MP for Mount-Royal looked more like a tourist.

"Where is the library?" he asked the clerk of the House of Commons who had just sworn him in.

Legend has it that on his first visit to the Parliament Buildings the security guards demanded proof of his identity: they couldn't believe that this dandy represented the stolid bourgeois burghers of the Town of Mount-Royal.

When Jean Marchand suggested that Pearson should take Trudeau under his wing as his parliamentary secretary, Trudeau waffled for three weeks. "I didn't come to Ottawa for that," he finally told a dumbfounded Pearson.

No one really knows whether he was trying to hold out for something more or whether he simply wanted to cling to his freedom.

After all, during the summer of 1966 he disappeared on another of his wilderness canoeing expeditions. He descended the Coppermine River in the Northwest Territories to its mouth on the Beaufort Sea: 400 kilometres of hard paddling and strenuous portages; up at five in the morning to avoid the swarms of ravenous blackflies; whole days spent huddled in a minuscule tent buffeted by a raging blizzard. When he finally got back to Ottawa his hands were swathed in bandages, and his fingers thick with calluses.

If there is one chunk of its British heritage to which English Canada steadfastly clings, it is the stilted tone and antiquated traditions of Westminster, the mother of Parliaments in London. The stones of the Victorian edifice that dominates the heights overlooking the Ottawa River are perhaps less ancient, the Speaker may no longer wear a wig, and the sergeant-at-arms does not always affect the solemn demeanour of an English peer, but there is still the daily formal procession through the corridors of Parliament led by the Speaker on days when the House sits, and the Viceroy still arrives on Parliament Hill in a ceremonial landau to open the Parliamentary sessions.

Pierre Trudeau, however, was insufficiently impressed to readily abandon his silk ascots, his fringed buckskin jackets, and his leather sandals. When he opened his mouth, it created shock waves.

"Who the hell is the member for Burnaby Seymour?" he shouted at the opposition benches one day.

"Fuck off," he yelled in English another time.

Fortunately members of the House of Commons may revise official record of what they have said in the House before it is printed for posterity in Hansard. But the microphones and the TV cameras never lie.

"What would you tell Quebeckers who criticize you for appointing two anglophone experts to conduct a constitutional reform study?" asked one daring reporter after Trudeau had been appointed justice minister.

"I'd tell them to go to hell," Trudeau retorted. (*Je leur dirais merde!*) Later he chewed out his press secretary when the quote showed up in large letters in *La Presse*.

In this and other instances when he resorted to vulgar French expressions Trudeau suffered from the vicissitudes of translation. Use of the word "*merde*" in French is not nearly as scatological as is its literal translation in English. When Trudeau told the Lapalme strikers on Parliament Hill to "*mangez de la merde*," it was, in the context of Québécois slang, only a slightly coarser way of telling them to get stuffed. But its literal translation (modified to "eat excrement" in some of the more squeamish newspapers) turned stomachs across Canada.

The funniest translation incident occurred when Trudeau told a Hamilton TV interviewer in Ontario that Quebeckers speak "lousy French." As transmitted to Quebec's newsrooms by La Presse Canadienne, the French-language service of the Canadian Press, it came out that Quebeckers speak "*du français pouilleux*," which Larousse translates as "lousy" in its exact sense, that is, flea-ridden or verminous. As could be expected, there was an uproar in Quebec.

Two days later, Trudeau explained himself in French. He had not said "*pouilleux*," but "*négligé*." (According to Larousse, "*négligé*" means careless or untidy, slovenly at worst.)

Trudeau's clarification was recycled to the newsrooms of English Canada by the Canadian Press.

"Lazy French, not lousy French," said the headline in the next day's *Globe and Mail*.

The many press secretaries who exhausted themselves over the years trying to explain Trudeau's remarks had one great fear: his explosions of temper. Despite his legendary cool, he was, in fact, easy to provoke, and some of his adversaries, notably Réal Caouette, could drive him up the wall.

One day, on the Prairies, one young demonstrator kept heckling him throughout his speech and threw handfuls of wheat at him.

"Cut that out or I'll come down and kick your ass," Trudeau snapped at him from the podium.

On the other hand, some of the shots from the media landed below the belt. The day Trudeau appeared at the portals of the House of Commons in his sandals, wearing a casual silk ascot instead of the de rigueur tie, the reporter from the eminently respectable *Ottawa Citizen* closed his article with the observation, "the justice minister is said to be a moderately gay bachelor."

Such allusions, like a placard held aloft by one young demonstrator on which Trudeau's myopic gaze could make out the words "Thank you — I'm homosexual," pained Trudeau more than they angered him. But on this occasion at least, he was able to jolly the media and his detractors into coming onside.

"I think everyone agreed when I said that the state has no place in the bedrooms of the nation," he said. "But you could also say that the nation has no place in the bedrooms of the state. At least the press doesn't."

Though he often talked a good fight, Trudeau never actually got directly involved in actual fisticuffs. However, there were times when his bodyguards had to protect him from himself.

This is what happened the day he got into a now-notorious dust-up with his old school chum Michel Chartrand in a corridor of the Parliament Buildings.

At the time some four hundred drivers for the Lapalme trucking firm of Montreal had been laid off because the Canadian Postal Service had cancelled its delivery contract with Lapalme in order to take over the delivery job itself. The drivers hung in for a lengthy protest, which became a political *cause célèbre* with echoes of the asbestos strike of '49.

As president of the Montreal council of the Confederation of National Trade Unions, Chartrand had accompanied a group of the Lapalme drivers as their spokesman for a demonstration on Parliament Hill. Chartrand, who has never backed off from a confrontation, or a provocation, encountered Trudeau and three of his ministers in a hallway where he unfurled a banner that read: "*Fédéral mon Q* [cul]." (Federal my ass.)

"You're a buffoon," Trudeau hissed into Chartrand's ear as he passed close to him.

"I'm never the biggest buffoon when you're there," Chartrand retorted.

The security guards who were on the scene quickly realized that the two were looking for a fight. There was tension in the air as they stood side by side in the corridor. Chartrand accused Trudeau of having imprisoned a young demonstrator in Vancouver a few months earlier.

"You're inventing that," said Trudeau.

"Now you're calling me a liar! You're nothing but a bunch of whores, though whores are more respectable than you people—at least they provide a service."

"You really are a weirdo," Trudeau shot back.

"I'm not a weirdo, but you're out of your mind, my friend," said Chartrand, his hands dangerously close to the back of Trudeau's jacket.

The security men tried to move Trudeau down the hall.

"So that's it," sneered Chartrand. "Your goons have to escort you away."

Trudeau wheeled around, clenched his fists and began bringing them up in front of him.

"I don't need any guards to protect me from you, Michel," he said fiercely.

In the end the guards managed, with diplomacy and their special training, to separate the two before the confrontation became physical, thereby sparing the country the spectacle of a grudge match in the corridors of Parliament dating back to the schoolyard showdowns in the little bilingual primary school in Outremont almost half a century before.

Trudeau would deliberately cut loose with some crudity on occasion, either to put one of his ministers in his place or to lighten up the atmosphere of a discussion that had become too strained. "The art of pirouetting," as Father Roger Marcotte, his former teacher at Brébeuf, had said.

This is how Trudeau, as prime minister, finally put an end to the "Radio-Canada incident."

His ministers had been tracking down separatists in the corridors of the Crown corporation for some time, and Trudeau, who tended to believe them, had promised the Liberal faithful what they wanted to hear: that he would take the bull by the horns.

At the height of the crisis, Gérard Pelletier, then minister responsible for the Crown corporation, invited Radio-Canada's president, Laurent Picard, to a private lunch at Rideau Gate, the government guest house across the street from the prime minister's official residence.

When Picard arrived and saw all the Quebec ministers around the table, including Marc Lalonde, who was still Trudeau's principal secretary at the time, he realized immediately that the talk was going to be spicier than the main course. Just then Trudeau arrived, seated himself at the table and opened the proceedings.

"Laurent, I think there are some people here who have something to say to you," he said, casually unfolding his napkin.

That opened the floodgates. Like the sound of a pack of hounds loosed on the trail of a fox, the baying rang across the dining room and through the swinging doors into the kitchen where it drowned out the noise of the pots and pans. Laurent Picard took advantage of the long half-hour during which the ministers vented their respective spleens to eat his lunch.

The prime minister finally reined them in and gave the floor to Picard. He, in turn, launched into a vivid rebuttal, angrily putting the likes of André Ouellet, Jeanne Sauvé, and even Lalonde in their places.

"Listen, Marc," he said. "If one of your ministers scratches his balls in the middle of a press conference, do you think I can stop my reporters from showing it on the air?"

"Laurent," Trudeau said without a pause, barely raising his nose from his plate, "if Radio-Canada can show me that even one of my ministers *has* any balls I'll take my hat off to you."

There was a momentary stunned silence as forks stopped halfway between the plates and mouths of the assembled ministers. When it passed, laughter rang around the table, though it rang a bit hollow for some. Jeanne Sauvé, who assumed that the remark wasn't aimed at her, laughed the loudest of all.

But from then on the incident was effectively closed. And the ministers understood it was time to stop taking potshots at Radio-Canada. It was Trudeau's way of underlining the ridiculousness of the situation and of putting an end to it without really seeming to do so.

Though Trudeau could be mean spirited and boorish in public, the democrat that slumbered within him always defended Radio-Canada's independence in the privacy of the cabinet room. And the sensitivity that hid behind his tough-guy demeanour often led him to soften a somewhat hurtful attack with a kind word.

"Trudeau would never apologize," said a close friend. "When he made a mistake he would rather live with it than lower himself to that."

In any case, most English Canadians, with the exception of a few bigots, were not unduly offended by Trudeau's occasional vulgarity. Mostly they laughed along with him. After all, wasn't he of the same race as General Cambronne, who had said *"merde"* to their ancestors at Waterloo?

This did not, however, benefit the folks back home, where Trudeau's wrath was not vented only on hecklers or those who penned vicious attacks against him. Though he was elected in Quebec, he continued picking fights with his compatriots, not seeming to mind and never apologizing when his sweeping statements flattened innocent bystanders.

It didn't take Trudeau much more than a year to become the bogeyman of the intellectual class of which he had once been a part and which had been so greatly awed by his intellectual superiority. To this day Trudeau still complains that the Quebec intellectuals always suspected his intentions. But then he often gave them cause for suspicion.

On November 23, 1966, the "three wise men" decided to celebrate the first anniversary of their entry into politics with a public meeting in Mount-Royal, where they gave a summary of the past year.

"There is nothing to suggest that the venture we have undertaken together has been in vain," said Marchand cautiously.

Pelletier, already embittered and ready to offer his resignation, let his hard feelings show. "The federal capital behaves as though French Canadians do not exist," he said.

Pierre Trudeau returned to the theme that would soon become his obsession: "We must overcome the conditions that allow Quebec to exercise its right to opt out. The provinces would then all be on the same footing: there would be no more special status."

During the course of the evening, Gérard Pelletier, who had recently been named parliamentary secretary to External Affairs Minister Paul Martin, talked of his dream of a worldwide commonwealth of francophone countries. It was a suggestion that Quebec's education minister, Paul Gérin-Lajoie had floated in Paris, in February 1965, and which had been picked up a few months later by Léopold Senghor, the president of Senegal.

Somewhat naively, Pelletier expressed the hope that this would also be a way to reconcile the federal government with French Canadians. But little did he reckon with the ingrained stubbornness of the anglophone bureaucracy or his friend Pierre's cold reason.

That very same evening friend Pierre let it be known where he stood. Ottawa would retain its prerogatives in foreign affairs, he said, even in areas of provincial jurisdiction.

"And if some ambassadors don't understand that, they should get out of the country."

The drums were already sounding, calling the politicians to the red carpet wars to come.

Trudeau was not yet a cabinet minister. His only international experience in government had been as part of a delegation to the United Nations during the winter of 1966. In January 1967, Lester Pearson put his talent to the test by sending his new parliamentary secretary on a special mission.

For some years now, Quebec had been making its presence felt on the international scene. Though he had yet to unleash his thunderbolt from the balcony of Montreal's city hall, General de Gaulle was encouraging this development with an increasing lack of discretion. And the federal bureaucracy was getting more and more annoyed.

When it was announced that the prime minister's parliamentary secretary would undertake "a tour of Africa to demonstrate Canada's interest in the French-speaking countries of Africa," there were knowing smirks in the ministerial suites in Quebec.

A parliamentary secretary in Ottawa had about as much power as the minister's chauffeur. One look at Trudeau's itinerary—Togo, Cameroon, Ivory Coast, Senegal, and Tunisia — persuaded them that he had simply been smitten by wanderlust again, nothing more.

But before long the reports filtering back from l'Agence France Presse turned the smirks to frowns in the provincial capital. In Senegal, Trudeau met President Senghor. In Tunis he was received by President Bourguiba, and he spoke with some insistence about the "considerable" participation of francophone Canadians outside Quebec in scientific and technical African aid projects.

In Paris, on February 10, 1967, he spread his cards on the table. The humble parliamentary secretary met the minister for international cooperation, Jean Charbonnel, and made sure that the very official AFP passed on his message:

"The constitutional position of the Canadian government is henceforth clear: foreign affairs are a federal prerogative."

Lester Pearson was happy. His parliamentary secretary had the right stuff, and he told the *Toronto Star*'s Norman DePoe, one of English Canada's leading journalists: "I'm impressed by his knowledge of constitutional law. We're into a period where that's important and we'll be dealing a lot with Quebec. Pierre is a Quebecker, and seems to be the kind of qualified person we need."

One year later, the colourful Joey Smallwood, then premier of Newfoundland, would put it in a somewhat cruder perspective. He was dining with Pierre Trudeau at the time, then the minister of justice.

"If you want my opinion," said Smallwood, "I say for Quebec: nothing, nothing, nothing. I don't mean almost nothing. I mean nothing whatsoever. Quebec should have nothing that Prince Edward Island or Newfoundland doesn't have. But for the French people in Canada, anywhere in Canada, everything, everything that English Canadians have. Everything, I said . . . "

Trudeau interrupted: "You've just said what I think, and I only wish I could have made my views so clearly."

On April 4, 1967, Trudeau made a splashy entrance into the cabinet, being named to the frontline post of minister of justice. And before he became engrossed in the Constitution, even Trudeau's worst enemies in Quebec conceded that he was a great justice minister.

It is noteworthy that he entered the cabinet on the same day as John Turner and Jean Chrétien, two Quebeckers (Turner represented a Montreal riding at the time) who later battled to succeed him. Claude Ryan noted their accession in *Le Devoir* with a twinkle in his eye.

"Mr. Chrétien is a good practical type, Mr. Trudeau is a thoroughbred intellectual, and Mr. Turner is somewhere in between."

Trudeau's first months as justice minister were a peaceful interlude in his relations with Quebec. He was largely preoccupied with

The Brébeuf student, 1938

The autonomist, 1957

1960: Where was Trudeau? Off in China with Jacques Hébert.

The 1965 press conference at which the three wise men announced that they
would join the Liberal party: "Let's see if they have the nerve to refuse."
Left to right: Maurice Lamontagne, Trudeau (partly hidden), Jean
Marchand, and Gérard Pelletier

Trudeau, Canada! Trudeau, Canada! The 1968 Liberal leadership
convention

The heyday of Trudeaumania. At left, in Stratford, Ontario,
a Pied Piper in sandals.
Above, with Miss Grey Cup 1969.

With Margaret Trudeau, "extending Trudeau's honeymoon with the country."

The end of the honeymoon: Trudeau campaigning in 1979.

Making history, 1982: "Her Majesty the Queen affixed her royal signature to the Constitution before an audience huddled under dripping umbrellas." Trudeau and Pitfield (right) look on.

Five days in November 1981. Above left, Lévesque and Trudeau; below left, Chrétien and Trudeau.

A gathering of hawks: with Michael Pitfield in 1982 (top)
and Marc Lalonde in 1983 (bottom)

The three wise men in 1986: Jean Marchand, Trudeau, Gérard Pelletier.

At the Meech Lake conference in 1987:
"I believe Quebeckers will turn the page and look to see
who won last night's hockey game."

Jean-Marc Carisse

"He 'returned' to Quebec without knowing for sure if Justin, Sacha, and Michel would ever call themselves Québécois, French Canadians, or 'citizens of the world.' "

The gunslinger rides again:
Trudeau at the launch for *Towards a Just Society* in 1990.

a series of progressive legal reforms and did not have time to focus on constitutional affairs. In fact, he was still unsure about the position he wanted to take on federal-provincial relations.

The social reforms that Trudeau introduced in Parliament made him popular in the eyes of the great majority of his fellow Quebeckers. In Ottawa, the Quebec MPs generally tended to be in the forefront of any revolution involving social mores or personal values.

In 1986, for example, when the Mulroney government set out to liberalize all federal legislation to take sexual orientation into account, thereby asserting the fundamental rights of homosexuals, Newfoundland's John Crosbie, then justice minister, discovered to his great relief and delight that he could count on the Quebec members to support him against the homophobes in his own party. Similarly, Mulroney was able to rely on his Quebec contingent to block the campaign to reintroduce the death penalty. Their weight, as the single largest group in the caucus, allowed him to appear "progressive."

The same was true in 1967 when Pierre Trudeau became justice minister. For reasons which are still obscure (except perhaps because he was ill at ease with the Quebec question, and justice took in constitutional affairs) Pearson named a succession of French Canadians to the justice portfolio: Lionel Chevrier, Guy Favreau (who was his Quebec lieutenant at the same time), Lucien Cardin, and Pierre Trudeau.

According to Maurice Sauvé, however, Trudeau benefited greatly from spadework done by his predecessors when he took over the portfolio. The famous divorce bill, for instance, had been prepared by Lucien Cardin, and all Trudeau had to do was defend it in the House of Commons.

Even so, his speech on December 5, 1967, on Bill C-187, the bill concerning divorce, was noteworthy. When the anglo-Protestant majority in English Canada heard this French Canadian, a devout Catholic to boot, defending the right to divorce on such all-purpose grounds as "marriage breakdown," they recognized a quality they have always appreciated in their leaders — a "truly liberal" spirit of tolerance.

But that was nothing to the frenzy that followed two weeks later when Trudeau introduced his "omnibus bill" — a bill, in Parliamentary jargon, that amends a whole range of legislation.

Canada, which had just celebrated its centennial at Expo '67 in
Montreal, was being catapulted into adulthood in one fell swoop.
The bill legalized lotteries, allowed for therapeutic abortions, and
tolerated homosexuality "in private between consenting adults."

There was laughter when Trudeau, with the Julius Caesar hair-
cut he sported at the time, declared: "The state has no place in the
bedrooms of the nation." But at the same time, all of Canada,
including Quebec, saw in him a truly modern leader.

"I couldn't see him as prime minister, but he was an excellent
justice minister," conceded Pierre Bourgault.

But it would not be long before certain Quebec intellectuals began
voicing reservations on the subject of Pierre Trudeau. This began
when he turned his attention to constitutional matters. Already relations between Ottawa and Quebec were becoming strained.

At the time no one paid much attention to a poll taken among
Quebeckers between the ages of twelve and eighteen. The three
politicians the group most admired were Pierre Trudeau (30.6 percent), René Lévesque (25.3 percent), and Ted Kennedy (12.6 percent). And since Trudeau was both himself and a sort of Kennedy
at the same time, he figured he overshadowed Lévesque by a two-
to-one margin.

Trudeau did not let the grass grow under his feet while he was
justice minister. Even as he shepherded his predecessors' bills
through Parliament, he found time that summer to bring his constitutional reform plan up to date.

During a Canadian Bar Association convention in Montreal in
1967, Trudeau played his hand with consummate arrogance. Special status as far as he was concerned was nothing more than
"bullshit." But not everyone found his crude references amusing
this time.

"Trudeau is a French-Canadian puppet king in a sports jacket,"
exclaimed René Lévesque.

"The cobra is poised to strike," said the Union nationale's
mouthpiece, *Montréal-Matin*.

"French Canadians should beware of the minister of justice's
non-nationalism," said Robert Cliche, then leader of the Quebec
NDP.

"I'm afraid that Pierre's antinationalism has become too dog-
matic," André Laurendeau confided to Gérard Pelletier a few
months before his death.

In Ottawa, the French-Canadian ministers held back. They recognized the fight that Trudeau was trying to pick with his own
province. Some of them were hoping he'd get his teeth kicked in.

English Canada, long in search of a political messiah who could
lead the nation into its second century without too much turbulence
in French Canada, looked on with interest.

Since May 1966, Lester Pearson had known that he suffered
from cancer of the optic nerve. He suggested to Marchand that he
serve as interim leader until a convention could be held to choose
his successor. Marchand replied that he would rather form a committee that would choose a successor in case of an unexpected
vacancy in the prime minister's office.

From time to time that summer, Edgar Benson, Judy LaMarsh,
Walter Gordon, Lawrence Pennell, Trudeau, and Marchand met
at the Cercle universitaire on Laurier Street in Ottawa. No one
thought Pearson's departure was imminent. When talk did turn to
a Québécois successor, in keeping with the Liberal tradition of
alternating English- and French-Canadian leaders, the names that
came up most often were Guy Favreau, Jean Marchand, and Jean
Lesage, rather than Pierre Trudeau.

On December 14, 1967, Jean-Pierre Goyer, the young Liberal
MP for Dollard, was on his way to the University of Montreal
where he still gave courses. As he drove along in his car, he absently
listened to the radio.

"The Prime Minister of Canada, the Right Honourable Lester
Pearson, has announced his resignation as leader of the Liberal
party, and has asked for a leadership convention to be held next
spring."

On the old Route 17 between Ottawa and Montreal, a car
screeched abruptly to a halt, did a quick U-turn, and headed back
towards the nation's capital with a squeal of tires.

13

"It's Your Turn"

When the young MP for Dollard breezed into the justice minister's office, no one thought to challenge him.

For some months now, Jean-Pierre Goyer had made a habit of dropping in at Pierre Trudeau's office, though his name was not on the minister's agenda. He was one of a small group of Quebec MPs who got together from time to time, "informally," as they say in Ottawa, which is a way of turning a blind eye to all manner of plots. It was vaguely known that they spoke about "Quebec problems" at their gathering.

It was a day of feverish excitement in the federal capital, of the sort that always accompanies the departure of a major figure from the political scene. Be it by death or resignation, the effect is the same. Those still in the fray are immediately consumed by the prospect of the weeks, maybe months, of intrigue to come.

"This is it. This time it's your turn," said Goyer, taking a seat in front of the minister's heavy desk.

"Are you mad?" said Trudeau.

But once again the minister's eyes had betrayed him. The muscles of his face did not twitch, but the look he threw his colleague spoke volumes about what had been running through his mind all morning. His phone had not stopped ringing.

"Go on! . . . Do you think . . . ? It's too soon to talk about that. . ."

And then: "We'll have to talk to Marchand first."

Was Pierre Trudeau surprised? A little. He hadn't expected such an avalanche of urgent calls.

Was he worried? Very much: he had a horror of political machines wherein he discerned far more ambition than sense of duty.

But above all, he was flattered. For the first time, perhaps, Pierre Trudeau realized that all of Canada was falling for him. And he loved it.

A few hours later, the minister of justice was in a luxurious Rockcliffe apartment. The aroma of the coffee mingled with the opening strains of Beethoven's Eroica symphony, and the fine Napoleon brandy gave off an amber glow in the Baccarat crystal snifters. Michael Pitfield was hosting another of his glittering soirées to which all Ottawa sought entrée.

To one side, Roy Faibish, the Ottawa producer for the CBC's show, "This Hour Has Seven Days," was deep in conversation with Pierre Trudeau. One could guess at what they were talking about from snippets of the conversation. "Noblesse oblige . . . " "For the good of the country . . . " "The Trudeau generation . . . "

The ink was barely dry on Lester Pearson's letter of resignation, and already English Canada's intellectual élite, not to mention its TV networks, were fawning over Pierre Trudeau.

We will never know if Lester Pearson, a seasoned diplomat accustomed to the corridor intrigues of international conferences and of the United Nations, foresaw what would happen. But in retrospect, the timing of his resignation could have had no other result than to propel Trudeau to the leadership of the Liberal party.

On September 13, 1967, at a convention held in Toronto, the Conservatives had elected a new leader, Robert Stanfield, the former premier of Nova Scotia. It was a leadership race from which the party emerged divided. Their new leader, though intelligent and charming, did not measure up to some of the more forceful provincial premiers, notably John Robarts of Ontario and Quebec's Daniel Johnson. Those two had recently made waves in Toronto with their "Confederation of Tomorrow" conference, at which the federal government was relegated to the cheap seats with mere observer status.

In Ottawa it had already been arranged that the winter session of Parliament would wind up with the introduction of a Criminal Code reform bill and a major speech by the minister of justice on the new values — liberal, of course — of Canadian society.

Another constitutional conference was scheduled for early February, and the minister of justice would once again be the relief pitcher. And Marc Lalonde, whose talents had been spotted by Pearson who had installed him as his executive assistant a few months earlier, convinced his boss to send Pierre Trudeau on a tour of provincial capitals in January to "break the ground." Pearson understood this to mean that he would be preparing the way for constitutional reform. But Lalonde had something else in mind.

Meanwhile, the Quebec MPs and ministers were in search of a contender. Few of them had any faith in Paul Martin (already beaten by Pearson in 1957), and they knew that if they let "their turn" go by, it would be seven to ten years before they would have another.

"We didn't come to Ottawa for that," fumed Marchand.

"We'll talk about it after the holidays," Trudeau told him.

The minister of justice had other things on his mind. For one thing, he was feverishly preparing his December 22 speech on Criminal Code reform. There were times when he allowed himself to smile distractedly, but none of his staff guessed that he was, in fact, thinking of the Club Med ad he had recently clipped from a newspaper. It promised Tahiti for $599.95. "All-inclusive," noted Trudeau, little dreaming that Tahiti would be the place where the first chapter in the story of the most celebrated couple of the early seventies would be written.

The Sunday following Lester Pearson's resignation, Trudeau was relaxing at the family home on McCulloch Street when Jean-Pierre Goyer dropped by once more, accompanied by some of the party's young Turks who had decided to go for broke.

"You've been a catalyst for the rest of us," said Goyer. "You're the most articulate, the one with the brightest future. At least let us look around and see if it's possible." Trudeau did not reply; his young visitors took it as an encouraging sign.

There was Pierre Levasseur, the party's executive director for Quebec, who immediately forsook his job and his family in Montreal to look for an apartment in Ottawa. There was Gordon Gibson, an upwardly mobile type from Vancouver, who was well connected in upper-class circles on the West Coast, and who served as executive assistant to Treasury Board Chairman Edgar Benson. There was Jim Davey, a British-born computer whiz who had come to Canada during the 1950s to work on the Avro Arrow combat fighter project. Unemployed ever since Diefenbaker torpedoed the program, Davey had recently lent his talents to a Montreal consulting firm, and through it to the Liberal party.

While Pierre Trudeau was in Tahiti introducing Margaret Sinclair and her two sisters to the joys of scuba diving, Jean Marchand spent Christmas in Florida with his wife and Louis de Gonzague Giguère. In the plush salons of the St. Andrew's Club at Delray Beach, the senator introduced the little guy from Cap Rouge to everyone as the "future prime minister of Canada."

In Ottawa, Marc Lalonde and Michael Pitfield were looking for the opportune moment to finesse the Trudeau card. While all of Toronto was still thinking of Jean Marchand as the "logical" successor to Lester Pearson, Pitfield and Lalonde were working the capital cocktail circuit. They knew that the federal bureaucracy plays a crucial role in any leadership campaign. By letting it be known, albeit discreetly, with whom they would most like to work, the senior bureaucrats influence the opinion makers, most notably the columnists, who then pass the message on to the party rank and file. (This is how John Turner finally beat Jean Chrétien in 1984.)

The Davey-Gibson-Goyer-Levasseur group had quickly come to the realization that it was going to be tough to sell Trudeau to the party membership. Too many of them remembered his scathing polemics in *Cité libre*, and the most conservative elements in the party found him too iconoclastic.

As a result, they planned to dazzle the Toronto intelligentsia: writers, artists, musicians, above all the so-called "poll makers," people who set the trends and can launch an idea like a fashion.

Here they had a head start. Peter Gzowski, editor of *Star Weekly* magazine, Norman DePoe, the CBC's best-known political reporter, and Roy Faibish, a producer with considerable clout in the Crown corporation, already knew Trudeau.

People have often wondered how the whole Trudeau phenomenon could have been whipped up in a mere three months. In reality it was quite simple: the people who run all the major media outlets in English Canada live in Toronto, and together they quickly crowned Pierre Trudeau. And, as invariably happens when a Que-

bec "star" is consecrated outside the province — even in English
Canada — the Quebec media hastened to fall in line.

What seduced English Canadians most of all was Trudeau's
evident intellectual capacity. Not only was he a French Canadian,
something that was generously accepted in the spirit of "alternation," but he also didn't mangle the English language like Jean
Marchand, for example, or Jean Chrétien.

And his face fascinated them. "The perfect mask — a charismatic
mask . . . he has the face of a North American Indian," opined
Marshall McLuhan in some Rosedale salon.

"My God!" English Canada exclaimed in one voice.

While Trudeau's younger supporters went after the Toronto
intelligentsia, Donald Macdonald took on the upper bourgeoisie.
Like Pelletier, he was a parliamentary secretary to Paul Martin.
"Big Mac," as he was nicknamed on account of his imposing six
foot plus, represented the wealthy riding of Rosedale in Toronto.
The Toronto millionaires, perhaps through some natural empathy,
felt at ease with the member for the high-rent Mount-Royal riding.
These were not, of course, the barons of Bay Street, who were
lavishly funding one of their own in the Liberal race, Bob Winters.
Those attracted to Trudeau were the new guard of Ontario's business establishment, younger, more modern in outlook, and greatly
impressed by the justice minister's reforms.

Trudeau's backroom promoters executed their strategy bril-
liantly during the winter of 1967 as they went out and knocked on
all the right doors in English Canada. Jean Marchand discovered
this, to his dismay, only a few days after he returned from Florida.

The Liberal party has generally had some rainmaker in its ranks
who pulls the strings behind the scenes. In 1967, his name was
Walter Gordon.

A wealthy chartered accountant (he founded the firm Clarkson
Gordon), a modern theoretician of English-Canadian nationalism,
a guru of the economic reform movement, the former finance minister and father of the Auto Pact with the Americans was the leading
power broker to be reckoned with in Toronto. He could make the
sun shine or the rain fall on any given parade. At least until 1968.

In the early days of 1968, Gordon withheld his support from
Trudeau, saying that he was "not a nationalist." And, to Jean

Marchand's misfortune, he let it be known that Marchand was "someone with whom one could agree."

But by then Gordon's star had flamed out: he had already announced that he would not be running in the next election. As usually happens with grey eminences after their prime, resentment against Gordon began rising to the surface. Far from serving Marchand's candidacy, Gordon's support had the effect of discrediting him in English Canada.

"We need a contender, but it can't be me," Marchand finally told his Quebec colleagues. "Physically I don't have the strength, and outside Quebec my poor English would be too much of a handicap. Trudeau is the one who should go."

Trudeau still seemed to hesitate, but those who knew him well were not unduly worried. It was typical of him: "I never liked to be a leader in anything," he told his official biographer. "I never liked to be responsible; I never sought to be chief of a boy scout troop, or if we were a gang off hiking, I never tried to be the first one. I'd sort of rather follow on my own and go off . . . I never had contempt for leaders. I don't think it's a useless function. But I didn't aspire to be one myself. Let's be honest: there was probably an element of not wanting to assume responsibility."

In mid-January, Trudeau embarked on his tour of the provinces. Before leaving Ottawa, he allowed the different groups promoting his candidacy to put together the framework of an organization. But on one condition. "Nothing is to be made public before the constitutional conference in February," he warned them. "I want to debate Johnson, but if it's known I'm running for the leadership, I'll lose credibility."

It would be the first constitutional conference televised across Canada. Its impact would be enormous, and Trudeau, who had missed out on the dawn of the TV age in the early 1950s, would make up for lost time.

On Tuesday, February 6, the entire country was mesmerized as it watched the justice minister put Daniel Johnson in his place. "Your problem, Mr. Johnson, is not with the federal government. It is with federalism."

English Canada seemed to like this, according to all the signs. Johnson, already weakened by a series of heart attacks, made the mistake of taking on Trudeau on his own ground when he started to trade barbs with him.

"Lord Elliott," he sneered, referring to Trudeau.

"The minister does not know his history very well," Trudeau shot back. "He seems not to know that Lord Durham affirmed the existence of two nations, whereas I do not subscribe to this thesis."

"The representative of Mount Royal," said Johnson in his thickest Irish accent, using the English name of Trudeau's riding.

"The member for Bagot," Trudeau answered the premier of Quebec, with pointed disrespect.

The press ate up the exchange, particularly some of the English ears who perhaps understood "bigot" for "Bagot," the premier's home riding.

Exactly one week later, Trudeau was still dithering. He sounded sincere as he poured out his reasons for not running to Marchand and Pelletier. Dumbfounded, the two said nothing to anyone.

But that evening, he met Lalonde and Pitfield in his office on Parliament Hill. The two hawks no doubt knew better than Marchand and Pelletier what arguments to use on Pierre Trudeau. Before the night was over, Trudeau had made up his mind. Early on Wednesday, February 14, the "three doves" met for breakfast in the parliamentary restaurant.

"I'm in," said Trudeau simply.

While Trudeau was preparing for his showdown with Daniel Johnson, the jostling began in earnest. The Quebec caucus of fifty-five MPs was ready to explode.

Jean Marchand had his share of enemies there. A number of them complained that he was too "bossy" with his Quebec colleagues, and now that the leadership race was on, his authority was greatly diminished.

When Trudeau got back from Tahiti, he saw that Jean-Pierre Goyer had done his job: his candidate could count on the support of at least twenty of the Quebec members. But it wasn't enough to convince Maurice Sauvé, who, along with another group of Quebec MPs, aligned himself with the Paul Martin organization. Bob Winters, a powerful businessman, got some Quebec support through the Quebec Liberal leader Jean Lesage, with whom he had become acquainted during the Labrador hydro negotiations.

Finally, Jean Chrétien, who had got his first leg-up in Ottawa as parliamentary secretary to Mitchell Sharp, who was also a candidate, convinced a small residue of Quebec members to rally to his former boss. At the same time, however, he was negotiating his eventual support for Trudeau with Lalonde in case Sharp's candidacy fell through, as it subsequently did.

On March 22, the flame reached the powder keg. The chaos at the Quebec caucus meeting was indescribable. That morning, Maurice Sauvé had announced his support for Martin. It was a severe blow for Trudeau, who had hoped at least to have the support of all the Quebec ministers.

"Some weeks ago in my office," Marchand wrote to Sauvé afterward, "in the presence of Marc Lalonde, Gérard Pelletier, Pierre Trudeau, and yourself, we discussed Pierre's candidacy. You had some reservations about the timeliness of such a candidacy, but you were moved to add that if Pierre were to decide to run, you would support him with all your strength.

"You understood, you said, that we were of the same generation, that we were friends. There would be no question that you would refuse your help. And you added that we had to be careful not to get stuck with 'Old' Martin."

In short, Marchand was calling his colleague a mountebank and a traitor. "He always wanted to play several hands at the same time," complained Marchand. "And he wanted my job as Quebec lieutenant. I know, because Pearson told me about it."

Word of this reached Sauvé, who dispatched a written reply via Commons messenger the very same day.

"I said I would support Trudeau if, before February 15, the majority of the fifty-five Quebec members had declared in his favour. But only twenty of the fifty-five have declared themselves. It was therefore evident that a majority of the caucus did not support Trudeau; hence I felt completely freed from the position I took in caucus.

"As I continued to reflect," Sauvé went on in his March 22 letter, "events led me to conclude that Paul Martin deserves my support. My friendship for Pierre, which goes back thirty years, leaves me in no doubt about his many fine qualities. But we now have to choose a leader for the party, and I think that under the circumstances, Paul Martin is the best candidate. This is not to say that Pierre and the other candidates are not competent. It's just that I believe Paul Martin is more so."

In Pierre Trudeau's camp, this caused a certain amount of consternation. They had counted on a majority of the votes from Quebec, but more than half the elected members from the province were refusing to get on side, at least not openly. Had they been equipped with better polling information, they would have known about the formidable wave that was building up in English Canada, particularly in Ontario. It was a wave that would sweep away all resistance to Trudeau, including the reservations of many Quebeckers.

As it was, Pierre Elliott gave English Canada more than it bargained for.

When Trudeau campaigned in the west, the big Toronto newspapers feasted on his declarations. In Winnipeg, for example, "Quebec's candidate" compared Quebec independence to a "form of African tribalism that even the Negro kings don't want for themselves."

Even in Quebec, Trudeau couldn't resist lashing out at his compatriots. During a Quebec Liberal convention in Montreal on January 26, he went a little too far. He even told a few leaden jokes about France, whose misfortune at the time was to be flirting a little too openly with Daniel Johnson.

"Masters in our own house?" Trudeau declared. "That's fine with me. But our house is all of Canada, from Newfoundland to Victoria, with its immense riches which belong to all of us, and we shouldn't give any of it up. Our young engineers won't stop at Manic [Manicouagan, where Hydro-Québec was installing its first northern power station]: they will soon look to the Athabaska tar sands, or the potassium deposits in Saskatchewan if they are not already."

"We're looking at the next prime minister of Canada," cried MP Gus Choquette in a "spontaneous" outburst that Jean-Pierre Goyer had had something to do with arranging.

The more lucid Quebec Liberals were worried. They knew that in certain parts of English Canada, people would not be at all averse to finding a leader who could put Quebec in its place. Pierre

Trudeau gave the impression that he was a little too eager to do the job.

This earned him the distrust of one of Mitchell Sharp's senior advisers, Neil Morrisson, who knew Quebec well, having served as chief of staff to André Laurendeau, and who had been the only anglophone manager at the CBC to support the Radio-Canada producers' strike in 1959. Sharp had recruited him in part for his knowledge of Quebec, not wishing to rely too greatly on Jean Chrétien's sometimes simplistic ideas.

"Trudeau refuses to acknowledge the existence of two societies in Canada, and that worries me," Morrisson told Gérard Pelletier at the outset of the campaign.

Douglas Fisher, a former New Democratic MP, since become one of the most influential columnists on Parliament Hill, also objected. "The problem with Mr. Trudeau's position," he wrote, "is that it rests on an absolutely erroneous concept of English Canada."

"I don't approve of Trudeau tackling Quebec head on," said Maurice Sauvé.

Four days before Trudeau was elected leader, the Liberal caucus chairman in the Quebec National Assembly openly deplored Trudeau's attitude, seeing it as a threat to Canadian unity: "If the next leader of the Liberal party hardens his attitude towards Quebec, it will be a catastrophe," he predicted. His name was Pierre Laporte.

In his personal diary, which he had been keeping since the beginning of Trudeau's campaign, Gérard Pelletier noted: "The only real question is whether Trudeau, as prime minister, will cut us off even more than we are from Quebec's younger generation—or whether, on the contrary, he will be able to unite us with the part of that generation that is not separatist."

14

Political Genocide

"J.R.," as they called him in the streets of Vanier, a district of Ottawa, only minutes away from the Civic Centre, was standing quietly amid the surging crowd acclaiming his new leader. He had tears in his eyes.

A young professional, he had been active in Franco-Ontarian education movements for about ten years. Jean-Robert Gauthier had just voted for Pierre Trudeau. "Pierre," he said, "understands the French-Canadian minority better than Paul Martin or any of the other candidates."

The night before, the "Just Society" candidate had declared: "French Canadians should refuse to let themselves be boxed into Quebec precisely because they are a tiny minority in North America."

"I would have become a French Canadian by adoption had I not been one by birth," he had written in the introduction to a collection of his essays published under the title *Federalism and the French Canadians*.

On the Ontario side of the Ottawa River, where the provincial government had tried to outlaw French teaching in Catholic schools in 1912, Pierre Trudeau was regarded as a saviour who would undo more than half a century of injustice. The "Just Society" would also have a cultural dimension.

But on this evening of April 6, 1968, it was easy to be taken in. Trudeau had been a fairly late convert to the virtues of constitutional reform, but once his appetite had been whetted, he piled double portions on his plate.

At the time of his first federal election campaign in the fall of 1965, Trudeau had put his ambitious *"Cité libriste"* projects on hold. In Quebec, on October 25, no doubt inspired by the spirit of the Quiet Revolution wafting across the Plains of Abraham, he had urged Quebeckers to treat constitutional questions with supreme indifference.

"This is not the time to reopen the constitutional debate," he said. "Asking for a new constitution would mean blocking the current devolution of powers to the provinces, at a time when the fire has gone out of the centralist dragon."

The time that would be spent on constitutional wrangles would be better spent on changing the social status quo, he suggested.

Trudeau wasn't kidding — after all he was in an election campaign — and he seemed content that the balance was tipping in favour of the provinces. The dream of "functional politics" that he had nursed with Marc Lalonde and Michael Pitfield the previous year appeared to have faded.

"If the centralizers want to change the rules of the game, let them try," said Trudeau.

Trudeau cited Quebec as an example of a provincial government that was taking its role seriously, and thereby forcing the federal administration to follow suit: "Because of the enormous progress Quebec has made, it is lending new prestige to the French fact in the other provinces," he said.

As such, it was time for Ottawa to get involved.

Six months later, Pierre Trudeau was Lester Pearson's parliamentary secretary, and the prime minister asked him to prepare a brief for the constitutional committee then holding hearings in Quebec. At the time Trudeau still did not see any need to embark on a constitutional reform process — he regarded social and economic issues as more important — save for one consideration: to ensure the equality of French language rights "everywhere in Canada."

In practice, Trudeau explained on March 13, 1966, where there are francophones in sufficient numbers to form a school (or university) population, they should have the same rights to education in their mother tongue as anglophones throughout Canada.

Of course, noted the young MP from Mount-Royal, we will have to determine what constitutes a "sufficient number," but he was confident that judges would be inspired by "a century of applying a similar notion in the far-flung regions of Quebec where there is a sufficient number of anglophones."

Jean-Robert Gauthier and his colleagues on the Ottawa-Carleton School Board were encouraged. But one small sentence in Trudeau's brief may have escaped them. "In the provinces, in principle, only the majority language will be official. However, if there is a French or British minority greater than, let us say, 15 percent, or half a million inhabitants . . . " If that was to be the criterion measuring a "sufficient number," it would take in only Quebec and New Brunswick, leaving Ontario with the short end of the stick.

On April 4, 1967, when Pearson named him justice minister, Trudeau was still stubbornly resisting any suggestion for a constitutional debate. "Daniel Johnson and John Robarts can agitate all they want," he said. "We have fifty-five members from Quebec, who know what the province wants." And so Pierre Trudeau threw himself into Criminal Code reform with the fervour of a young jurist just out of law school.

When Gordon Robertson proposed to the cabinet that the constitutional file be reopened, Trudeau reacted angrily.

"It's a can of worms," he said. "We don't want to get into that."

"We had so many problems with Jean Lesage," replied Robertson. "And things aren't working out with Daniel Johnson. There are all sorts of social and economic questions that can't be settled without constitutional reform." Lester Pearson, a former mandarin himself, sided with Robertson and ordered Trudeau to begin studying the question.

Trudeau grumbled, but he did so discreetly. He went ahead and recruited Ivan Head, a University of Alberta law professor, and Carl Goldenberg, who had made something of a career of royal commissions, through whom he had got to know Michael Pitfield in 1962. The token French Canadian in this small group which was to draw up a new Canadian constitution would be Pierre Trudeau himself. And when Quebeckers raised their eyebrows at this turn of events, Trudeau told them to go to hell!

During the summer of 1967, the ministerial jets and limousines shuttled between Ottawa and Montreal. Anybody who was anybody wanted to be part of Expo '67. But not Pierre Trudeau. Trudeau visited Expo only once that summer, dressed in sandals and jeans, leaving the officials at the Romanian pavilion wondering how such an important Canadian minister could go around dressed like a hippie.

But then the minister of justice was busy with other things. Things that became clear over the Labour Day weekend. In keeping with tradition, the minister had been invited to address the annual Canadian Bar Association convention, which was being held in Montreal that year. Trudeau took the opportunity to drop a small bombshell.

Without any warning, he unveiled a detailed constitutional reform plan. Ivan Head and Carl Goldenberg had done their work thoroughly. Trudeau, the champion of civil liberties who had founded the Human Rights League in Montreal with Jacques Hébert, chaired all the working sessions.

When all the provinces, not just Quebec, began demanding constitutional amendments, they had in mind new power-sharing arrangements between Ottawa and the provinces. Trudeau not only slammed the door on their illusions, he padlocked it.

Since they had to begin somewhere, he proposed that Ottawa and the provinces should first agree on a Charter of Rights. The idea was that you had to get married before divvying up the household tasks.

"I propose," said Trudeau, "a declaration of rights that will act as a brake on all levels of government, federal and provincial."

Canadians would never lose their colonial status if they had to go cap in hand to London to get approval for the charter. Therefore a new amending formula was called for.

And since it would be the courts, not Parliament and the legislatures which would henceforth interpret whole new areas of Canadian law, it would also be necessary to reform the Supreme Court of Canada.

Trudeau's plan was strikingly clear. He would stick to it until April 17, 1982, when, with a sudden rain squall, Her Majesty the Queen affixed her royal signature to the document proclaiming it the law of the land before an audience huddled under dripping umbrellas.

In September 1967, the Parti québécois had not yet been born. So it fell to the leader of the Quebec Liberal party to comment on the plan put forward by big brother in Ottawa. "The federal minister ostensibly refuses to identify with the opinion of a great majority of his compatriots whom he represents in Ottawa," thundered Jean Lesage. What was eating him?

The answer was obvious. Most citizens' rights were under provincial jurisdiction. Trudeau was proposing to put them under double lock in the Canadian Constitution, forcing Quebec to go to the Supreme Court for permission to make any changes. "Are we Quebeckers going to give up rights we now have by virtue of the constitution in favour of a central tribunal?" Lesage fumed.

His deputy, Pierre Laporte, proposed a temporary alliance of all provincial parties against Ottawa's proposal. This would come about fourteen years later, in December 1981, when all parties in the National Assembly rose up to denounce Trudeau's final constitutional initiative.

But at the time activity on the constitutional front was stalemated by the sudden death of Union nationale leader Daniel Johnson, Jean-Jacques Bertrand's interim succession, and the jostling to replace Liberal leader Jean Lesage. The political picture in Quebec was shifting, and Trudeau was hoping for the election of a more docile government in Quebec that would be more receptive to his constitutional intentions. If necessary, he would meddle in the provincial Liberal leadership campaign.

Before the Bar Association convention in September 1967, Trudeau noted that "language is the foremost of instruments necessary for the conservation and development of a people's cultural identity . . . I say we need a broader definition and greater guarantees to ensure the recognition of official languages."

Everyone, French Canadians in particular, understood that Trudeau was talking about linguistic communities. But the federal government was paralyzed by the refusal of the provinces to go along with its constitutional reform proposals, and for the time being it was content to act only within its own jurisdiction. As such, the Official Languages Act adopted by Parliament on July 9, 1969, did not apply to the provinces.

Canada became a country with two official languages, but not a bilingual country. It was an important nuance.

Elsewhere, as when he was courting the Ukrainian vote in Winnipeg during his leadership campaign, Trudeau freely said that *any* language could become official in Canada, as long as it was spoken by a sufficient number of Canadian citizens.

"I am quite ready to admit that if a third large linguistic group were to want to communicate with the state in its own language, it would have to be recognized. Maybe even a fourth; Switzerland, after all, has four official languages."

Neil Morrisson, the former secretary on the bilingualism and biculturalism commission, couldn't disagree more categorically: "Our recommendations were based on the principle of the equality of two dominant societies — French and English — not on the equality of official language minorities."

"If that's the way we want to go," replied Trudeau, "we'll first have to recognize the Indians and the Eskimos." The only reason he gave French official-language status is that French Canadians constituted a quarter of the population.

In light of the way he had played with words during the campaign, it became obvious from the day he was elected as head of the federal government that the electorate's rush to embrace Pierre Trudeau had been based on a misunderstanding.

"What Trudeau will do in government will be brilliant, reminiscent of John Kennedy's reign as president, but his policy for a united Canada will not allow for the resolution of cultural differences which persist on the linguistic level," warned Claude Ryan.

And in the other Canada, Southam News commentator Bruce Phillips, later to become Brian Mulroney's communications director, flatly asked: "Who voted for bilingualism?"

English Canada was already beginning to suspect that Trudeau had purposely avoided talking specifically about the country's bilingual character during the election campaign. "What Trudeau is proposing is a great leap forward in the instruction of French across large parts of the country," warned Phillips. Sure enough, six months later there was the tempest over French on cereal boxes. "Trudeau wants to ram French down our throats," cried the western rednecks.

The sponsor of the Official Languages Act was the new justice minister, one John Turner. Trudeau hoped that Turner himself would go out west to defend the government's language policy. He was fluently bilingual, and the English-Canadian media adored him to the point where they had already anointed him Trudeau's heir. But Turner had other ambitions. As was the case for Trudeau with the Constitution, bilingualism threatened to become Turner's "can of worms." Turner had also left his Montreal constituency in 1968 for a riding in the national capital region, and his civil service voters were getting dangerously restless.

"Turner didn't have the guts to defend the official languages policy, and we had to send Gérard Pelletier, who was secretary of state, in his place. That only made it worse," said Keith Spicer, the first official languages commissioner. It was like pouring oil on the fire. Pelletier brought with him the frustrations of several years of living in "a capital that behaves as if French Canadians did not exist." And the English Canadians complained that sending a French Canadian to extol the virtues of bilingualism was sheer provocation.

French Canadians outside Quebec hunkered down and waited for the storm to pass. "Trudeau talks about a bilingual country," explains Jean-Robert Gauthier. "But that was never our ambition. We had enough trouble preserving our language. It wasn't one of our priorities to have the federal government spend millions to bilingualize government services and their functionaries."

The paradox of Pierre Trudeau's policy is that while the use of French was extended, those who spoke it became increasingly assimilated.

While Ottawa was building expensive language schools and filling them up with anglophone bureaucrats with little interest in learning another language, while it paid an annual eight-hundred-dollar bilingualism bonus to civil servants incapable of dictating a letter in French to their secretaries, the little back-country schoolhouses remained closed to French Canadians, their recreational clubs got the bottom of the subsidy barrel, and the greatest boost for the French language came from Vatican II when it abolished the Latin mass.

Worse yet, the provincial premiers learned from the warning Trudeau got in the 1972 election, when he came within two seats of losing power. It frightened them into putting the brakes on any initiatives aimed at recognizing francophone minorities or at assuring them even a semblance of the services already available to the anglophone minority in Quebec.

"Make a gesture, surprise me for once," Trudeau told his left-hand neighbour at the federal-provincial conference table in Ottawa in 1981. He wanted René Lévesque to allow all English-speaking Canadians — not just anglo-Quebeckers — to send their children to English schools in Quebec. But he never had the political energy — or courage — to ask his right-hand neighbour, Ontario Premier William Davis, to make a parallel gesture.

Trudeau came to office by reducing the Quebec problem to one of language and by promising that his official languages policy would reduce tensions between English and French Canadians. But in fact, the situation only got worse. During the bilingualism in the air crisis, a.k.a. the "Gens de l'air" crisis, when French-speaking pilots asked to be allowed to communicate in French with their control towers as they did with their post offices, Trudeau withdrew and came out in favour of the English majority after a phone call to his transport minister, Otto Lang. He did not even raise the subject at a cabinet meeting.

The sixty Quebec members met when a rumour began to circulate that Jean Marchand was about to quit. Some, like Francis Fox, begged him to stay. "Whether you like it or not, your resignation will assume significant proportions," he told him. "Gérard Pelletier is already gone [he had recently been named ambassador to Paris]. And now you. Of the three wise men, only Pierre will be left. It's starting to look like a rout."

Trudeau, who already had Marchand's letter of resignation in his pocket, asked him to "reconsider his decision." But not strongly enough, perhaps. (Robert Bourassa always suspected that Marchand was sacrificed — maybe even by Trudeau himself — to calm down the Quebec nationalists. Francis Fox all but confirmed it: "Marchand told us that his resignation would probably be best for the party.") "Impossible," Marchand finally murmured, with tears in his eyes. "I came into politics with certain fundamental principles. It wouldn't be honest to stay, because it would be incompatible with my principles."

Principles? Trudeau had principles. But in practice, for instance, he would never allow translators into cabinet meetings. A bilingual minister would have to sit beside a unilingual francophone minister, like Marcel Lessard from Chicoutimi, to keep him abreast of what was going on. Joe Clark allowed the translators in when he won in 1979, but when Trudeau returned less than a year later, he turfed them out again.

Again in 1979, Joe Clark was the one who set up a standing Senate-Commons joint committee on official languages. Up to then, Liberals like Jean-Robert Gauthier, Serge Joyal, and Pierre De Bané had been lobbying Trudeau in vain for such a committee.

Like Marchand, Jean-Robert Gauthier would cry on the afternoon of December 2, 1981. The House of Commons had just adopted a new constitution. While his colleagues rose in a rousing chorus of "O Canada," he remained seated. "Where numbers warrant," he thought ruefully. "We're going to wind up being put on reserves, just like the Indians."

But Henri Bourassa's old dream, which Trudeau co-opted in 1969, was caught in a whirlpool generated by two opposing currents. Since 1968, the Quebec government had created its own commission to inquire into the state of French and linguistic rights (the Gendron commission), which would wind up putting Quebec on the path of French unilingualism. Meanwhile, English Canada stewed in its old prejudices, refusing to make the gesture its minority was waiting for.

Trudeau had said he would have become a French Canadian by adoption had he not been one by birth. When he left politics, there seemed to be no more French Canadians. His compatriots became "Québécois." The others became "francophones outside Quebec" or merely "francos." Worse, they split up among themselves, becoming "Franco-Ontarians," "Franco-Albertans," "Franco-British-Columbians" or "Franco-Saskatchewaners," while the Acadians from the eastern provinces united under a red, white, and blue banner emblazoned with a yellow star . . . like the Jews.

Fortunately, Pierre Trudeau always resisted defining French Canadians as a "people." Otherwise he might have stood accused of "political genocide."

On December 22, 1982, Pierre Elliott Trudeau would thumb his nose one last time at his native brethren whom he did not want to see boxed up in Quebec.

A Senate vacancy occurred in the constituency of Ottawa-Vanier. A district where the numbers warranted the nomination of a French Canadian, thought Jean-Robert Gauthier. "Pierre," he told Trudeau, "the Liberal party hasn't named a Franco-Ontarian senator for fifty years, while John Diefenbaker named two [Horace Cho-quette and Rhéal Bélisle] in six years."

Roger Guindon, rector of the University of Ottawa, was thought to be available and prepared to accept. But Pierre Trudeau was carrying a grudge. In the 1979 election, the Franco-Ontarians had abandoned him to vote for Joe Clark. "I don't get enough support from you," he reproached Gauthier. Moreover, during the referendum campaign, some leaders of francophone associations outside Quebec had committed the grievous affront of coming out in favour of the Yes side. Trudeau decided they had to be punished.

The new senator for this area of the national capital, where the numbers clearly warranted a francophone, would be named Michael Pitfield. A minority for a minority: an Anglo-Quebecker to take the place of a Franco-Ontarian.

15

No More Mr. Nice Guy

The echo of the fervent chanting at the Ottawa Civic Centre—
"Trudeau, Canada! Trudeau, Canada! Trudeau, Canada!"—
had barely faded, lost amid the noisy bustle of eleven weeks of
Trudeaumania, when already another chant began to arise.

"*Trudeau au poteau! Trudeau au poteau!* [Trudeau to the
stake!]" It is a time-honoured Québécois expression of disenchant-
ment with a politician.

A few days earlier, the new prime minister of Canada had compared "the FLQ terrorists" to Robert Kennedy's assassin. It infuriated the independentists, notably Pierre Bourgault, who promised
Trudeau "a surprise" if he dared show his face at the St. Jean
Baptiste parade in Montreal.

On June 24, 1968, in Lafontaine Park on Sherbrooke Street,
Pierre Trudeau, Daniel Johnson, Jean Drapeau, the Archbishop of
Montreal, and a host of supporting dignitaries were on the review-
ing stand awaiting the parade.

Pierre Bourgault, who as a provincial party leader (of the Rassemblement pour l'Indépendance Nationale) was on the official
invitation list, had instead called on the populace to show its
displeasure.

"Trudeau has no business coming here," he fumed, refusing to
join the others on the reviewing stand. "I'm staying in the street."

But not for long. There was a stir in the crowd; hostile shouts
began to ring out. "*Trudeau au poteau!*" The police, some on
horseback, who had been eyeing the scene nervously, suddenly
charged, with nightsticks swinging. A clutch of RCMP officers in
civilian clothes grabbed Bourgault and hoisted him to their shoulders. Amid the confusion, his friends thought he was being carried

triumphally, and began to applaud. Bourgault got out his official invitation card, thinking they were going to deposit him at the foot of the reviewing stand.

Instead he was deposited into the hands of the municipal police, who hustled him into a paddy wagon, as they did with 289 other demonstrators that night. When word of Bourgault's arrest spread through the crowd, people started to throw Coca-Cola bottles at the reviewing stand. The dignitaries fled, all save Pierre Trudeau, who stood his ground at the railing, his arms up to protect his face, alone on a stand covered with overturned chairs. He emerged unscathed. Not so the eighty-three civilians and forty-three policemen who were taken to hospital. Fourteen horses were dispatched to the veterinarian, and a dozen cars needed body work.

Within hours of casting its ballots in the federal election, English Canada was watching its idol defying a mob of separatists. Was it simply a matter of enhancing his leadership image? Or was his gesture intended to show his Quebec adversaries the contempt he felt for them? Whatever the case, the image of Trudeau confronting a hostile mob, staring down a street riot, registered deeply in the collective soul of English Canada. "Just watch me!" he would say two years later, at the height of the October crisis. And a confident English Canada would take him seriously, having already watched him at work, that day in 1968.

The next morning, at Dorval Airport, the prime minister of Canada shook hands with the motorcycle cops in his escort, offering a word of sympathy for their colleagues injured the night before. Not a word, though, for the battered civilians. That same evening, in the Château Laurier, he savoured his first election victory as a party leader. The Liberals would form a majority government, with 155 of the 264 seats in the House of Commons, including fifty-six from Quebec.

Pierre Elliott Trudeau's first mandate as prime minister was heralded by a mounted police charge and the sound of billy clubs breaking heads. Some attributed this relatively minor outbreak to the epidemic of violent protest that swept the western world that summer of 1968. But in Quebec the hard feelings would linger.

In June 1969, three bombs went off in the Quebec Coliseum during the convention that confirmed Jean-Jacques Bertrand as leader of the Union nationale and premier of Quebec. In October of that year the Montreal police went on strike for a day and the downtown area was pillaged by roving mobs. Shop windows were smashed in St. Catherine Street and cars overturned in St. Leonard. More than twenty thousand young people marched on McGill University, and fifty thousand on the National Assembly, demanding a French Quebec.

Ever since Pierre Bourgault had dissolved his Rassemblement pour l'Indépendance Nationale in October 1968, the Parti québécois had become the channel for "sovereigntist," "independentist," and outright separatist sentiment in Quebec. The PQ was preparing the posters and buttons for its first election campaign that would be fuelled by the slogan: "*Oui!*"

In Ottawa, the prime minister modified his basic line from month to month. Henceforth his speeches would use a new equation: "independentism" rhymed with "fascism," and "independence" with "violence."

At the beginning of the 1960s, there was a succession of minority governments in Ottawa, while in Quebec, Jean Lesage was solidly entrenched with his "*équipe du tonnerre*," and piling up brownie points for Quebec.

In 1968, this power alignment was reversed. Pierre Trudeau reigned as the undisputed master in Ottawa, while Quebec became the weak sister. The Union nationale was showing signs of senility, while the Liberals were in search of new ideas and a new leader. The balance was tipping towards Ottawa, which began attracting the up-and-coming federalist political talent from Quebec. Others, attracted by the dream of independence and Lévesque's charisma, went into opposition back home.

Pierre Trudeau did not hesitate to take advantage of the situation, and for good reason. One year after his election, his greatest concentration of admirers by far was in Quebec. Polls taken in 1969 showed that among his compatriots, Trudeau was seen as the most "intelligent, honest, and likeable" political leader in the country. But the soundings also showed that he was seen as the most "rigid" and "reactionary" leader as well. It seemed that the polarization had already begun.

For two years the prime minister of Canada had two main bogeymen: Jean-Jacques Bertrand and Charles de Gaulle. Beyond the personality conflicts, there was sharp disagreement about Ottawa's jurisdiction over regional economic development and international relations.

At the same time as the official languages policy was being introduced, Ottawa created its own Department of Regional Economic Expansion, whose first minister would be Jean Marchand. It was part of the "Just Society": poorer regions would benefit from special programs designed to attract new industry.

When Trudeau assumed control of the government, he inherited the trench warfare with Quebec over the construction of a new international airport in the Montreal area. The Quebec government wanted it on the south shore, close to Drummondville; the federal government wanted it at St. Scholastique, north of Montreal; the Ottawa bureaucrats wanted it to straddle the Quebec-Ontario border. In the end, the federal government had its way: the new airport would be built at St. Scholastique and rebaptized "Montreal-Mirabel International Airport."

Quebec claimed it had the final say on land use in the province, but Ottawa curtly replied that it knew where Quebec's interests lay as well, if not better, than the provincial administration. The exchange grew more heated, and Trudeau became angry. "That's not how it's going to be while I'm here," he declared at the door of the House of Commons. "Mr. Bertrand is exaggerating and saying provocative things just to boost his chances for the Union nationale leadership."

In the fall of 1969, the prime minister used a speech at a fundraising dinner at the Queen Elizabeth Hotel in Montreal to draw his bottom line: if the Quebec government was unable to maintain order on its own, he was prepared to see to it himself. "No crisis will find us absent from any part of the country, particularly not from Quebec. *Finies les folies*! (Enough foolishness!) It has gone on too long in recent years."

In situations like this, before a friendly partisan crowd, Pierre Trudeau has an annoying habit of putting aside his written notes to shoot from the hip, standing with his thumbs hooked in his belt loops in what has become known as his "gunslinger" pose. That evening he also took a few potshots at French foreign minister Jean de Lipkowski, who was visiting Quebec, and who had committed the unpardonable sin of coming to Quebec without first making a diplomatic stopover in Ottawa. Mr. de Lipkowski's Quebec tour, joked Trudeau before three thousand Liberals, who roared with laughter, was topped off by the donation of 185 volumes of *La*

Pléiade (a collection of French literary classics) and a cine-bus "of the kind that Canada regularly gives to underdeveloped countries."

"As for French investments, they don't go to Quebec, but to Nova Scotia." (France's biggest tire manufacturer, Michelin, had just announced that it would build its Canadian plant not in Quebec, but in Nova Scotia, which had passed anti-union legislation tailored to the French company's demands.) With his allusion to the Michelin project, the prime minister introduced a theme that became a regular feature of his speeches: if Quebec's economic situation was deteriorating, it was because of the bombs and the violence.

And he wasn't far wrong. To the Michelin example he could have added Péchiney, which chose the state of New York over Quebec's north shore, or the Marcel Dussault aircraft firm which decided against investing in Quebec at the last moment. Or Renault, which was quietly withdrawing from Quebec. The least one could say at the time was that French businessmen did not share the Gaullist enthusiasm for Quebec.

Ever since the infamous balcony incident at Montreal's city hall — or did it go back to the year he wasted at university in Paris in 1946? — Pierre Trudeau had shown a suspicion of France that at times bordered on paranoia.

For his part, General de Gaulle was only too happy to heap provocation upon provocation. Even in his New Year's messages to the people of France, he always had a few words of sympathy for those whom he called "the French of Canada." On January 1, 1969 he went so far as to offer the wish that Quebec would be able to take its destiny into its own hands.

Pierre Trudeau was so furious that the next week he skipped a session of the Commonwealth conference being held in London to telephone Marc Lalonde back in Ottawa. Trudeau excused himself, saying he had to deal with "urgent internal problems." Everyone anxiously speculated about what political crisis could have broken out in Canada. In reality, the prime minister spent the evening and a good part of the night discussing with his principal secretary the composition of the Canadian delegation to a conference of education ministers from French-speaking countries to be held in the Congo the following week.

At the time, the "James Bonds" in the federal bureaucracy had even detected what they believed was a French "agitator" on a "clandestine mission" in Canada. During the summer of 1968, a low-level functionary from the prime minister's office in Paris, a certain Philippe Rossillon, had visited a francophone group in Manitoba. "Without asking permission or notifying us," declared a greatly offended Pierre Trudeau. "Nothing hurts minorities more than the involvement of outside agitators." His entourage recalled that this mysterious Mr. Rossillon had also been seen sniffing around Acadia and in the company of Quebec nationalists at the time of the de Gaulle visit in 1967.

As it turned out, the whole affair was a red herring. Far from being on a "mission" to Canada, Rossillon had simply accepted an invitation from the Manitoba group, who wished to reciprocate for having been so politely received by the French authorities on a visit to Paris the year before. The senior diplomats in Ottawa, for whom Trudeau generally showed little respect, had come close to provoking a rupture in Canadian-French relations over a mere trifle.

The African governments found these quarrels between "the big white chiefs" quite amusing, but knew that there was nothing to be gained for them in these little spats. In 1969, despite this bidding contest between Ottawa and Quebec, Canadian aid to francophone African countries totalled barely thirty million dollars, which was less than what Peru gave.

As a result of these tensions, Quebec ministers who travelled abroad on official business were shadowed by federal chaperones. Marcel Masse, then Quebec's intergovernmental affairs minister, was particularly suspect.

As minister of state for education, Masse had struck up a personal friendship with his French counterpart, Alain Peyrefitte. Trudeau suspected that the two had plotted together during Expo '67 to have Gabon extend an official invitation to the "state" of Quebec. The letter went directly from Libreville to Quebec (thanks to Canada Post) without going through the External Affairs Department in Ottawa as required by normal diplomatic practice. The ultimate affront was that it invited Quebec's education minister, Jean-Guy Cardinal, to "represent French Canada."

"We called it our 'oxygen,'" recalls Masse, now minister of communications in Ottawa. "Thanks to this glorious era, we saw the

emergence of great French-Canadian engineering firms like Lavalin." These firms grew rapidly out of contracts awarded in French
Africa.

(One of history's little ironies is that after his retirement from
politics, Trudeau was not above representing Lavalin's interests as
a private emissary on the firm's behalf in places like the Soviet
Union, China, and Thailand, as he did during the summer of
1989.)

In January 1970, Marcel Masse was invited to give a speech at
the university of Louvain in Belgium. It was a high-minded speech
—in keeping with the setting and the minister's personality—on the
respective roles of Quebec and Canada in international affairs.
Masse used the occasion to remind his audience of a series of incidents that had punctuated the relationship between Ottawa, Quebec, and Brussels, pointing out that the friction between Quebec and
big brother in Ottawa was not limited to relations with Paris. The
Union nationale minister went so far as to question Ottawa's ability
to represent French Canadians, since Ottawa also had to take into
consideration the interests of Canada's English majority.

On January 23, 1970, Pierre Trudeau set a historic precedent
that may be unique in the annals of federal-provincial relations: he
took the trouble to write Quebec Premier Jean-Jacques Bertrand a
personal letter, warning him about his young minister's crypto-
separatist tendencies.

It is interesting that Pierre Trudeau's dislike of France, and the
tasteless jokes by which he expressed it, was not widely shared by
his fellow Quebec MPs. Was it the influence of the Canadian diplomatic community — still very British in manner and orientation
at the time—or was it a personal obsession on the prime minister's
part? Whatever it was, it certainly embarrassed Gérard Pelletier,
who was named ambassador to Paris seven years later.

"I don't understand how Trudeau could treat the subject of relations with France so carelessly," Pelletier wrote in his journal. "If all
he does is make jokes (and God knows, they're easy to make), he's
giving the impression that France-Quebec relations are unimportant.
When Pierre talks about France seriously, knowing the way he
thinks, I'll be happy. But I don't understand the insensitivity he's
displaying in this matter, or the contempt he's showing for other
people's feelings. Maybe he's giving in to his impatience . . . "

What bothered Trudeau, in fact, was that this "oxygen" that Quebec was breathing in Europe and in Africa was feeding the nationalist flame. When it finally went too far, he sounded a warning to foreign governments: "Hands off!" "Do I tell de Gaulle that he has an untenable constitutional regime in Martinique?" asked Trudeau.

When the federation of St. Jean Baptiste societies came out squarely in favour of Quebec independence, Trudeau warned foreign diplomats in Canada, asking them not to participate in the traditional June 24 parade.

By the end of the summer of 1969, Pierre Trudeau thought that his troubles were over. Jean Lesage had resigned, and the opportunity arose for the prime minister of Canada to choose his next Quebec counterpart. He was determined to seize it.

Of all the candidates in the race to succeed Lesage — Robert Bourassa, Pierre Laporte, and Claude Wagner — Pierre Laporte was probably closest to Trudeau and Pelletier; their friendship went back to the days of *Cité libre*. But Laporte, a minister in the Lesage government, had become a "nationalist."

Pierre Trudeau had already met Robert Bourassa informally at Carl Goldenberg's house (Goldenberg playing the go-between once again). At the time, Bourassa, a young economist, was working as an adviser to a Quebec commission on fiscal matters. They had also met at a federal Liberal conference in Kingston, Ontario. However, the two didn't really know each other very well.

Robert Bourassa had a bad reputation among federal Liberals. When he was close to René Lévesque, Bourassa had tried until the last minute, during a series of discussions in the basement of his home, to keep Lévesque in the Liberal family. When the Quebec Liberal party was oscillating between Paul Gérin-Lajoie's "special status" and René Lévesque's "sovereignty-association," he stayed dangerously perched on the fence. "He's driving us crazy," said Raymond Garneau, Lesage's chief of staff. "We don't know where he's going." Bourassa finally committed himself, but not quickly enough to suit federal big brother.

When Pierre Trudeau presented a white paper on federal spending power, Robert Bourassa made some disturbing comments. The young member of the National Assembly for Mercier spoke of a "reorganization of powers," particularly in the area of family allowances. "I am ready to see what we can take from the Pandora's box of federal spending power that Mr. Trudeau has had the nerve to open," he said. "But Quebec Liberals must be prepared to push the logic of federalism to its limits, and some of them may well catch their federal counterparts off guard."

"What's that young whippersnapper trying to do?" said Trudeau.

In Ottawa, Louis de Gonzague Giguère had settled into the Senate and was overseeing the federal party's Quebec affairs on a full-time basis. "Robert is a little young, he's still learning," the Senator told Jean Marchand.

Two of the three "wise men" were already becoming restless in Ottawa. Gérard Pelletier was considering not running again and was being mentioned for the Paris embassy. Jean Marchand, who had always dreamed of a career in Quebec politics, was making himself available.

Pierre Trudeau himself admitted that his Quebec lieutenant was seriously thinking of leaving him in 1969 to join the Quebec Liberal leadership contest. "Marchand would have liked to have been a candidate himself," he said some years later. "And if we could rewrite history, I suppose it would have changed the course of history. But we were still pretty weak in Ottawa . . . We just couldn't dispense with Marchand. That's why we tried to hold him back when the crucial moment might have been for him to do it. The timing was off."

In fact, the polls taken by the federal Liberals were harsh and irrefutable: Quebeckers wanted a leader who would stand up to Ottawa, someone reassuring, who promised economic prosperity and political stability.

Quebeckers were also, no doubt, fed up with having their premiers die in office. It appeared that age was a decisive factor in the eyes of the electorate. All of a sudden Robert Bourassa's thirty-five years became an advantage, against older men like Jean Marchand, Pierre Laporte, Paul Gérin-Lajoie, Claude Wagner, or anyone else.

"We tried hard to beat you, Robert," Marchand himself told Bourassa in 1970. "But we knew the lie of the land and saw that we didn't stand a chance. We were bound to lose."

"I suppose the federal Liberals had doubts about the depth of my federalist convictions," says Bourassa today.

Trudeau, being a good sport, congratulated Bourassa on his victory at the convention. "He was cordial, nothing more," Bourassa recalled.

In any case, an election was soon called, and the federal Liberals rolled up their sleeves. Better a slightly "lukewarm" federalist than a hard-line nationalist like Jean-Jacques Bertrand. Especially since some of Bertrand's ministers like Mario Beaulieu and Marcel Masse were threatening Quebec independence if Ottawa failed to come up with the several million dollars that Quebec was demanding.

Against all expectations, the Union nationale collapsed, and the Parti québécois took its place as the official opposition and began gaining in the polls. There was panic in Ottawa, and the federal government decided they had to get involved. For the first time — but certainly not the last time, for it was merely a rehearsal for what would come after 1976 — federal members began going around Quebec with a brochure, entitled *What's New?*, which listed in detail every federal expenditure in Quebec.

Twelve hours before the polls opened, Pierre Trudeau himself went on television to talk about Quebec's place in Confederation.

And down Highway 401, between Montreal and Toronto, rolled a convoy of Brinks trucks, in case anyone had missed the message.

"It got a little heated," said the Quebec MPs, breathing a sigh of relief as the Liberals took seventy-two seats in the 108-seat legislature.

Trudeau was cautious in his response to the election of a Liberal government in Quebec and a premier who believed in "profitable federalism." "It will be the end of blackmail politics," he said hopefully. "I have the feeling that the dialogue will be more polite, rather than a dialogue based on threats . . . "

But as the euphoria of the moment began to subside, it was replaced by fresh worries. "The problem now," said Marchand, "is that to vote against the Quebec Liberal government, you have to vote for the separatist opposition."

René Lévesque certainly had every reason to claim a moral victory. Six months earlier, Trudeau had dismissed the Parti québécois as an upstart rump, making a joke with the party's name (Parti-Q or *"particule,"* a derogatory diminutive) and freely predicting that it would never elect a single member. Yet here was the PQ with 24 percent of the vote and seven seats in the National Assembly. The all-powerful Union nationale had to make do with 20 percent, and the Créditistes took 12 percent. In other words, the dissatisfied vote was now going to the Parti québécois.

From the spring of 1970, the PQ became Ottawa's arch-enemy. Even when Bourassa reached the zenith of his glory in the next election three years later, winning 102 of the legislature's 108 seats, Trudeau wouldn't stop talking about the separatists. It was not hard to understand why.

All during the late 1960s the federal Liberal rhetoric itself contributed to the deterioration of the social climate in Quebec. "The situation in Quebec has reached a stage at which the disorder that reigns is comparable to the civil war in Northern Ireland," Trudeau told a group of Liberals. "The violent climate is the product of the political debates of the past ten years," he said, referring to the St. Leonard language riots after the Union nationale introduced a Bill 63 forcing immigrants to attend French classes. "Now imagine what Montreal would be in an independent Quebec. It's not a pretty picture."

"Don't let yourselves be pushed around," the member for Mount-Royal told his anglophone constituents from Hampstead. "We're not going to let a small bunch of terrorists push us around." A few months later, in a speech to the Montreal B'nai B'rith society, he flatly advised his Jewish audience to "get off the fence and stand up for your rights."

"It takes a Chicken Little like Trudeau to stir up the Jews when they're already nervous," fulminated René Lévesque. "It comes down to insinuating that we're all racists and anti-Semites, that we're a threat to them. It's a low blow, the subliminal slander of a hypocritical rabble-rouser."

"I can even sympathize with the nationalism of yesteryear, because it was a defensive nationalism," sighed Trudeau nostalgically. "It was the phenomenon of a small, besieged people defending itself as best it could . . . "

In 1970, Quebec nationalism was not hunkered down in a defensive posture any more. It was on the march. Bourassa was talking about "cultural sovereignty." And on election night, on April 29, René Lévesque sniffed the air at the jam-packed Paul Sauvé arena and said, "I smell gunpowder."

Part Four

"We Are Going to Make History" (1970-1981)

"Because force is just when it is necessary."
Machiavelli

16

The October Crisis

Sunday, October 19, 1969. The leader of the Liberal Party of Canada was telling three thousand of the party faithful gathered at the Queen Elizabeth Hotel in Montreal: "No crisis will find us absent from any part of Canada, particularly not from Quebec." Pierre Laporte, the member of the National Assembly for Chambly, was among those attending the fund-raising dinner.

Friday, October 24, 1969. Pierre Trudeau tells the House of Commons that he will not let himself be impressed by "Robin Hoods and revolutionaries disguised as *taxi drivers* . . . We will use the powers bestowed upon us to ensure respect for the law."

Monday, October 5, 1970. At about 6:30 a.m., Marc Carbonneau arrives at a Diamond taxi stand at the corner of St. Denis Street and St. Joseph Boulevard in Montreal. At 8:20 a.m. two armed men push a British diplomat into the back seat of the taxi parked in front of his home.

Saturday, October 17, 1970. Shortly before midnight, the phone rings at the Simard residence in Sorel, where Robert Bourassa is spending the weekend with his in-laws. The body of Quebec's deputy premier, Pierre Laporte, has been found in the trunk of a green Chevrolet, licence number 9J-2420.

Twenty years later, the full story has yet to be written about this "crisis" that the authorities chastely call "the events of October."

Even before he was sworn in as prime minister, the RCMP began devoting more energy and manpower to ensuring Pierre Trudeau's safety than they had deployed for any of his predecessors. Trudeau readily provoked people, and sometimes the reactions were excessive, particularly in Quebec, where the bombs had started going off. As party leader during an election campaign, Trudeau liked to mix with the crowds. Fond of his self-image as a "brawler," he would sometimes brush off his bodyguards with an irritated gesture.

On June 4, 1968, the RCMP announced that "following the assassination of Robert Kennedy, the prime minister's security has been considerably reinforced." On June 23, several newsrooms got calls from people claiming to be with the FLQ who announced that Pierre Trudeau would be assassinated during the St. Jean Baptiste Day parade. Jean-Paul Gilbert, Montreal's police chief, informed the RCMP, as they were responsible for protecting the prime minister and the diplomats who had been invited to sit on the reviewing stand as guests of honour. Neither the premier of Quebec nor his justice minister nor the Quebec provincial police were told. No one approached the St. Jean Baptiste Society or the parade organizers about changing their plans.

On February 14, 1969, Pierre Elliott Trudeau attended the winter carnival festivities in Quebec City. The night before, during a reception at the Reform Club, Jean Marchand told a small group of people that there had been a death threat against the prime minister. "I got an anonymous call telling me they were going to put twenty-five bullets in his head," he said. The minister added that one thousand policemen had been assigned to protect Trudeau during the carnival. "We can't take any chances," said Marchand. "We don't want another Dallas on our hands."

The minister later denied he had said this. It was a private occasion and his conversation was perhaps influenced by the generous flow of cocktails that evening. But what is certain is that from that moment on, paranoia increasingly pervaded the newspapers. And the police made themselves more and more visible. At the carnival's St. Valentine's ball on Friday night, RCMP agents surrounded Trudeau when he hit the dance floor with the carnival queen, holding back the other dancers. The next day he was in his home riding of Mount-Royal, where another police spokesman made allusions to "special precautions." At a news conference during the days preceding the first anniversary of the St. Jean Baptiste parade riot, the reporters flatly asked the prime minister: "Do you feel you could be assassinated in Quebec?"

For months now the police had been leaking information about the extraordinary security measures surrounding the prime minister, and reporters began falling more and more under the spell of a political terrorist psychosis.

The incidents piled up throughout 1969. A police strike in Montreal turned into a riot on October 7, and the Quebec government asked for help from the army to restore order. Pierre Trudeau was sympathetic: "The Montreal police have a difficult job," he said. "Of late they have been subjected to criminal violence and political violence. They have been harassed and treated like the Gestapo. It is understandable that they would want to know what place they have in society."

At the same time, verbal violence was becoming increasingly common. "The greatest artisan of violence in Quebec is Mr. Trudeau," declared the Ligue d'Action nationale, calling Trudeau's statements "extremist." "This is how heads of state become oppressors," charged Patrick Allen, the LAN spokesman. "They use the violence they themselves provoke to justify the creation of a police state."

At the time, "the Events" were still fifteen months away.

"I'm tired of being insulted for everything and nothing," declared Jérôme Proulx, the "sovereignist" member of the National Assembly for St. Jean. And the Confederation of National Trade Unions was now talking about Trudeau's "intellectual terrorism."

One year to the day before Pierre Laporte's death, René Lévesque took a run at Jean Marchand, who made a habit of linking terrorist agitation with the independence movement in general. "As soon as there's a broken window — and often it's a lot more serious than that — it's the separatists in English and the independentists in French. It's factitious propaganda, considering that we've been working like dogs for more than a year to promote the need for change in a democratic manner, maybe even to be a lightning rod, as much as we can, against violence."

Was it a hunch? A sudden awareness that things were going too far? On Friday, October 2, Trudeau was touring Quebec's north shore. "Canada," he told a thousand Quebeckers assembled in the Sept-Iles arena, "is neither trap nor treason nor swindle. It is a hope, a promise, an ambitious challenge that we can take up only

if we believe, if we find within ourselves enough passion and confidence, enough energy to put an end to quarrels and age-old secular
animosities and to work together, hand in hand, like men and like
human beings."

Pierre Elliott Trudeau had already responded to the FLQ manifesto forty-eight hours earlier. But it was too late by then. The
manifesto had been written days before, and it had now been
printed. Thirty-five men and women, of whom seven were prepared to take part in political kidnappings, had already gone
underground.

The political climate was so poisonous that nothing further
could surprise public opinion in Canada. On September 28, the
RCMP commissioner authorized the formation of a special section,
"exclusively assigned to deal with problems related to separatist/
terrorist [*sic*] activities in Quebec."

Pierre Trudeau's personality and his prejudices about Quebec
explain the rest.

His contempt for the army was well known. For him a uniform
was a uniform; sending the army to reinforce Montreal would be
akin to deploying the Corps of Commissionaires, the aging war
veterans who guard the doors on Parliament Hill. He did not fore-
see the impact of what was for him a simple operation intended to
maintain order.

The jurist deep inside Pierre Trudeau always made him respect
a strict separation of powers. He never wanted to meddle in legal
and police matters, particularly not during a crisis. But this time
he would systematically close his eyes, even if it made the civil
libertarian in him uncomfortable.

When he was a "*Cité libriste*" he had thought that democracy
was not well anchored in Quebec. Had he not written in 1962 that
"democracy has just been born in Quebec"? And he added, evoking
Hitler's rise to power: "It is impossible to say whether democracy
has been born alive, or what its chances are for survival." Trudeau
didn't have much difficulty convincing himself that democratic
power was seriously threatened.

Neither Trudeau nor his ministers had much confidence in Robert Bourassa. They thought he was too young and sometimes irres-
olute. At the height of the crisis, Marc Lalonde would exclaim
before witnesses: "That Bourassa, he has no balls!"

The October Crisis unfolded in four distinct phases, an evolution which can be explained both by the nature of the events, and by the personalities of the people involved.

1. For one week, from the time British diplomat James Cross was kidnapped until Quebec Justice Minister Jérôme Choquette's refusal to negotiate with the kidnappers, the federal government was in control of events, Ottawa being solely responsible for the safety of foreign diplomats.

2. When Pierre Laporte was kidnapped, Robert Bourassa and his ministers became personally involved. The premier, the prime minister, and certain ministers in both governments had a direct emotional involvement: Laporte had been Gérard Pelletier's boss at *Le Devoir* and he was also a member of the original *Cité libre* group.

3. At the beginning of the second week it became obvious that the police were in over their heads, that the investigation was lagging, and that negotiations with the FLQ were going nowhere. The RCMP, which maintained excellent relations with the senior brass in the Montreal police force, indicated its readiness to send in reinforcements. Rumours of a coup d'état grew steadily.

4. The call for the army and the imposition of the War Measures Act, two events which tend to be confused with each other today, though they were strictly distinct from one another, had become inevitable by this time.

During the hours that followed the James Cross kidnapping on October 5, Trudeau himself spoke with Bourassa by telephone.

"It's serious, and we're worried. We have to coordinate our actions," he said.

During the following two weeks the normal channels of communication between Quebec and Ottawa were modified. In keeping with tradition (and unlike Brian Mulroney's method today), Trudeau generally did not deal directly with his provincial counterparts. Instead it was his principal secretary, Marc Lalonde, who handled liaison with the premiers.

During the crisis, however, Trudeau and Bourassa communicated directly, several times a day. Marc Lalonde, meanwhile, was in direct contact with Julien Chouinard, the secretary to the provincial cabinet. And it was the minister of external affairs, Mitchell Sharp, rather than Justice Minister John Turner or Solicitor General George McIlraith (who was in charge of the RCMP), who dealt with Jérôme Choquette: at the time the affair was still being treated as a "diplomatic incident."

This explains why Robert Bourassa went ahead with a scheduled trip to New York after the Cross kidnapping. Not going would only have served to dramatize the events back home.

Of the demands put forward by James Cross's kidnappers, there were two which, for Trudeau, were non-negotiable: the release of twenty-three "political prisoners" and the release of the name of the informer who had betrayed FLQ members to the police in June. The imposition of a $500,000 "voluntary tax" and the rehiring of the Lapalme postal drivers were two other conditions that were never seriously considered.

On the other hand, Ottawa immediately contacted the governments of Cuba and Algeria, where the kidnappers could be taken if they released their prisoner. And there was heated discussion in cabinet about broadcasting the FLQ manifesto over Radio-Canada as the liberation cell had demanded.

This gave the appearance that Ottawa was prepared to negotiate, and the reading of the manifesto became inevitable after Louis Fournier, a reporter for the Montreal radio station CKAC, got hold of a copy and began broadcasting excerpts on Wednesday night.

Ottawa discreetly set up a special group — the Strategic Operation Centre — which included two of the young Turks from Quebec who had played a major role in Pierre Trudeau's rise to power. They were Jean-Pierre Goyer, parliamentary secretary to Mitchell Sharp and then to Trudeau himself, and Jim Davey, who was Marc Lalonde's assistant in the Prime Minister's Office. Both were under direct orders from Lalonde. The group was assigned to analyze the political situation in Quebec, and one of their "antennas" was Gérard Pelletier, who stayed in Montreal during most of the crisis. Afterwards, the group would conduct a lengthy witch hunt in the ranks of Quebec society.

Pierre Trudeau was personally against broadcasting the FLQ manifesto on the national television network, but the diplomats at External Affairs, no doubt acting out of a sense of solidarity with one of their own, insisted. Trudeau has since been criticized for what was widely interpreted as an error. "He showed that he was ready to make quite humiliating concessions," said Robert Bourassa.

The manifesto repeated, in inflammatory prose, all the frustrations of the Quebec labour movement. It enumerated the labour conflicts that were dragging on in the province and pointed the finger at some of the big bosses, like Steinberg, Paul Desmarais, the Bronfmans, the Simards (Robert Bourassa's in-laws), and so forth. The feeling that that spring's provincial election had been "stolen" from the Parti québécois came through in references to the Brinks caper (when trucks were rushing down Highway 401, the night before the election, to scare voters) and to the "big shots" in Westmount and the "Town of Mount Royal."

But above all, the FLQ vented its contempt for the political leaders of the day: "Rémi Popol, the cat-o'-nine-tails (Rémi Paul had been the justice minister in the Union nationale administration), Drapeau the dog, Bourassa the Simard canary, Trudeau the faggot . . ."

It was the two final paragraphs which had the greatest impact on public opinion:

"Make your own revolution in your neighbourhoods and in your workplaces," declared the FLQ. "In the four corners of Quebec, those who have been treated disdainfully as lousy French and alcoholics are vigorously taking up the fight."

To the federal government's great surprise, there was a wave of sympathy for the ideas put forward by the FLQ, particularly among young people and union activists. In the heat of the excitement, the francophone media betrayed a certain complicity with the kidnappers, who fed them with "scoops" by sending their communiqués directly to reporters.

The FLQ had set Saturday, October 10, 6:00 p.m., as the deadline for the execution of James Cross. That morning Jérôme Choquette was prepared to offer the ultimate compromise by resorting to a tactic common to Crown prosecutors throughout Canada: he would recommend that a number of the so-called political prisoners be given parole.

But Pierre Trudeau resisted for two reasons. For one thing, he didn't want to hear any talk of "political prisoners." To him members of the FLQ were "common criminals" and they had already received one favour too many by having their manifesto broadcast over the state airwaves.

"But above all," said Robert Bourassa, "there were things on which he didn't want to negotiate, and I have to say I agreed with him. He was particularly intransigent on the principle of not giving way on anything that went beyond the separation of powers, by which I mean taking measures that would affect the functioning of the justice system."

While brothers Jacques and Paul Rose, and Francis Simard, and Bernard Lortie, members of a second FLQ cell (Chénier), waited in their hideout in St. Hubert, several hours of dramatic negotiations ensued between Quebec and Ottawa, complicated by the fact that Bourassa was caught between two planes in New York.

At 5:30 p.m., Jérôme Choquette announced the governments' position on television. It was now evident that there would be no more concessions other than safe conduct for the kidnappers.

At 6:00 p.m. Pierre Laporte went out in the street to throw a football with his eighteen-year-old son Claude in front of their home on Robitaille Street in St. Lambert. He seemed to be unaware of the tense talks between Ottawa and Quebec, and the fact that he was casually playing in the street showed to what extent the kidnapping was still being taken fairly lightly. For Quebec, the Cross kidnapping was an isolated incident which had embarrassed the federal government more than anyone, since it involved a foreign diplomat, and thereby tarnished Canada's international reputation.

At 6:18 p.m., the crisis took a whole new turn. This time a Quebec minister had been kidnapped, and everyone felt directly involved.

Robert Bourassa, who had returned to Quebec incognito by this time, was immediately informed of Laporte's kidnapping. He asked Julien Chouinard and the assistant cabinet secretary, Paul Tellier, to discreetly call the cabinet ministers to meet in Montreal. "We didn't want to add to the panic by organizing a convoy of ministers between Quebec and Montreal," explained Tellier, who drove to Montreal on Sunday morning in a car with two ministers, Bernard Pinard and Gérard D. Lévesque.

The cabinet met on Sunday afternoon at Hydro-Québec's headquarters, where Robert Bourassa had an office that he used when he was in Montreal. Everyone was in a state of shock as a result of the latest developments, and the general feeling now was that they were dealing with a well-organized plot. One kidnapping could be the action of a few extremists. Two kidnappings were something else entirely.

In mid-afternoon, Marcel Saint-Aubin, the Montreal Urban Community police chief, arrived at the Hydro building with "an important message for Mr. Bourassa." Paul Tellier left the cabinet room and opened the envelope. It contained a personal message from Pierre Laporte. "Read it aloud," Bourassa told Tellier, to avoid having to circulate the note around the table.

> My dear Robert,
> I am convinced that I am writing the most important letter of my life. . . . We are in the presence of a well-organized uprising which will end only with the freeing of the political prisoners. After me there will be a third and a fourth and a twentieth. Better to act right away and thereby avoid a blood bath. . . . It should be done quickly because I do not see why, by taking more time, you should allow me to die slowly in this place where I am being held. Decide if I will live or die. . . .

Ten months earlier, Pierre Laporte had been a candidate in the leadership race against Robert Bourassa. Some of the ministers present at Hydro-Québec that afternoon were very close to him. Bernard Pinard and Gérard D. Lévesque were particularly distraught.

Everyone was aware of the gravity of the situation: the life of a friend and colleague hung in the balance. Remarkably — and it would be so throughout the crisis, during which no one resigned — the ministers reached a unanimous agreement.

That evening Pierre Trudeau himself felt the full impact of the drama being played out in Montreal. "But," said Bourassa, "he understood that my position was more difficult than his."

Finally the premier of Quebec emerged from the caucus meeting with a statement that was a masterpiece of ambiguity. The CBC and *Le Devoir* concluded that he was ready to negotiate, while Radio-Canada commented: "Bourassa has said no to the terrorists."

In Ottawa, Marc Lalonde's Strategic Operation Centre and the RCMP moved to take control of the operation. Their resolve to do so was heightened by an event that appeared quite innocuous to those familiar with the habits of Claude Ryan, publisher of *Le Devoir*, but which was blown out of all proportion in Ottawa and in the minds of Montreal's municipal leaders.

On Sunday afternoon Ryan called a meeting of his closest colleagues at *Le Devoir* for a "high-level reflection," as he often did in grave circumstances, on what the paper's editorial line should be. He had already spoken to Robert Bourassa and Lucien Saulnier, chairman of the Montreal Urban Community, and had determined that the authorities were in a state of "utter confusion."

At the meeting with his colleagues, Ryan put forward three hypotheses: (1) Bourassa would yield to pressure from Ottawa and call for the immediate imposition of the War Measures Act. (2) Bourassa would show himself incapable of dealing with the situation, and the formation of a provisional government composed of representatives from all parties and different elements of Quebec society would have to be considered. (3) Bourassa would opt for a negotiated solution and stay in control of the situation. Consciously or otherwise, the three scenarios were based on a single premise: that Bourassa was the weak link.

As was often the case, Ryan did not limit his musings to his circle of *Le Devoir* collaborators, but spoke of his "hypotheses" to Lucien Saulnier, chairman of the Montreal Urban Community and responsible for the community's police forces. In less than twenty-four hours Ottawa had been informed that Claude Ryan was openly discussing the formation of a "parallel" government.

The only one who did not believe in this "plot" was Gérard Pelletier, and with good reason: he had run a newspaper himself, and he was quite familiar with Ryan's habits. In any case, the next morning the publisher of *Le Devoir* appeared to be satisfied with Bourassa's overtures, for he wrote an editorial fully supporting the Quebec government position. The following Thursday, Ryan even endorsed the decision to call in the troops. "The police forces have been on twenty-four-hour call for two weeks now, and are on the brink of total exhaustion. The government of Quebec . . . has decided that its duty is to call out the armed forces. And it was right to do so."

But the rumour of a coup d'état did not surprise Pierre Trudeau unduly: he had always feared that Quebec's "fragile" democracy could be swept away by a "fascist" group. And Trudeau, who had no reason to like Claude Ryan (Ryan did not support his leadership and was often critical of his government), remembered that he had once worked for the Catholic Action movement, which had mixed feelings about national-socialist movements in Europe.

※   ※   ※

Negotiations began between Robert Demers, who was close to the Liberal party and a personal friend of Bourassa, and Robert Lemieux, the lawyer for several of the FLQ militants who had been arrested prior to the kidnappings. "The reports I was getting from Robert Demers indicated that the negotiations weren't very serious," recalled Bourassa.

Moreover, it appeared that the police were incapable of dealing with the situation. Every time the provincial police wanted to make a search they had to inform the premier, because the kidnappers had said they would kill Laporte if the police intervened. One day, after Bourassa had given provincial police director Maurice Saint-Pierre permission to raid a house where "suspects had been seen with rifles," it turned out that the "suspects" were merely a group of law-abiding hunters just back from the bush. Instead of admitting their mistakes, the heads of the provincial police and the Montreal police force reinforced the conspiracy theory to explain their problems. "Look, Mr. Bourassa," the senior policemen kept saying, "we're up against a brick wall. They must be really well organized if we can't find them!"

Meanwhile, the police forces had been keeping a night-and-day watch over public buildings, the homes of politicians and their relatives, and the businessmen directly named in the FLQ statements, and they were showing signs of exhaustion.

On Thursday, October 15, the Quebec government officially asked for army support. In keeping with the National Defence Act, a combat regiment based in Valcartier, near Quebec City, was dispatched to Montreal.

Meanwhile, the proclamation of the War Measures Act had been discussed in the greatest possible secrecy since the beginning of the week. "After two or three incidents in which it was clear the police had no idea where to turn, I decided it was time to act," said Bourassa.

On Wednesday, the premier had warned Ryan that there would be a "small turn" towards greater force. René Lévesque was also aware of the imminent recourse to the War Measures Act. The same evening, the PQ leader assembled a group of fifteen people at the Holiday Inn to study the text of a joint statement.

The Cross-Laporte affair is, above all, a Quebec drama . . .

The rigid, almost militaristic attitude of Ottawa, in our opinion, threatens to reduce the Quebec government to tragic impotence.

This is why, leaving aside the differing attitudes we have on a number of subjects, conscious only of being Quebeckers and thereby vitally involved, we offer our most pressing support for negotiations leading to the exchange of the two hostages for the political prisoners. And this against all obstruction from outside Quebec, which would require the positive concurrence of the federal government.

There were those who detected both Claude Ryan's apprehensions and his style in this statement. The appeal from René Lévesque, the leaders of the large labour centrals, and Alfred Rouleau, the widely revered chairman of the Desjardins credit union movement, generated a great wave of sympathy in the population. Students went on strike and occupied administration offices in universities and junior colleges.

A few hours after the army was deployed around Montreal's major public buildings, a crowd of three thousand assembled at the Paul Sauvé arena.

They were supporters of FRAP, a left-wing coalition that stood as the only organized opposition against Jean Drapeau in that fall's civic election. "The FLQ is every one of you," declared Pierre Vallières, who had been invited to address the rally. "It is every Quebecker who stands on his feet."

The crowd leapt to its feet, chanting and giving the clenched-fist salute: "F-L-Q! F-L-Q! F-L-Q!"

"I had real reason to believe that the inclination of opinion leaders in Quebec to obey their legitimate government was crumbling," Trudeau explained some years later. "They signed this manifesto saying that the Quebec government and the federal government should free the 'political prisoners'. . . . To my dying day I'll think that's where the turning point lay. To me, that is, I'd almost say, the dying shame of very eminent people in Quebec, to sign that manifesto."

In fact, the federal government did not wait for prominent Quebeckers to sign their statement before acting. On Tuesday, October 13, fully forty-eight hours before Bourassa announced the "small turn," Trudeau had informed the Soviet ambassador in Canada that he would have to cancel a trip to Moscow scheduled for the following week. And the RCMP had already begun drawing up lists of "suspects to be arrested." On Wednesday, October 14, the federal police force asked for the lists to be reviewed by the cabinet. Trudeau designated Marchand and Pelletier to go over them on the federal government's behalf, while in Quebec City, the task fell to provincial ministers: Social Affairs Minister Claude Castonguay and Finance Minister Raymond Garneau.

The first list drawn up in Ottawa included 158 names. In Quebec the Quebec police added another fifty. By the end of the week the list had grown to 465 people who would be detained.

"I don't know any of these people. I can't make head nor tail of this," Raymond Garneau told provincial police chief Maurice Saint-Pierre as he looked over the lists.

"I remember that there were certain names that made me raise my eyebrows," said Robert Bourassa. "I remember that Trudeau was wondering about some of them too. We talked about it." (Pierre Trudeau confirmed a few years later that among other names he was astonished to see that of singer Pauline Julien on the list. Bourassa remembers that one of the names that made his eyebrows twitch was that of poet Gérald Godin.) But Trudeau and Bourassa did agree on one point: there was no question of interfering in police business. "It's not up to me to pick the names," Bourassa told the heads of the provincial police force. "Carry out your duties and come up with proof."

In the early afternoon of Thursday, October 15, the Quebec government officially asked for the proclamation of the War Measures Act. But Ottawa disagreed with the way the request was drafted. The day before Jean Marchand had come to Quebec and secretly met with Bourassa at the Clarendon Hotel, across the street from Quebec's city hall. "I wondered why we couldn't just meet in my office," Bourassa recalled. "But Marchand told me, 'Robert, this is serious.'"

According to Marc Lalonde, Trudeau was not personally in favour of the imposition of the War Measures Act. Yet he became the only prime minister to invoke it outside of wartime. "If that's what you want," Trudeau told Bourassa, "you'll have to ask me formally and say that you are faced with a state of potential insurrection."

Marc Lalonde flew to Quebec City and met with Bourassa in the provincial government's Executive Council Office in an annex to the National Assembly building. The letter was negotiated by Lalonde and Julien Chouinard, and jointly drafted by the federal and Quebec governments. It was signed first by Robert Bourassa in Quebec City, then by Jean Drapeau and Lucien Saulnier, whom Lalonde visited later that night in Montreal.

Nevertheless, Bourassa offered the kidnappers a final compromise. The number of jailed FLQ members who would get a "favourable" recommendation to the parole board would be increased from five to twenty. He also promised that a plane would be ready to take the kidnappers out of the country as soon as they released their hostages. He gave the FLQ until 3:00 a.m. on Friday, October 16, to respond.

At 3.30 a.m. a Privy Council officer woke up Governor General Roland Michener and had him sign the proclamation of the War Measures Act.

"The most pessimistic say that there are three thousand members of the FLQ," Jean Marchand told the House of Commons by way of explaining the government's decision. "We know one thing for certain: that an organization exists that has thousands of guns, rifles, machine guns, and bombs and close to two thousand pounds of dynamite—enough to blow up downtown Montreal."

It took another few years before Gérard Pelletier admitted that the pool of FLQ extremists numbered "between forty and fifty people, maybe a hundred."

Jean-Luc Pépin would try to explain, from his point of view, how panic had seized the Trudeau entourage in Ottawa: "I think we were all thinking about ourselves. We were a very small group: Trudeau, Pelletier, Marchand, Lalonde, Chrétien, myself, and a few civil servants, maybe fifty in all, committed to bringing off a revolution in Ottawa. We were a 'revolutionary' group. We were also well-organized, though our means weren't the same."

Less than thirty hours after the imposition of the War Measures Act, Pierre Laporte's body was found in the trunk of a green Chevrolet, parked near the St-Hubert airport on the south shore, only a short ride from where he had been abducted.

James Cross was freed on December 3, and his kidnappers took refuge in Cuba.

On December 28, members of the Chénier cell, who had jointly declared their responsibility for Pierre Laporte's death, were arrested near the village of St. Luc, also on Montreal's south shore.

On January 1, 1971, the last of the suspects arrested in the sweep that had followed the proclamation of the War Measures Act were freed, with the exception of their "leaders": Michel Chartrand, Charles Gagnon, Robert Lemieux, and Pierre Vallières.

On January 4, 1971, the army withdrew to its barracks. Neither Pierre Trudeau's nor Robert Bourassa's popularity suffered as a result of the October crisis. The two governments had collaborated throughout, and it is difficult to say whether or not one was manipulating the other. "There may have been differences of style, but not of substance," said Bourassa.

On the other hand, both leaders sustained irreparable damage to their reputations, and two decades later they are still paying the political price. On the international level, Pierre Trudeau's reputation as a champion of civil liberties was badly tarnished. And Quebec acquired a reputation as an unstable region best avoided by prudent investors. Within the province, Robert Bourassa came away with the image, often unjustly invoked, of a leader who was too weak to protect his "sovereignty" against Ottawa's strong-arm tactics.

As for Pierre Trudeau, his actions during the crisis cut him off irrevocably from at least one part of Quebec. "He is our biggest peacetime war criminal," said one of his former colleagues from the Rassemblement démocratique. "They fabricated a crisis," charged René Lévesque. "It was coldly calculated by Trudeau's group in Ottawa . . ."

"Just watch me," Trudeau had told a reporter at the height of the crisis when asked how far he was prepared to go. He also let it be known that he had no time for "bleeding hearts" and "wet hens."

"Mr. Trudeau is a statesman, not a sentimentalist," Robert Bourassa still says.

17

Quebec Scores Points

During the early months of 1971, while Canada was recovering from "the Events," a number of new faces appeared on the Canadian political scene. It was a sort of changing of the guard, though no one noticed it as such at the time.

In February, Bill Davis replaced John Robarts as premier of Ontario. In March, New Democrat Allan Blakeney brought down the curtain on a seven-year Liberal reign in Saskatchewan. And before the summer was out, a certain Peter Lougheed took over the premier's chair in Alberta.

On March 4, Pierre Elliott Trudeau and Margaret Sinclair were married in a private ceremony at St. Stephen's Church in Vancouver. On the church steps there were a few bigots who whispered knowing comments about "age difference," but there were others who suggested that this trendy prime minister would have no trouble keeping up with his young bride.

At the time, English Canada thought the identity crisis that had torn the country for the past five years was over. There was still some gnashing of teeth over the Official Languages Act, to be sure. But as a consolation there were the RCMP raids on Quebec "revolutionaries" which were occurring with increasing frequency. It made little difference if the raids were against the PQ or the FLQ; it was all the same thing.

In 1968, Canadians had implored Trudeau to settle the Quebec question once and for all. Three years later he had not only put down an apprehended "coup d'état" by the Quebec intelligentsia, but he was promising them a new constitutional agreement.

On February 9, 1971 it appeared that a breakthrough had been achieved in the constitutional negotiations that had been lagging for the past three years, ever since that day in 1968 when Canada had discovered a justice minister with steel in his spine who could put "the member for Bagot" in his place. "After a pregnancy, it is only normal that the birth should take place, and so it shall be," sighed Trudeau, inspired, no doubt, by his own impending marriage. "At the rate things were going, it looked like we might lose some of the players." Perhaps his overconfidence about his ability to deal with Quebec was prompted by the knowledge that he was up against a provincial government which had been forced to beg for help from his army and his police. In any case, Trudeau thought that once the matter was settled, no one would oppose his proposals.

But in Quebec, the nationalists in the government were digging in their heels. Claude Castonguay, Bourassa's minister of social affairs, was calling for the National Assembly to assert its "sovereignty" in the area of social policy. Jean-Paul L'Allier, the minister of communications, shored up the foundations of "cultural sovereignty" with an attempt to get jurisdiction over cable TV.

Trudeau didn't seem to be paying attention. He was busy putting the finishing touches on the "Magna Carta," the new Constitution drawn up during the summer of 1967 that would carve him out a place in the history books. "Why can't you write me a preamble like the one in the American Constitution?" he grumbled to his aides, already taking himself for the Thomas Jefferson of the Great White North.

The problem was that Jefferson, who had founded the antifederalist party, had had all the powers of a strong central government behind him. Trudeau, on the other hand, had a constitutional obligation to bargain with the provinces.

As it turned out, the greatest objection to the federal initiative was not over the preamble, which guaranteed fundamental political rights. In fact, Trudeau's proposal was almost perfect. It was remarkably generous towards the French-Canadian minority and towards Quebec. It was all there: language rights, Supreme Court reform, an amending formula with a Quebec veto, and even, as in the Meech Lake accord of the distant future, the promise of an annual conference of first ministers.

The federal bureaucrats were somewhat less optimistic than their political master. Quebec was not the only province kicking up a fuss during the preparatory meetings in the spring. Bill Davis, the new Ontario premier, himself a former education minister, was unhappy about the obligation to guarantee rights for his francophone minority.

Was Trudeau's overconfidence inspired by the success of his hard line during the October crisis? Whatever the case, Trudeau chose to play the heavy, particularly with Quebec.

He claimed what was, in effect, federal power to set up Ottawa's own social policy: old age pensions, family allowances, youth allowances and manpower training. He agreed not to invade the jurisdiction of provinces that already had programs in these areas. But if they did not, Ottawa could move into the vacuum on ninety days' notice.

The trouble was that Quebec already had some ideas of its own on the matter. A year earlier, the provincial Castonguay-Nepveu Commission had drawn up the outline of a Quebec family income policy. Some provincial civil servants, Claude Morin in particular, warned that "Trudeau's Charter" would cut into the province's room to manoeuvre in the social policy field.

Unfortunately for Trudeau, the eleven governments agreed—as they did at Meech Lake in 1987—that constitutional reform would be an all-or-nothing proposition. The new Charter would be adopted unanimously or not at all.

The first ministers scheduled a meeting in Victoria on June 14, 1971. "It is in Quebec's best interest to come to an agreement," said Trudeau. "There is a broad consensus on a range of subjects. Will it fall through if there is no agreement on certain aspects, such as the division of powers? I've no idea."

There was a feeling of euphoria in Victoria. The constitutional question was finally going to be settled, and the country could move on to serious things, like the economic woes that were piling up. Everyone seemed to be on the same wavelength, except for Quebec, which was still worried about family allowances.

During the evening of June 15, Claude Castonguay's mood became surlier by the hour. "Wacky" Bennett, the Social Credit premier of British Columbia, had commandeered a provincial ferry for a high-level reception. As everyone else swilled cocktails and munched on canapés, admiring the gorges of Juan de Fuca Strait or the comely young Mrs. Trudeau in her yellow pantsuit, Quebec's social affairs minister remained aloof, strolling around the deck with Claude Morin.

In what could have been a dress rehearsal for that other night in November 1981, the federal bureaucrats resorted to all manner of devious tricks in an effort to isolate Castonguay from his adviser and keep the Constitution afloat. Trudeau went so far as to brandish a cheque for $60 million, the amount Quebec families would stand to gain under *his* family allowance scheme.

Nothing worked. On the morning of June 16 Robert Bourassa was more hesitant than ever. This did not stop Trudeau and his ministers from letting it be understood after the conference that Quebec had given its agreement in principle to the new Charter. "That's not true," says Robert Bourassa. "I asked for ten days to reflect on it. The very fact that I asked for a delay shows that I hadn't yet made a decision."

Even so, Trudeau hoped that his colleague would force his cabinet and caucus into line, as he would have done under the circumstances. "I will evaluate the situation," Robert Bourassa promised as he left Victoria. "After all, it's barely six months since the October crisis. Nationalism is bubbling over in Quebec: I cannot take the risk of setting off another seven or eight years of political violence. The political climate doesn't allow me to take any uncalculated risks."

Bourassa's situation at home was even more precarious than it was on the shores of the Pacific. On June 22, at about 7:00 p.m., his caucus was divided down the middle, "half for, half against."

By 9:00 p.m., most of the ministers were against "the Victoria Charter" as put forward by Trudeau.

At 11:00 p.m. Robert Bourassa called Marc Lalonde. "Warn Trudeau," he said. "I'm going to meet the press, and the answer is no." Fortunately for the premier, Lalonde hung up before saying what he thought of this.

The next day, the eve of the St. Jean Baptiste Day celebrations, the premier was given a standing ovation by all members of the National Assembly. Péquistes, Unionistes, and Créditistes applauded along with the Liberals. Everyone present felt moved. It was like a stroke of revenge: Quebec had finally regained its unanimity. But ten years later it would pay dearly.

On June 24, the prime minister of Canada threw a garden party at his official summer residence at Harrington Lake. The buzz among the ministers and senior advisers was mostly about Quebec's rejection of the Victoria Charter. Pierre Trudeau himself concluded that it would never be possible to reach an agreement with Quebec. Therefore, if there was going to be a constitutional agreement, it would have to happen without Quebec.

Henceforth, the premier of Quebec would be perceived as a coward in English Canada. In 1981, Jean Chrétien would have little trouble convincing his colleagues, starting with those in Ontario and Saskatchewan, and moving on to those in the rest of English Canada, that a Quebec premier could not be taken at his word. And the federal bureaucrats made a note of the fact that it was best not to let their Quebec counterparts sow confusion among the other provincial delegations.

For Pierre Trudeau, Victoria remains the single greatest failure of his political career. "If only Quebec hadn't been so greedy," he would keep sighing.

The failure of the Victoria Charter signalled the beginning of a protracted period of guerilla warfare between Ottawa and Quebec that would continue until the election of the Parti québecois.

In the fall of 1971, Quebec demanded a seat as a participating government in the Agence de coopération culturelle et technique, an international cooperative organization whose membership includes most of the world's French-speaking countries. "It's reached the point where people are wondering if Quebeckers should have ambassadors, if they should be independent, if they should have diplomatic pennants on their limos," grumbled Trudeau.

To soothe English Canada, which had been antagonized by the Official Languages Act, Pierre Trudeau presented a white paper on multiculturalism. "This clearly contradicts the mandate of the Royal Commission on Bilingualism and Biculturalism," replied Bourassa. "It divorces culture from language. To me that sounds like a dubious proposition."

In 1972, Quebec Finance Minister Raymond Garneau lit into federal foreign investment control policy. Labour Minister Jean Cournoyer accused the federal government of being incapable of running the national ports system. He added insult to injury by doing a crude imitation of Trudeau's nasal voice in the National Assembly.

When Robert Bourassa came forward with a new federal-provincial fiscal sharing proposal, Trudeau sent him packing like a panhandler. "If you need money," he told him, "raise your taxes."

The provincial government's new immigration program angered Trudeau to the point that he came within a whisker of calling Bourassa a racist. "I hesitate to criticize any provincial government's immigration policy, whatever it may be, but I fear Quebec is less receptive to the rest of the world than other parts of Canada. That mentality has not disappeared. It stems from the eagerness of some of Quebec's new élites to make *joual* the official language."

This did nothing to deter Bourassa. A few months later, fresh from an electoral triumph that gave him 102 of the 108 seats in the National Assembly, his government introduced Bill 22, the first Quebec language law to place restrictions on the use of English in the province. In doing so, Bourassa showed little concern for big brother in Ottawa, who was in the midst of a difficult election campaign.

Since the summer of 1971, everything had gone badly for Pierre Trudeau. That August, U.S. President Richard Nixon had slapped a 10 percent surtax on all American imports. The move threatened 100,000 jobs in Canada. Trudeau could plead for "special status" all he wanted but the White House remained intransigent. There were already 700,000 unemployed in Canada, a half-baked fiscal reform initiative was going badly in Ontario, and the west was becoming increasingly reluctant to swallow any more "bilingual" cereal.

On October 30, 1972, Trudeau was virtually defeated. And Jean-Luc Pépin, his minister of industry and commerce, lost his seat, though a counting error involving a few dozen votes in the riding of Drummond made it appear he had been re-elected for a few hours. Trudeau was able to cling to power, but for the next two years he had to negotiate his every move with David Lewis's New Democrats, who became more and more demanding as time went on.

At the beginning of 1973 the international oil crisis gave Quebec a few months of respite. Alberta Premier Peter Lougheed, assisted by his energy minister, Don Getty, became the new *enfant terrible* of Confederation. With a ringing cry of "No Kuwait in Canada," the federal mandarins mounted an assault on "the blue-eyed sheik's" oil wells.

Pierre Trudeau won his majority back in the federal election on July 8, 1974, but his run of bad luck continued.

In 1975 he lost his secretary of state, Gérard Pelletier, who went to Paris, leaving behind him the shambles of an increasingly controversial language policy. John Turner defected, slamming the door behind him, and recycled himself as a conservative Bay Street businessman and Trudeau critic. James Richardson went back to Winnipeg to launch a flurry of bitter recriminations about "French power." The Sky Shops Affair, in which Senator Louis de Gonzague Giguère was accused of having reaped excessive profits from the new duty-free stores at Mirabel airport, blew up in Jean Marchand's face at a time when the transport minister was already fading as a political force in Ottawa.

Trudeau not only lost seven ministers in the space of a few months, but found that his leadership was being challenged within his own party. In a leadership review vote at the party's 1975 convention that November, 418 Liberal delegates, almost one in five, voted to oust Trudeau from the top job.

It was not surprising, then, that Pierre Trudeau was in a foul temper on March 3, 1976. When Trudeau arrived at Robert Bourassa's "bunker" on Grande Allée in Quebec City, he encountered a pack of reporters lying in wait for him. Some even had the nerve to mention the marital problems he was having at the time. He wanted to get away as quickly as possible, and when one of them asked what he and the premier would have for lunch, Trudeau shot back, without turning his head: "I don't know. It seems he eats hot dogs."

Earlier, at the airport, Trudeau had noticed a pile of copies of the magazine *L'Actualité*. The front page carried a full-colour picture of Bourassa, about to bite into a grilled hot dog. Trudeau meant it as nothing more than a harmless joke. Since then, however, Trudeau's careless hot-dog crack has been widely construed as a vicious insult by his opponents, including René Lévesque and Brian Mulroney, who have referred to it as an example of Trudeau's contempt for Quebec.

But it was another incident that really aroused "Lord" Elliott's fury. "There were a dozen other topics on the agenda," recalled Bourassa, "but all he wanted to talk about was the Constitution." With his leadership under fire within his own party and the country in the grip of escalating economic problems, Trudeau knew he would have to act quickly. One last time he wondered if he might not be able to realize his dream of "decolonizing" Canada.

"What will you do if we patriate unilaterally?" he asked Bourassa.

"It's politically unacceptable," replied Bourassa. "I wouldn't be able to explain it to the population."

Quebec's premier had more pressing things on his mind that day. The Olympic Games were scheduled to begin in Montreal in three months, the stadium was still unfinished, and the Olympic debt was skyrocketing. Again and again Bourassa tried to steer the conversation around to economic problems, but Trudeau wouldn't listen. His sole preoccupation seemed to be the Constitution.

"Listen," Bourassa finally told him, "I have enough on my hands with the Olympics, and I don't want to get into another constitutional fight right now."

"Fine! I'll prepare my speech," snapped Trudeau, throwing his napkin on the table, although they hadn't finished lunch.

Fearing the worst, Bourassa murmured in Trudeau's ear just before he was swallowed up by the elevator on his way out: "Be careful, Pierre. Watch what you say, and think of the way it's going to be interpreted by the journalists."

"Nobody takes journalists seriously," said Trudeau with a shrug.

But the whole province heard, and took it seriously . . .

That evening Trudeau addressed a convention of the federal Liberal party's Quebec wing at the Quebec City convention centre, a block from Bourassa's office. If Bourassa wanted to talk about the Olympic deficit, he would get a run for his money. In his speech Trudeau spelled out why Ottawa could not pay a share of the Games deficit, telling the assembled Liberals: "Think about it for twenty-four hours and you'll understand why. As for the premier, I'm not sure if he'll be able to understand in twenty-four hours, so I've given him three days."

Trudeau's aides wondered what was eating the boss. The Quebec press corps, engaged in a running feud with Bourassa over his attempts at news management, sniggered gleefully. The Quebec Liberals were devastated.

"Why the vicious attack, and why such arrogance?" wondered Raymond Garneau.

"That's our thanks for holding the vote against his leadership below 20 percent," said one Liberal organizer who took Trudeau's statements as a personal insult.

The next day, Marc Lalonde tendered apologies in his master's name.

Bourassa responded pragmatically: "I'd rather live with the prime minster's anger than another constitutional debate while I've got the Olympic stadium on my hands."

In Ottawa, Trudeau was stymied. He had no choice but to wait for a more opportune moment. But while he was at it, he took advantage of the Western Economic Summit in London to make discreet inquiries as to whether British Prime Minister James Callaghan would go along with a unilateral patriation move when the time came.

The Olympic flame had barely been extinguished when Trudeau was back in Quebec again. It was a more sombre visit this time; he was there for the funeral of Albanie Morin, the Liberal MP for the Quebec City riding of Louis-Hébert. Once more, Trudeau and Bourassa met, this time in secret at the Hilton Hotel. Bourassa laid out the problems he was having: his popularity was sagging, Anglo-Quebeckers were in an uproar over Bill 22, and the air traffic controller crisis was whipping nationalist sentiment into a froth. Trudeau, however, was distinctly unsympathetic. After all, if Bourassa hadn't concocted Bill 22, Quebec pilots wouldn't have had the preposterous notion of speaking French to their ground controllers.

It was as though Trudeau was thinking: "Too bad! For me, nothing is more important than patriating the Constitution. I don't intend to sacrifice myself just because history will judge you harshly."

"This time it's serious," Bourassa told his aides. "Trudeau is serious about patriating unilaterally, and if he does it in spite of my opposition, my government will go down in history as a laughing stock."

Bourassa's only avenue of escape was to call a provincial election. Trudeau agreed that it was a good move; at the time no one envisaged the worst. A reduced majority, or even a minority government, would make Bourassa far more conciliatory.

Three of Trudeau's men, Jean Marchand, Bryce Mackasey, and Roland Comtois, came over to shore up the tottering Bourassa team. But Trudeau's repeated attacks against the premier after the 1970 October crisis had completely destroyed Bourassa's credibility. After six years in office, his administration reeked of exhaustion and corruption.

On November 15, 1976, even Parti québécois leader René Lévesque was surprised by the magnitude of his election victory. English Canada went into a state of shock.

The only person who did not seem unduly upset was Pierre Trudeau. For a while, he seemed almost content. "I enjoy a good fight," he told the *Montreal Star* in an interview, "and René Lévesque is going to give us a run for our money. Deep down it may be a good thing for the country that someone of his calibre will force Quebeckers and Canadians to make up their minds."

Publicly Trudeau proclaimed that he would refuse to negotiate "any form of separatism with any province." In the privacy of his party's caucus room, he warned his MPs: "The Péquistes can't be trusted. If we make the slightest move to negotiate, we'll be caught in a trap. It's time to stop this constitutional striptease."

Playing to the gallery, and to English Montreal in particular, Trudeau compared an independent Quebec to a Pakistan or an Ireland, where people are killed for their race or religion. In Washington, Trudeau spoke of a threat even graver than the Cuban missile crisis of 1962, when the U.S. and the Soviet Union had stood on the brink of a nuclear war. "Stay in Quebec to bury Lévesque," he told Sun Life shareholders after the company noisily announced it would move its head office from Montreal to Toronto because of the growing nationalist menace in Quebec.

A good sport nevertheless, he assumed part of the blame for Bourassa's defeat. In Winnipeg a few months later, he admitted that the bitter controversy over the use of French in aviation had contributed to the Parti québécois victory.

Putting old grudges aside, Trudeau hailed the emergence of Claude Ryan as the leading candidate for the leadership of the Quebec Liberal party. English Canada felt reassured. Marshall McLuhan, the guru of the Toronto intelligentsia, issued a comforting prophecy: "Trudeau has the face of a North American Indian, and that gives him an enormous advantage over René

Lévesque. Indian blood has been strong in Quebec ever since the fur traders started marrying Indian women."

Until the PQ victory, Trudeau's popularity had been dropping precipitously in the polls. After the provincial election he surged back to 51 percent, more than enough to win another majority. It was almost "Trudeaumania" all over again.

For the next two years, Ottawa and Quebec would play a cat and mouse game. The federal government was hoping that the Péquistes would put their cards on the table by calling the referendum they had promised. Trudeau even tried to shame them into holding it as soon as possible. But the Quebec government knew that time was on its side. In 1976, Trudeau had only three years left in his mandate; Lévesque had five.

At times it was difficult to keep the panic among the Liberal ministers and MPs in check. Shortly after the election, Trudeau created a special strategy committee that included Marc Lalonde, Michael Pitfield, his new principal secretary Jim Coutts, and Gordon Robertson, Ottawa's senior federal-provincial relations bureaucrat.

"We need somebody who can work on this full time," Trudeau decided that Christmas.

"Why me?" asked Paul Tellier, when he was selected for the task.

"You've remained a Quebecker," he was told. "You go home every weekend."

After the October crisis, Tellier had left the provincial government to come to Ottawa where he joined the newly created department of urban affairs. "I joined the Trudeau school," he explained. "Being a francophone didn't give me an inferiority complex. If anything, I felt superior."

Still, Tellier was bothered by the amount of English his children were tracking into the house in Ottawa, so he began spending every weekend at a cottage in the Laurentians. For months, Tellier used his Quebec connections with people like Jean-Paul L'Allier, Maurice Pinard (of McGill University), and Arthur Tremblay. He also sounded out people like William Johnson, the *Globe and Mail*'s fervently federalist Quebec columnist, with whom he had "a number of long dinners."

The "Tellier Group," as it became known, ran a flurry of polls. On the political level, the federal Liberals began seeking a *rapprochement* with their provincial cousins. The objective was to avoid frictions within the federalist camp before the coming referendum campaign. "Our role was to make sure that there wouldn't be another squabble like the airline pilots business. That and to take advantage of whatever opportunities presented themselves."

As such, Trudeau's first reaction to the introduction of Bill 101 was to rush to the barricades. "It takes us centuries into the past," said Trudeau, evoking the dark days of Duplessis. But six months later, he would decline to invoke his power to disallow the PQ language legislation. "I don't intend to let Mr. Lévesque choose the time, nor the weapons," he explained.

Some years later, Lévesque would wonder if this initial triumph was not, in the end, a Pyrrhic victory. Assured of their "French state," Quebeckers felt less of a pressing need for independence.

But attacking Quebec became an increasingly difficult proposition for Trudeau. At federal-provincial conferences, ministers from other provinces found themselves sympathizing with these Quebeckers, who turned out not to be terrorists after all. Instead, early Quebec initiatives, like public auto insurance, electoral reform, agricultural zoning, and above all a constructive fiscal policy, made the PQ look more and more like the good government it had promised to be. The squabble over the federal government's sales tax gambit, which the Tellier Group was powerless to prevent, provided a shining example of the new government's polished image.

Jean Chrétien, then minister of finance, had proposed that the provinces should lower their sales taxes by 3 percentage points. It appeared that even Jacques Parizeau thought it was a good idea. Convinced that he had pulled a smart move, Chrétien announced the good news to the taxpayers in his budget. But suddenly a communiqué arrived at the Ottawa Conference Centre, where the media were previewing the budget documents: the negotiations with Quebec had hit a snag.

It seems that Parizeau had not been playing straight with his federal counterpart, but then the opportunity was too good to pass up. A reduction of only 3 points in the sales tax would primarily benefit Ontario industries. Someone at the Quebec finance department had come up with the ingenious suggestion of removing *all* sales tax from selected items like shoes, clothing, and hotel rooms, which would be of greater benefit to Quebec business.

Parizeau's calculations were less than flawless, and his arguments were somewhat convoluted, but he won the battle of public opinion. Not one of Chrétien's provincial colleagues, not even Ontario's Darcy McKeough, lifted a finger to help him. Ottawa had been taught its lesson: it didn't pay to play fair with the Péquiste devils. But the sales tax scrap also caused problems within the Liberal ranks. Serge Joyal and Pierre De Bané were furious with Chrétien and threatened to defect to the NDP.

While all this was going on, Trudeau lost another of his ministers. This time it was Solicitor General Francis Fox, whom Trudeau regarded as his heir, and who was being meticulously groomed by Marc Lalonde. But he resigned when it came to light that he had signed a false name to a certificate authorizing an abortion for a former lover.

On the whole, 1978 had been a bad year for Trudeau. In a moment of euphoria, Lévesque went so far as to threaten to send his minions against Trudeau in the next federal election. To finish him off, no doubt!

"If Lévesque wants a black eye in the next federal election, let him send his troops," Trudeau retorted. "If that's what he wants, he's welcome to it. After that we won't need a referendum."

18

Trudeau Bails Out

"The universe is unfolding as it should."

In the ballroom at the Château Laurier Hotel in Ottawa, Liberal workers from the capital region, secretaries, assistants to members and ministers, and even a few civil servants had tears in their eyes. It was May 22, 1979, and the bells in the Peace Tower had just rung an end to a memorable day. It was shortly after midnight when the announcement came that British Columbia had given nineteen of its twenty-eight seats to Joe Clark and the Conservatives.

Since 7:00 p.m., Trudeau and his circle of advisers, huddled at the prime minister's residence, had been jotting down calculations on scraps of paper. Quebec had held fast, giving the Liberals sixty-seven of its seventy-five seats, but Ontario had swung massively to the Tories, giving Joe Clark fifty-seven of ninety-five seats.

By the time the Prairie vote was in, Trudeau was assured of 113 seats in the House of Commons, while Joe Clark had racked up 117. Trudeau knew that things could only get worse in B.C., and he was prepared to call his opponent to congratulate him on his victory. But Jim Coutts wanted him to hold off: "The NDP already has eighteen seats, and there are still six of Fabien Roy's Créditistes in Quebec. We could win enough to form a coalition . . . " But by 11:00 p.m., when the early B.C. results came trickling in, it was obvious that Trudeau's magic had been no more effective on the western slope of the Rockies than it had been in the rest of English Canada.

"Well, well," René Lévesque said to his brother-in-law, Philippe Amyot, who was watching the results come in along with the rest

187

of the family in the premier's office in Quebec. "We've just won *this* referendum."

"No! Don't go!" the Liberal faithful cried out to their leader that night.

But the hard reality was that the Conservatives had won 136 seats and the Liberals only 114. To stay would mean clinging to power, and Trudeau had no stomach for that. Like all political leaders, he felt somewhat relieved that destiny had finally ended a fight that had lasted for fourteen years.

"The universe is unfolding . . . " he said philosophically.

But this wasn't the first time he had felt like getting out.

Three years earlier, Trudeau had come very close to quitting politics then and there. Not that the voters had turned against him. On the contrary, at the time he was more popular than at any other time since 1968. But he had a premonition about the scandals that were about to blow up in his face, and his main concern was to protect his three sons from the fallout.

His aides may well have wondered what was eating him in Quebec that Friday night in March 1976 when every sentence in his speech was laced with venom. What no one knew was that Trudeau's sudden rush to complete his constitutional patriation plan was primarily motivated by his desire to leave politics in order to save his marriage to Margaret.

"He had his problems," said Robert Bourassa, recalling the strained meeting in his office that day. "Trudeau didn't talk about it, but I got the impression that the time frame for achieving his political *raison d'être* had been determined by family considerations."

At the beginning of 1977, not long after the PQ victory, Trudeau spent three hours closeted with René Lévesque. He spoke at length about his wife and his hope that he would be able to get out of politics before a separation became inevitable.

"Dammit, I've got to get out," he told Lévesque at one point in the conversation. "Margaret cried the night you won. She knew what it meant . . . "

"René must have been touched," said Corinne Côté-Lévesque. "After his meeting with Trudeau, he told us: 'Christ, does he ever love his wife.'"

"Margaret was very unhappy about the Lévesque victory," Trudeau confided to his official biographer. "Because she instantly said, 'Now you're never going to be able to get out of politics,' and she saw herself locked into this thing for time indefinite, whereas until then both she and I had sort of kept our options open. . . . Suddenly that freedom was much less within reach . . . So it's a little bit like the fates cornering me in the very execution of the task that I got into politics for."

"Maggie" was born in September 1948, in Vancouver. Her father, James Sinclair, had been a British Columbia MP since 1940, and he served as fisheries minister in Louis St. Laurent's last cabinet.

Margaret Sinclair had barely turned nineteen when she met Pierre Trudeau for the first time on a beach in Tahiti. Two years later, in 1969, during an intimate dinner at the Grouse's Nest in the Rocky Mountains, where he had registered her under the name of "Miss Patterson," Trudeau first broached the subject of marriage.

At Christmas that year, Trudeau invited Margaret to Montreal to meet his mother. And at Easter he travelled secretly to Vancouver to ask the Honourable James Sinclair for his daughter's hand in marriage. During the fall and winter of 1970, Trudeau and Margaret regularly spent time together, though the country knew nothing about it. Their wedding on March 4, 1971, was such a secret that the couple was off on their honeymoon before the rest of the world found out.

Trudeau's instinctive aversion to responsibility applied to romance as well as to politics. "Why did I get married so late?" he mused one day. "I always say it's because I liked to enjoy my freedom and so on. But there was probably the feeling that I wasn't ready to bear that responsibility."

The couple's first years of marriage extended Trudeau's honeymoon with the country. Two years apart, in 1971 and 1973, Margaret bore him sons on Christmas Day. "Creation is a constant marvel," said Trudeau of his sons. "I guess the best thing for me is that I'm laughing all the time when I see these human beings develop. I'm just amazed, you know—mankind is always attracted by beauty or truth, a beautiful sunset, beautiful woman, a beautiful symphony, and here you see these human beings, they're right there and they're doing things. It just makes you feel great. It's seeing beauty and it's seeing reality in the making."

During the 1972 campaign, Trudeau was adamant that his wife and son would play no part in it. But in 1974, when all the stops had to be pulled out to regain the Liberal majority, Trudeau allowed his organizers to talk him into taking Margaret along on the campaign trail. She was a hit unprecedented in the annals of Canadian politics. She was young, beautiful, and high-spirited; it was as though she allowed Canadians to rediscover the Pierre Trudeau of 1968. With the emergence of our very own "Jackie," Canada rediscovered its Kennedy.

In 1972, Trudeau had come close to being chased from office by an electorate that found him cold, distant, and arrogant. "None of that is true," Margaret told crowds in town after town. "In fact, he's shy and modest and gentle. . . . He taught me about love!" And Trudeau would lower his eyes in embarrassment.

At twenty-six, Margaret discovered that the whole country adored her, particularly the reporters, who would crowd around her on the campaign plane. The members of the Parliamentary Press Gallery, then more than now, were mostly men, and highly chauvinistic men at that. They liked prime ministerial wives like Margaret or Mila Mulroney, who didn't mind playing the role of dutiful spouse. They tended to be far less receptive to independent-minded women with unabashedly feminist views like Joe Clark's wife, Maureen McTeer.

But during the summer of 1974, Margaret, along with the rest of the press corps, suffered from what Ottawa denizens call "the post-election blues." After the adoring crowds, the long flights aboard the campaign plane, and the feverish atmosphere of election night, it was back to earth again and the crushing boredom of watching the government, and, for Margaret, her husband the prime minister, plunge back into those heavy briefing books, more inaccessible than ever. Margaret tried to find things to do to fill the time, but when she landed an assignment to take pictures for *Chatelaine*, it caused such an uproar that she had to give it up. When she felt like riding her bicycle in the park around Rideau Hall or along the Rockcliffe parkway leading to the Ottawa River, two RCMP officers, also on bicycles, would follow her all the way, and photographers would be lurking at every bend.

In an effort to dispel the depression she had fallen into, she fled to Paris without a passport. She came back two weeks later in the throes of a nervous breakdown. She was treated at the Allan Memorial Institute, the psychiatric wing of Montreal's Royal Victoria Hospital, whose director at the time was Dimitrije Pivnicki. His daughter Mila was married to Brian Mulroney.

After her treatment, she tried to go back to her role as wife and mother, and gave Trudeau a third son, Michel. At the time, Trudeau could still have made her happy and kept her close to him. But as he had said: "I've never liked responsibility . . . "

Besides, he was wrapped up in his work as prime minister, which didn't leave him a lot of free evenings. "We'll have to change that, get out and see people," he was forever telling Margaret, who wanted to organize dinner parties for their friends. But he was always coming home with what she called "those damned brown boxes," briefcases full of Privy Council documents that had to be studied each night. In 1979, Michael Pitfield calculated that though Trudeau put in at least fifty-two hours a week at the office, he never had more than an hour a day to reflect or to work alone while he was there. Even on nights that he didn't bring home any of the "damned brown boxes," he still felt the need to isolate himself in the small office at the official residence.

A discouraged Margaret began to stray from the straight and narrow again, getting involved in escapades that attracted the attention of reporters. They, at least, found her funny. In fact, all they were doing was chasing scandals. As soon as Trudeau stopped being prime minister, people would stop paying attention to her.

Trudeau was getting angrier and angrier as certain Conservative MPs, not to mention the gossips in the press gallery, began making open references to his marital problems. One day, when Calgary MP Harvie André, now a Mulroney cabinet minister, made a particularly pointed insinuation, Trudeau exploded: "You son of a bitch!"

"Must have touched a nerve," the Tories snickered.

For a year the country watched Margaret's follies with a mixture of fascination and embarrassment. Some newspapers went so far as to publish details of alleged extracurricular liaisons on the part of "the prime minister's estranged wife" as they now called her.

On May 27, 1977, the prime minister's press office issued a curt two-paragraph communiqué:

Pierre and Margaret announce that because of Margaret's
wishes, they shall begin living separate and apart. Margaret
relinquishes all privileges as the wife of the Prime Minister
and wishes to leave the marriage to pursue an independent
career.

Pierre will have custody of their three sons, giving
Margaret generous access to them. Pierre accepts Margaret's
decision with regret and both pray that their separation will
lead to a better relationship between themselves.

It was from all of this, as well as the constraints of power, that
Trudeau felt liberated on the night of May 22, 1979. He kept up
his bluster for the benefit of the press, such as when the president
of the press gallery made the inevitable slip and called him "Mr.
Prime Minister" at his first post-election press conference on July
19, 1979.

"Not yet," Trudeau replied. "But in my opinion, I'm still the
best."

At that press conference, Trudeau confirmed that he would stay
on as Liberal leader.

After that he went on holiday, taking his sons to Nova Scotia,
where they stayed with MP Donald Johnston's parents. Johnston
was the MP for St. Henri-Westmount and a minister in Trudeau's
final term, but also a longtime personal friend and confidant.

At the height of the election campaign, Margaret had published
a book entitled *Beyond Reason*, in which she disclosed intimate
details of her life with Trudeau and her escapades with the likes of
the Rolling Stones and a prominent American politician who was
widely presumed to be Ted Kennedy. On a number of occasions,
Trudeau told Johnston and his family how much he wanted to
protect his children from scandal. "What hurt him most," said a
friend, "was the thought that someday his sons would be old
enough to read that book."

At the end of the summer, Trudeau once again felt the call of the
wild and embarked on a canoe trip in the Northwest Territories.
In September he left for China and Tibet, where he let his beard
grow.

Meanwhile, Margaret had moved back to Ottawa that summer,
setting up house a few blocks away from Stornoway, the opposition
leader's official residence. Trudeau knew he could never distance

his sons from their mother as long as they all lived in the same city, so he asked a real estate agent to find him a house in Montreal. It was far enough away, and it was, above all, French: both served to keep his sons away from Margaret.

At 9:00 a.m. on November 21, Trudeau assembled his staff in the office on the third floor of Parliament's Centre Block. It was the same office he had occupied as prime minister for eleven years, and Joe Clark had had the grace to let him keep it.

"There is no easy way, nor an ideal moment to go," he told them. "At any given moment one must follow what one believes to be one's destiny." At 10:00 a.m. he told the same thing to the few MPs who showed up for the weekly caucus meeting. "We feel orphaned," they said. The Quebec members were particularly affected by the news. They had been trying to get him to stay for the referendum that would be held in the spring. But Trudeau convinced them that he could be heard just as well as an ordinary Quebec citizen as he could as prime minister should he be called upon by Claude Ryan, head of the "no" forces in the referendum campaign.

Trudeau then made his way to the theatre of the National Press Building where he had given so many press conferences during the past fourteen years. He read a short statement, in French and in English, then got up to leave. The assembled reporters broke into spontaneous applause. Trudeau wheeled around, looking slightly surprised.

In the House of Commons at 2:00 p.m., Prime Minister Joe Clark expressed "the gratitude of the Canadian people for a man with his many years of distinguished service." All members of the House, Conservatives, Liberals, New Democrats, and Créditistes, rose to their feet and gave him an ovation that lasted for five long minutes. Trudeau sat in his seat, hiding his face in his hands.

In the National Assembly, René Lévesque and his ministers supported a Liberal motion paying homage to Trudeau. Only Gérald Godin, who had been imprisoned under the War Measures Act, could not forgive him: "I find it impossible to congratulate a man who, at a given moment in our history, allowed the establishment of a police state in Quebec."

When he finally left Parliament Hill near 4:00 p.m., Trudeau looked like a broken man: fatigue was deeply etched on his sixty-year-old features, his gaze was blank, and flecks of white foam had formed at the corners of his mouth.

This time it was really over.

There are those who maintained it was merely a feigned departure. But those who saw his stooped silhouette that afternoon, leaving the Hill for what looked like the last time under the despairing gaze of a handful of hard-core loyalists, knew that this was no charade.

"Conservatives out of danger," trumpeted the headline of the *Toronto Star* the next day. The emotional shock of Trudeau's departure had barely been absorbed when the line started forming to succeed him. A convention was scheduled for March in Winnipeg.

Joe Clark's Conservatives, feeling they had a period of grace before them while the Liberals cast about for a leader, began governing as though they had a majority. At 8:00 p.m. on Tuesday, December 11, Finance Minister John Crosbie presented the first Conservative budget in seventeen years.

It was indeed a "conservative" budget. In an attempt to reduce the federal deficit by half over four years, Crosbie increased taxes by close to $4 billion. In particular, he imposed a gasoline surtax of eighteen cents a gallon that would become the symbol of the Conservatives' subsequent electoral defeat.

"We will have to vote against the budget," said the leader of the opposition.

Since the beginning of the session there had already been two motions of nonconfidence in the new government, but neither had come close to toppling the Conservatives because not all the Liberals had showed up to vote. This time, Liberal House Leader Allan MacEachen ordered party whip Charlie Turner to summon every last Liberal MP to Ottawa. Two of them, who were in Brussels with External Affairs Minister Flora MacDonald at the time, fled home like thieves in the night, leaving Flora behind.

On Wednesday morning, MacEachen, who had been deputy prime minister under Trudeau, told his Liberal colleagues that it was time to bring down the government. Trudeau did not oppose the initiative, but let it be known that there was no question he would return as leader. "For that," he said, "the sovereign would have to come and ask me on bended knee, and ask me three times!"

At noon, John Crosbie met a Quebec reporter in the parliamentary restaurant.

"Do you have any idea what the Créditistes are going to do?" Crosbie asked.

"Are you telling me that nobody in your government is talking to Fabien Roy?" asked the incredulous reporter.

In the Commons, the Conservatives had 136 seats and the Créditistes had six. A coalition between the Conservatives and the Créditistes seemed natural. But they were stacked up against a possible alliance of 113 Liberals (Joe Clark had named a Liberal, James Jerome, as Speaker) and 26 New Democrats.

It was a thin majority—142 against 139—that could easily be whittled down to nothing by a few absentees, either off on a trip somewhere or sick in bed. This is exactly what happened the night of December 12, 1979: Flora MacDonald was at a NATO ministers meeting in Brussels, Alvin Hamilton was in hospital, and Lloyd Crouse was on holiday on the other side of the Pacific Ocean. In their absence, the House was divided 139 to 139.

It was time for the Conservatives to talk, and talk nicely, to the Créditistes. Especially since Quebec Finance Minister Jacques Parizeau had advised Fabien Roy to negotiate a price for his support. "Quebec farmers have to be exempted from the famous eighteen-cent tax on gasoline," Parizeau told him. This is exactly what Roy subsequently proposed in Question Period that afternoon. But no one on the Conservative benches bothered to pick up the earphone to catch the simultaneous translation of what the unilingually French-speaking Roy was saying.

That evening, the Liberals broke out the good cheer at their annual Christmas party on Parliament Hill. They presented Trudeau with a chainsaw "to cut down the government."

MacEachen approached Trudeau and whispered in his ear: "You should think about what you're going to do. I believe the government will be defeated."

"What am I going to do?" replied Trudeau with a smile. "Well, my duty, to be sure . . ."

On another floor of the West Block, Fabien Roy was alone in his office. With tears in his eyes he told a journalist that several of his MPs had already gone home to their ridings. It was too late to offer Joe Clark the deal that could save his government.

On Thursday morning, when the prime minister realized that he stood a chance of being defeated in the Commons, desperate calls went out to Flora MacDonald to get her back from Brussels. But all the flights to North America from Belgium had already left, and there was not enough time to make it to Paris to catch the Concorde to New York.

At 10:21 p.m. on Thursday, December 13, 1979, 139 Liberals and New Democrats voted against the budget, while 133 Conservatives voted in favour, and the six Créditistes abstained. One of the Liberal members, fresh from an extensive cardiac operation, was brought to the Hill in an ambulance, and his colleagues had to help him rise in his seat for the vote. White as a sheet, his pain-wracked features nevertheless lifted into a smile.

At that very moment, in Quebec City, cabinet secretary Louis Bernard was not smiling. On the contrary. His one-word response to the news that the Clark government had failed was: "Dammit!"

The next day, Allan MacEachen suddenly pulled out the results of a poll he had been carrying around in his pocket for a week. It showed that the Liberals had a large enough lead to win the election. With Trudeau as their leader, their chances would be even better. But it was another, even more secret poll that would finally convince Pierre Trudeau to "do his duty." He had not lost all contact with his friends in the Tellier Group, and they had informed him confidentially that in Quebec the "no" side of the referendum was only five points ahead of the "yes" option.

"In response to an urgent appeal from the national caucus and the Liberal party executive, I have decided to resume the leadership of our party in the election campaign now underway.

"This decision is, without a doubt, the most difficult I have been called on to make in my life. You are familiar with the reasons that led me to leave public life. My deepest wish was to leave politics and raise my family in Montreal.

"Nevertheless, in light of the serious problems confronting Canada, it was my duty to once again undertake the leadership of my party . . ."

On March 3, 1980, Pierre Elliott Trudeau, Canada's fifteenth prime minister, succeeded the sixteenth prime minister, Joe Clark.

(In Ottawa, as on the hockey rinks, prime ministers always keep the same number.)

Ironically, in seeking to manipulate the Créditistes, Jacques Parizeau was one of the instruments of destiny that allowed Pierre Trudeau and René Lévesque to square off once again, face to face.

19

Showdown with Lévesque

"Welcome to the 1980s," were the first words out of Pierre
Trudeau's mouth when he made his appearance at the Château Laurier on the night of February 18. This time the two thousand Liberal supporters who had descended on the hotel were in a
jubilant mood as they crowded into the same ballroom where Trudeau had philosophically swallowed his defeat nine months earlier.
What a difference between this night and that night in May 1979,
when the man Canadians had just rejected cast his lot with
"eternity."

While destiny may have played a part in Trudeau's dramatic
return to the forefront of national politics, it was greatly assisted
by the blunders committed by Joe Clark and his administration.
But destiny may have been on his mind as he trudged through a
snowstorm in his Rockcliffe neighbourhood on the night of December 17, pondering a question that a number of his intimates, including Marc Lalonde, Michael Pitfield, and Allan MacEachen, had
been asking him: "You, who have always said that no French Canadian since Laurier has been indispensable to history as it was made,
what do you think your place in history will be?"

It was not that Pierre Trudeau's eleven years as prime minister
had been wasted. His government had passed legislation like the
Official Languages Act, established the system of equalization pay-
ments from richer to poorer parts of the country, liberalized
regional development policies, and enhanced a range of social programs. At the end of the 1970s, Canadian society was indeed more
just than it was at the close of the previous decade.

But somehow, on the eve of the 1980s, the Trudeau record was
still less than spectacular.

The great dream of national reconciliation and unity, which English Canada had expected him to bring to fruition, had encountered a growing wall of resistance in Quebec. The referendum on sovereignty-association, which would be held in a few months, could leave the country facing the biggest deadlock in its history.

At the beginning of the 1970s, the federal treasury still had a surplus of revenues over expenditures, but after the petroleum shock of 1973, when the price of oil began to skyrocket, the government wandered into the wonderland of deficit financing. It started with a $2 billion deficit in 1974, which grew to $5 billion in 1975 and $10 billion by 1977. In 1979, Trudeau bequeathed the Conservatives a government that was on the verge of bankruptcy.

Unemployment was climbing dangerously above 8 percent, generally considered as the maximum acceptable level, and prices were spiralling upward despite the government's anti-inflation program.

Had Pierre Trudeau entered the history books on this night of February 18, 1980, instead of being granted the chance to write a few more chapters, Wilfrid Laurier might not have been all that proud to welcome him at the Pearly Gates.

But he had a rendezvous with history already scheduled for three months hence, and he had been preparing for it for a long, long time.

Trudeau had always been reluctant to face the nationalists on their own ground, in a referendum in Quebec. In 1969, shortly after René Lévesque had founded the Parti québécois, he had said: "If Quebec holds a referendum, and if it's close, I might want to get involved. But I'd prefer it to be otherwise."

When the PQ came to power in 1976, Pierre Trudeau took to playing the sophist. Contrary to what most people think, he did not wait until the panic of the final days leading up to the referendum to extend his promise of renewed federalism if Quebec would give him "another last chance," as René Lévesque put it.

Two days after his "resignation" in November 1979, Pierre Trudeau was in Montreal sitting in the living room of one Michel Roy, editor-in-chief of *Le Devoir*. "It has to be made very clear that 'no' voters in the referendum should know that 'no' means 'yes' to constitutional reform. It is an important consideration that I should communicate to English Canada."

In fact, Trudeau had been breaking the ground in English Canada since 1978 when he published his white paper on constitutional reform, *A Time for Action*. And he said over and over again that he would act unilaterally if necessary.

Though it had elected a nominally separatist provincial government, Quebec nevertheless gave Trudeau his crushing majorities on his home ground while the PQ was in power: sixty-seven seats out of seventy-five in 1979 and seventy-four in 1980, almost a clean sweep (save for Tory holdout Roch LaSalle). "The obvious paradox," said Trudeau, "is that in the last election Quebec gave us a mandate. Why, in the long run? To patriate the Constitution, unilaterally if we have to."

At the very least, no one was surprised by Trudeau's inclination to behave as though the Quebec government did not exist. "To say that Trudeau was consistent is almost to praise him," said Jean-Roch Boivin, Lévesque's chief of staff.

The Trudeau takeover from Joe Clark in 1980 took place quickly, almost with indecent haste. But then the news coming in from Quebec was getting gloomier by the day.

While Trudeau was in northern Ontario on December 19, 1979 getting his election campaign off the ground, René Lévesque was huddled in the bunker in Quebec City with his ministers, negotiating every comma of "The Question."

> The Quebec government has made public its proposal to negotiate a new agreement with Canada based on the equality of nations;
>
> This agreement would enable Quebec to acquire the exclusive power to make its laws, administer its taxes, and establish foreign relations abroad — in other words, sovereignty — and, at the same time, to maintain with Canada an economic association, including a common currency;
>
> Any change in political status resulting from these negotiations will be submitted to the people through a referendum.

On these terms, do you agree to give the Quebec
government a mandate to negotiate the proposed agreement
between Quebec and Canada?

The rest of the country paid scant attention as debate on "The
Question" began in Quebec. But the Tellier Group's polls confirmed
what everyone in Quebec already knew: if left to their own devices,
Claude Ryan and his brave band of survivors from the November
15, 1976, debacle would stand little chance against the formidable
PQ machine. Ministers and members of the National Assembly were
vigorously promoting the PQ line according to a closely tailored
script, and the various government branches vied to outdo each other
in coming up with advertising campaigns promoting "the cause."

When Trudeau held the first meeting of his new cabinet in March
1980, the bureaucrats brought along their latest polls from Quebec.
They showed the "yes" side out in front with 45 percent support
and the "no" with 43 percent. Another 11 percent of respondents
were undecided, which indicated that the "no" side had room to
grow. Still, the sovereignty option was getting dangerously close
to the critical 50 percent mark.

"René always thought that he could make up the difference with
a good campaign," said his widow, Corinne Côté-Lévesque. "He
was hoping to get a clear majority of the francophone vote, something like 75 percent." Lévesque was so certain that he could pull
it off with a good campaign that he took off to Bermuda for a few
days on the eve of the battle, along with his wife, his sister, and his
brother-in-law.

On the plane that took them back to Montreal, Lévesque found
a Quebec newspaper. It carried a story about how Lise Payette, the
minister responsible for the status of women, had given a speech
in which she lampooned the old Québécois schoolbook gender
stereotypes, "Guy" and "Yvette." Guy was the breadwinner and
the incarnation of the strong and silent type, while Yvette was the
docile housewife, cooking dinner and tending the kids, content to
live in her husband's shadow.

She drove her point home with a personal insult: "Claude Ryan,"
she declared, "is married to an Yvette."

As the plane made its approach to Mirabel airport, the Lévesques
and the Amyots laughed heartily at Payette's wit. High in the sky,
with the sun in their faces, "we found it funny," recalled Corinne.

But it turned out that there were a lot of women in Quebec who saw nothing wrong with being a devoted homemaker, and who were offended by Payette's cavalier, not to mention downright sexist, attack on Madeleine Ryan, a person of considerable substance in her own right. When they banded together, calling themselves "Les Yvettes," and filled the Montreal Forum to the rafters for a pro-federalist rally, a Canadian flag in one hand and a fleur-de-lys in the other, the laughter died abruptly in the PQ backrooms.

It was the boost that the "no" side needed to get its campaign rolling.

When he returned to power, Pierre Trudeau named Jean Chrétien justice minister and put him in charge of the federal troops in the referendum. This infuriated Claude Ryan, who took it to mean that the prime minister had little confidence in the intellectual debate he was planning to mount against Lévesque, and was sending in a populist to make the difference.

Ryan and Chrétien had known each other since 1964. At the time, the "little guy from Shawinigan" had asked the publisher of *Le Devoir* whether he should stay in Ottawa or join Jean Lesage's team in Quebec, which was looking for reinforcements.

"Your place is in Ottawa," Ryan had decided.

Later, in 1977, Chrétien had thought seriously about running to succeed Bourassa. He made the mistake of once again consulting the publisher of *Le Devoir*, who wasted no time leaking the information on the front page of his newspaper.

It didn't help that Chrétien had put his foot in it when Ryan confided his own interest in running for the provincial Liberal leadership. "You're a journalist," Chrétien told him flatly. "It's your life. You excel at a difficult and important trade. If I were you, I'd never get into politics, I'd stay publisher of *Le Devoir*."

Having the two of them on the same stage over the course of a sixty-day campaign was bound to generate friction.

Moreover, Robert Bourassa chose the referendum campaign as his opportunity to resurface and win back his stripes. But he deliberately kept apart from the official campaign. "I didn't want to be seen on the same stage as Trudeau, because the hot dog business was still fresh in people's minds," he said.

So the "no" campaign got off to a bad start, headed as it was by leaders who had trouble getting along with each other. Across the way, meanwhile, the "yes" camp was riding a wave of euphoria. A month before the vote, Trudeau was seriously worried: "I sensed there was something missing from the 'no' campaign," said Trudeau. "The PQ was quite clever at making people believe that all it took to vote 'yes' was a little pride. But even beyond the practical aspects of the question, Canada is a noble undertaking. Bringing together two of the most important cultures in the western world to live fraternally over half a continent is not a shabby undertaking. On the contrary, it is a noble cause to defend. This is the message I wanted to see delivered."

Claude Ryan was furious, and Jean Chrétien felt betrayed. Both accused Trudeau of torpedoing a boat that was already taking on water.

Trudeau decided the time had come to throw himself into the fray.

He had already warned Quebeckers in the House of Commons on April 15 that a "yes" vote would result in a deadlock. "When René Lévesque comes to me to negotiate, the answer will be, 'You don't have a mandate to discuss sovereignty because the question hasn't been asked clearly and simply in your referendum.'"

On April 25, Trudeau issued "An Open Letter to Quebeckers."

"I am not promising any miracles if the 'no' side should win," he wrote, "because a genuine breakthrough is not possible as long as the party whose goal is the destruction of federalism remains in power in Quebec. But I promise we will spare no effort to make constitutional reform possible."

"Whose constitutional reform?" Quebeckers wondered. Claude Ryan's or Jean Chrétien's? In his "beige paper," Ryan had proposed a far-reaching constitutional reform whereas Chrétien seemed to be upholding the status quo.

Trudeau did not respond directly, but his first speech of the referendum campaign in Quebec, to the Montreal Chamber of Commerce, eloquently demonstrated the panic that was overtaking the Ottawa end of the federalist operation. The "yes" militants were "cowards," he said, who were trying to get away with asking an "ambiguous" question. He praised the "courage" of the "true" independentists of the movement's early years who were not afraid to call a spade a spade.

He also took cover behind the declarations of several provincial premiers who had let it be known that they were not interested in negotiating an "association" with a "sovereign" Quebec. And he ridiculed the PQ strategy, comparing it to "historic" examples like Ireland, Algeria, Grenada, the Fiji Islands, and even Cuba and Haiti.

After that speech he was told he had gone a little too far, and he came close to tendering an apology in his next speech, this one before a crowd of six thousand in Quebec City. The "no" forces had been making plans for a mass rally in Montreal on May 14. They had considered holding it in the Velodrome next to the Olympic Stadium. But in the end they opted for the storied Paul Sauvé arena. It had the double advantage of being easier to fill, and having symbolic importance as a Péquiste shrine. Trudeau would make his final charge on enemy ground.

"If it is 'no,' we have all said that it will be interpreted as a mandate to change the Constitution and renew federalism. I'm not the only one who's saying it. There are also the seventy-four Liberal members of Parliament in Ottawa and the premiers of the nine other provinces.

"I am saying to Canadians in other provinces in all seriousness that we in Quebec are sticking our necks out when we tell Quebeckers to vote 'no.' We are telling you that a 'no' vote cannot be interpreted by you as a sign that everything is all right and that things can remain as they were before.

"We want change. We are staking our seats on those changes."

René Lévesque listened to Trudeau's speech apprehensively in the basement of the Sambo Restaurant on Sherbrooke Street, a short distance from the arena. Had he stepped outside, he could have heard the chant "Ell-i-ott, Ell-i-ott, Ell-i-ott" emanating from the building down the street.

"It was a damned good speech," Lévesque told some of his close advisers in the tone of a good sport. "It's going to hurt us, coming like this at the end of the campaign."

"What hurt him," explained Corinne Côté-Lévesque recently, "is that someone had told Quebeckers that they had nothing to lose by voting 'no.'"

The reason the "no" supporters at the Paul Sauvé arena were chanting Trudeau's middle name that night was because a few days earlier Lévesque had publicly questioned Trudeau's Quebec roots. "Yes," countered Trudeau, "Elliott is my mother's name. It's the name her ancestors carried to Canada two hundred years ago. My name is a Québécois name, but it is also a Canadian name."

When Trudeau talked like that, Lévesque found it difficult to contain himself. He would tell people in his circle how Trudeau's three sons would come down to say hello during first ministers' dinners at 24 Sussex Drive, and how it was all but impossible to get a word of French out of them, particularly Michel, the youngest. "I was shocked, and even more so because it's obvious that Trudeau is embarrassed about it," explained Lévesque. "I just can't understand why there's so little of the Québécois in Pierre."

In the end, on referendum night, Lévesque did not even get a majority of francophones (only 49 percent) to vote "yes." It wasn't even a moral victory of the sort that the PQ had got used to celebrating after its early election campaigns.

"Until next time," said Lévesque from the stage of the Paul Sauvé arena, before leading the singing of Gilles Vigneault's poignant song, "Gens du Pays," in a voice ravaged by sixty days of speechmaking and double his normally formidable consumption of cigarettes.

In Ottawa, Trudeau reached out to the referendum losers. "I cannot help but think of all the 'yes' supporters who fought with such conviction, and who have to pack up their dream tonight and bow to the majority verdict. And that takes away my taste for any noisy victory celebrations."

Claude Ryan was not quite so modest and conciliatory in his victory address in Montreal. He was determined not to share the triumphal stage with Chrétien, and they came close to staging a wrestling match before the TV cameras as a furious Chrétien tried to seize the microphone that Ryan was refusing to let go. All the votes had not yet been counted, and already the federalist coalition that had carried the referendum fight was dissolving into a family squabble.

"If we take into account broken friendships, strained affections, and injured pride, there is no one who does not have some wound to the soul to heal in the days and weeks to come," said Trudeau on television.

But there was at least one person who would not have time to put back on the fifteen pounds he said he had lost during the referendum campaign.

On May 21, 1980, Pierre Trudeau decided that he would take advantage of the relief in English Canada over the referendum result to play his cards as soon as possible. And he already knew what he wanted: it was all in his speech to the Canadian Bar Association in Montreal in September 1967.

But the English provinces who had been enlisted for the federalist referendum drive now turned up with shopping lists in their pockets.

"Go see what they want," Trudeau ordered Chrétien.

What followed was one of the most ludicrous cross-country odysseys ever undertaken by a federal minister in the name of federal-provincial relations. Even Senator Lowell Murray, in May 1990, did not break his record. Flanked by his faithful chief of staff Eddie Goldenberg—son of Carl, who had been advising Trudeau on constitutional matters since 1967—Chrétien set out on his tour of provincial capitals aboard a government Challenger jet. (Chrétien was proud of the little fleet of Challengers at the government's disposal. It was he who, as industry and commerce minister, had saved the plane's manufacturer, Canadair, from impending bankruptcy with a government buyout when the company's parent firm, General Dynamics, was anxious to unload it.)

On Tuesday night, Chrétien dined with Bill Davis at the plush Albany Club in Toronto. The Ontario premier could be counted on to be a strong ally, as long as no one forced his hand on the French-language issue in his backyard. In 1978, when he had blocked a Liberal bill to make the province officially bilingual, his office had been deluged by an avalanche of letters—at a rate of ten to one in favour of his decision. He knew where his interests lay.

On Wednesday morning, Chrétien had breakfast with Manitoba's Conservative premier Sterling Lyon. He wanted nothing to do with any charter of rights that would infringe on his legislative prerogatives. Lunch was with Allan Blakeney of Saskatchewan, and the topic was jurisdiction over natural resources. At teatime he was in Alberta with another Conservative, Peter Lougheed, and he made it to Victoria in time for dinner with British Columbia's Social Credit premier, Bill Bennett.

On Thursday morning, with the sun barely over the Rockies, he headed in his Challenger to Prince Edward Island where, because of the time difference, he arrived in time for tea. "The Mayor of Charlottetown" as some Ottawa wags called PEI premier Angus MacLean, was never hard to deal with. Later that evening in Halifax, over a plate of lobster, Nova Scotia premier John Buchanan spoke to Chrétien about offshore mineral resources.

The same topic dominated his conversation on Friday morning with Newfoundland's Brian Peckford, who had visions of Hibernia crude dancing in his head. In Fredericton, Chrétien met Richard Hatfield at the hotel the New Brunswick premier used as his official residence. Hatfield promised to help Trudeau.

When he got back to Ottawa on Friday night he had just enough time to pack a fresh suitcase before climbing back on another plane, this one to Florida for a long-promised vacation with his wife, Aline. For the time being, he wasn't needed back home.

Now Pierre Trudeau himself stepped into the breach. Michael Pitfield, who had exiled himself to Harvard during the Clark interregnum, had returned as Privy Council clerk after the Liberal victory in February, and had immediately busied himself cleaning house in the upper reaches of the bureaucracy. Most notably, Michael Kirby was put in charge of federal-provincial relations. Or, more accurately, federal-provincial "tensions."

A student of Machiavelli, Kirby did not believe in an agreement between Ottawa and the provinces. All that Ottawa had to do, he proposed, was to negotiate in sufficiently bad faith that the provinces themselves would break off the constitutional talks, thereby justifying an appeal to London for unilateral patriation.

Over the weekend — dispatch and efficiency had suddenly become paramount in Ottawa—Trudeau put the finishing touches on a letter to the provinces which he sent on May 28. "We are obliged to take advantage of the favourable new climate created by the referendum result," he wrote. "It is incumbent upon us to amend the country's constitution without delay."

Already Trudeau had stopped using the expression "to renew federalism," which he had brandished with reference to the Constitution at the Paul Sauvé arena two weeks earlier. And he warned his colleagues to "show a sense of realism."

But the language Trudeau used in his letter to René Lévesque was somewhat different. "The majority of Quebeckers have chosen the route of loyalty to Canada," he said, "and, according to your own terms, have decided to give *renewal* within the framework of the Canadian federation 'another chance.'"

Trudeau then called the ten premiers to a lunch at 24 Sussex Drive, and between the dessert and the cheese plate, he handed them a list of twelve priorities and gave them three months to reach an agreement.

In Quebec, Claude Ryan was beside himself. Trudeau's "list" included the predictable federal priorities, and a few of the points raised by some of the English provinces — notably those with an interest in natural resources. Quebec's traditional preoccupations were conspicuous by their absence.

Cultural policy, immigration, social policy, fiscal agreements, international relations: none of these things was discussed during the July 9 luncheon in Ottawa. Ryan foresaw "a disaster." René Lévesque spoke of "hasty federal tinkering" with the Constitution.

Just as Trudeau contributed to Robert Bourassa's defeat in 1976 by belittling him in the eyes of the Quebec people, this time he had a hand in Ryan's defeat by refusing to negotiate with Quebec.

On April 13, 1981, the Parti québécois was re-elected with a majority government, winning 49.21 percent of the vote in a provincial election.

"But who will be the spokesman for this renewal of federalism?" Trudeau had asked during the referendum campaign. "The PQ government wants to destroy federalism. So I repeat that even a 'no' vote may not necessarily lead to the new federalism that everyone wants . . ."

20

Five Days in November

The list of constitutional questions to be settled before patriation grew from week to week during the summer of 1980.

But this was predictable: every time the constitutional "can of worms" was opened, every premier would come to the table with a set of preoccupations, items which were dear to his own heart or which would allow him to score points. (In 1978, for example, the ten provinces submitted a list of twenty-nine proposals to Trudeau, of which about a third had no other purpose than to limit Ottawa's powers. A "non-starter," declared Trudeau.)

During the June 9, 1980, lunch, the first ministers assigned the impossible task of writing a new Canadian constitution to their justice ministers. After fifty-four years of failure, no one believed in miracles any more.

On July 7, a veritable travelling circus got underway at the Complex Desjardins in Montreal. It would take the eleven ministers and some fifty-odd civil servants to Toronto, Vancouver, and finally to Ottawa.

As usually happens in such circumstances, alliances developed, most notably between Quebec's intergovernmental affairs minister Claude Morin and Roy Romanow, his opposite number from Saskatchewan. The bureaucrats from British Columbia, Alberta, and Newfoundland in particular were impressed by the strength of the arguments put forward by the Quebec delegation. The federal bureaucrats, finding themselves increasingly isolated, struck up a special relationship with their Ontario counterparts.

The first ministers finally met in conference in Ottawa on September 8. It quickly turned into a disaster that would go down in the constitutional history of Canada as "Black September."

Problem number one was an overloaded agenda. Then a top secret federal strategy paper written by Michael Kirby — for ministers' eyes only — which outlined the various strategic scenarios envisaged by the Ottawa negotiators, somehow made its way to Claude Morin's mailbox in Cap Rouge, a suburb of Quebec City. At a dinner hosted by Governor General Ed Schreyer to open the proceedings Trudeau showed how inexplicably arrogant he can be. Finally, on Friday night, this time over dinner at the prime minister's residence, things came completely unstuck.

"If I have to choose between the prime minister's vision and that of the premier of Quebec, I prefer René Lévesque's," said Brian Peckford.

"I feel like throwing up," whispered Chrétien.

Nevertheless, Ottawa quickly learned its lesson. Every morning of the week of "Black September," the provincial premiers would meet for what was quickly dubbed the "consensus breakfast."

"It was Lévesque who kept himself apart from any joint action by the other provinces," said Chrétien. "He would always sabotage any possible agreement."

Four days later, Pierre Trudeau told his caucus that he intended to "go all the way," over the dead bodies of his provincial counterparts if that's what it took.

Earlier that summer, he had taken advantage of a stopover in London to warn Margaret Thatcher that she might be receiving a unilateral patriation request from Ottawa sometime in the near future. The Iron Lady was less than enthusiastic, but Trudeau told her: "Hold your nose and look the other way."

On October 6, Trudeau undertook the most difficult constitutional fight of his career. The Conservatives refused to approve any patriation of the constitution that did not have the approval of the provinces, in particular, the seven Conservative premiers who held Joe Clark's political future in their hands.

In Parliament, the Conservatives resorted to every possible delaying tactic to stall the Trudeau reform. They put forward endless petitions to force the government to hold televised hearings.

In the meantime, five of the premiers, and later what would grow up and be known as "the gang of eight," teamed up to contest Trudeau's initiative in the courts, even up to the Supreme Court, if necessary. The "gang" included all the provincial premiers except for Ontario's Bill Davis and New Brunswick's Richard Hatfield.

On April 16, 1981, three days after René Lévesque's re-election, the eight met to sign an agreement. Quebec gave up its right to veto future constitutional amendments, and in return his colleagues promised to help Lévesque obtain an "opting-out" provision that would allow a provincial government that did not wish to participate in a national program to be compensated with enough money or tax points to mount an equivalent program according to its own standards and priorities. (The proposed Meech Lake accord would give this "opting out" option to all provinces, which infuriates Trudeau.)

The case of the dissenting provinces made its way to the Supreme Court, which on September 28, 1981, pronounced its verdict. This Solomon-like judgement said, in effect, that Trudeau did not need the backing of "all" the provinces to bring about constitutional reform. "Morally," however, he could not proceed with the support of only two provinces.

At least this was Margaret Thatcher's interpretation of what the Supreme Court said. It so happened that at the time of the verdict, Trudeau and Thatcher were attending a Commonwealth conference in Melbourne, Australia.

The message from London was clear: Trudeau had to try one last time to reach an agreement with his colleagues.

That evening, Roy Romanow and his Ontario counterpart, Roy McMurtry, visited Jean Chrétien at his home on Bower Street beside the Rideau Canal in Ottawa. The Saskatchewan minister had lost the bet of a bottle of scotch on the Supreme Court judgement, and he had come to pay up.

All three hoped someday to succeed their leaders: Chrétien to replace Trudeau, Romanow to succeed Blakeney, and McMurtry to step into Bill Davis's shoes in Ontario. It was in their interests to get their leaders out of the constitutional impasse, thereby giving them an incentive to quit, and establishing a sound footing from which to launch their own leadership campaigns.

On the one hand, the gang of eight was clinging to the amending formula proposed by Peter Lougheed in 1978, which put all the provinces on an equal constitutional footing. On the other hand, Trudeau was insisting on his Charter of Rights and Freedoms.

If there were ever to be agreement between Ottawa and the provinces, it would have to turn on these two points: Ottawa's charter versus the provincial amending formula. The premiers decided that they would return to the bargaining table during the first week of November 1981.

This set the stage for an extraordinary five-day odyssey.

Saturday, October 31, 1981

First ministers' conferences in Ottawa resemble United Nations general assemblies. The delegations install themselves in their respective hotels, each with a contingent of secretaries, photocopiers, computers, if necessary, and a set of filing cabinets.

At the same time, the national media install their microwave transmitters on the hotel roofs, equip their reporters with cellular phones, and chase the premiers from the airport to their hotel lobbies and even as far as the corridors leading to their rooms.

Civil servants, ministers, and reporters form a small world of their own, linked by their own closed-circuit communications system. Rumours run rampant, and the least public statement is recorded and analyzed at great length; a single word can start a debate, create an impasse, or break up a logjam that has stymied the discussions.

The first rule is to know who the important people in every delegation are. Where are they staying? In what room? Do they have a cellular phone? A walkie-talkie? And at what number or what frequency can they be reached?

On this day, the gang of eight established its headquarters in the Château Laurier Hotel, an old Canadian Pacific hotel in the grand style at the foot of Parliament Hill. It has the advantage of being linked by underground tunnel to the old Ottawa railway station, which has been transformed into the government's National Conference Centre.

Saskatchewan's Allan Blakeney checked into the Château Laurier along with Manitoba's Sterling Lyon, Nova Scotia's John Buchanan, and PEI's Angus MacLean. Blakeney was one of the key players in the negotiations. A member of the gang of eight, he was nevertheless actively seeking a compromise with the federal government. He would act as the link between Trudeau and the gang, via Bill Davis.

As usual, the Ontario premier installed himself in the Four Seasons, a five-minute stroll from the Château. Under the same roof were New Brunswick's Richard Hatfield, Newfoundland's Brian Peckford, and British Columbia's Bill Bennett, who was the chairman of that year's premiers' conference.

Peter Lougheed was alone at the Skyline in a vast penthouse suite overlooking the Ottawa River. From his living room, he could see the red-brick façade of the Auberge de la Chaudière, the finest hotel in Hull. There René Lévesque was ensconced in the presidential suite, but his staff nevertheless kept a room across the river in the Château Laurier. Most of the time this room would remain unoccupied.

A number of the first ministers arrived over the course of the Halloween weekend, notably Richard Hatfield, who spent most of Saturday afternoon at the justice department building on Wellington St. The federal bureaucrats were drilling him on a proposal that he was to submit to the conference's opening session. The plan was to divide the Charter in two, and make one part subject to the approval of the provincial legislatures. In this way Trudeau hoped to show that he was being conciliatory, and thereby convince at least a few of the gang of eight that "Trudeau's charter" was not altogether sacred, and that an agreement could be reached.

Sunday, November 1
5:00 p.m. Bill Davis is an avid Toronto Argonauts fan. After watching the broadcast of that week's football game, he headed for Trudeau's residence. As his minister Roy McMurtry and Michael Kirby had advised him, Davis announced he was prepared to renounce his veto right on Monday morning, as René Lévesque had done before him. That left Trudeau the only defender of the old "Victoria formula." (Under this formula, the four "regions" of Canada would have a veto, thereby making Ontario and Quebec the only individual provinces with a veto of their own.)

7:00 p.m. Peter Lougheed was going over his files with his intergovernmental affairs minister, Dick Johnston. One note in particular advised him to prepare for the possibility that Quebec might refuse to sign an agreement. "There are precedents," said the note. "Lesage, who refused to accept the Fulton-Favreau formula after having agreed to it in 1964, and Robert Bourassa, who changed his mind after he returned home from the Victoria conference in 1971."

8:00 p.m. The gang of eight had its first dinner in the suite on the fourth floor of the Château Laurier that would serve as its headquarters for the duration of the conference. The eight premiers agreed that they would meet over breakfast at 8 a.m. every day for a strategy session. They also agreed to put forward no positions, to partake in no discussions, and to make no compromise that had not been approved by the group as a whole.

Monday, 2 November

10:15 a.m. Conference chairman Pierre Trudeau gavelled the meeting to order. There were some present who got a flash of déjà vu when Jean Chrétien sat down at his right, close to Bill Davis, while the taciturn Allan MacEachen sat to his left, next to René Lévesque. This first session, which was televised to an estimated audience of two million people, according to the television networks, produced nothing concrete. As expected, Trudeau sounded conciliatory: "We are here to listen to each other," he said. Bill Davis and Dick Hatfield made the overtures they had rehearsed with the federal bureaucrats the day before. Every premier took his turn speaking following the order in which the provinces had entered Confederation. René Lévesque was intractable, and, as though seeking revenge for May 20, 1980, he challenged Trudeau to put his constitutional proposal to the Canadian people.

(Pierre Trudeau had already given all the details of his patriation plan in a speech in Montreal on May 19, 1979, twelve days before he lost power. "I repeat," he had promised, "I will not act unilaterally. I will seek the consent of the provinces. Failing that, I will ask the consent of the population . . . " But nobody paid much attention to the speech at the time.)

Some observers began to drift off as John Buchanan launched into his speech. The reporters went for coffee, and munched the inevitable doughnuts that are served in press rooms on these occasions, when Angus MacLean began to speak. Sterling Lyon and Peter Lougheed were hardest on Trudeau. "You lost in the Supreme Court," they reminded him cruelly. The first overture from the gang of eight came when Bill Bennett sighed: "We don't need another Hundred Years War to solve our constitutional problems."

12:30 p.m. Trudeau offered to share the buffet he had ordered laid out in the fifth-floor room of the conference centre where all the closed-door conference sessions were held. Most of the premiers declined.

2:30 p.m. The first in-camera session began. Pierre Trudeau made it clear to everyone that this was indeed the "last chance." The premiers immediately fell to attacking the amending formula, and no one seemed to notice Bill Davis's grand gesture of renouncing his veto.

4:00 p.m. False alarm: Allan Blakeney hurried into the office reserved for his delegation asking for a pair of scissors. "Is it getting that serious already?" he was asked. But the Saskatchewan premier only wanted to cut an article out of a newspaper. There was no perceptible movement at the session: the participants mostly eyed each other's positions.

By the end of the day, the eleven players had aligned themselves in different groups which would have to be moved when the time came, like pawns on a chessboard. There were:
—the federal clan, including Trudeau, Davis, and Hatfield;
—the Gang of Eight;
— "the three Bs" (Buchanan, Bennett, and Blakeney), who were also nicknamed "the three doves" because they were the most disposed to reaching an agreement; and
— "the hawks," who included Lougheed, Lyon, and Peckford.

Angus MacLean was largely forgotten, which is "The Mayor of Charlottetown's" usual fate. René Lévesque, meanwhile, was nowhere.

Tuesday, November 3
7:30 a.m. Peter Lougheed had just been interviewed live on "Canada AM" on the English-language CTV network. "If Trudeau doesn't get the support of the provinces, he'll have to go to the people," said the Alberta premier. Such television interviews were important in that they would often lead to fresh discussions once word got back to the conference centre.

8:00 a.m. The premiers gathered over scrambled eggs and croissants made limp from half an hour on a hot plate. Bennett said he might have a proposal to put on the table, but Lougheed and Lyon were not interested. "Let's see Trudeau's cards first," they said.

Practically at the same moment, in the temporary office set up for the prime minister at the conference centre, Bill Davis announced for the first time that he was ready to propose a trade with the gang of eight: a charter for their amending formula.

9:30 a.m. The day's discussions started badly, recalling the worst moments of "Black September" in 1980. Trudeau was still resisting the provincial amending formula, particularly its "opting-out" clause.

"It is a bonus for separation," he repeated.

"So I guess the people will have to decide," suggested Lévesque.

"At least we won't rig the question," Trudeau shot back.

Hatfield, whose emotions could get dangerously out of hand at these conferences, accused Lévesque of retreating into his own little "Warsaw ghetto."

11:00 a.m. Trudeau called a coffee break to ease the tension. As usual, small groups formed, and Bill Davis began talking about his "exchange" with Allan Blakeney: "'Our' charter for 'your' amending formula."

When the session resumed, however, Davis's proposal aroused little real interest because it was vague, and because some of the premiers understood it to mean that only a "mini" charter would be imposed on them.

2:30 p.m. Hatfield and Trudeau, who had stayed at the Conference Centre with their aides, were surprised to see that no one had yet returned from lunch. As it turned out, the eight had invited Davis to hear Bennett's suggestion: the amending formula for a "mini" charter. Davis deliberately did not react because he had got what he was after — a counter-offer from the holdout provinces. Davis suggested that he should take Bennett and discuss the proposal with Trudeau. The group also sent along one "dove," John Buchanan, and one "hawk," Peter Lougheed.

"Is this a joke, or what?" said Trudeau when Bennett explained his proposal for a "mini" charter. "You're becoming René Lévesque's puppets."

There was anger at gang of eight headquarters at the Château Laurier when Bennett, Buchanan, and Lougheed reported back after the discussion with Trudeau. As he was leaving the Château, Lévesque broke his vow of silence: "Trudeau is being stubborn as usual," he said. "Davis is thinking of dropping him."

The rumour reached Richard Hatfield in the Cock and Lion, the downstairs bar at the Château Laurier where the premier had gone to catch a set by country singer Sneezy Waters. He tried to reach Trudeau or Chrétien, but both were in a special cabinet meeting.

8:00 p.m. During the evening, Bill Davis and Allan Blakeney and a few of their ministers and advisers ran into each other at Mama Teresa's, an Ottawa dining spot and watering hole favoured by political types. Restaurants, like hotel lobbies and television studios, play an important role in federal-provincial conferences. (Ottawa guidebooks even include a chapter on where the politicos hang out: Conservatives, for example, have breakfast at the Four Seasons, lunch at Hy's, on the ground floor of an office building that bulges with lobbyists' offices, and dinner at Les Saisons, the opulent dining room at the Westin Hotel. The Liberals can be found at Nate's on Rideau St. at lunchtime, or in the alcoves of the Canadian Grill. New Democrats tend to lunch in one of the Parliament Hill cafeterias, but in the evenings they occasionally step out to Le Soupçon, a French restaurant on Rideau St., which was a favourite of Ed Broadbent's.)

By chance, the Ontario and Saskatchewan delegations were at neighbouring tables at Mama Theresa's on the evening of November 3. (The Blakeney group had actually been given a table previously reserved by the British Columbia delegation.)

It was a significant coincidence, for this is where Romanow and McMurtry first discussed the idea of adding a "notwithstanding" clause to Trudeau's charter. This clause would allow the provinces to subscribe to one or several obligations in the Charter of Rights to the extent that they were prepared to respect them. The way it was conceived, it would be an "opting-in" formula instead of an "opting-out" plan.

Davis and Blakeney seemed interested, but they couldn't really discuss it as they were both ensconced at the head of their respective tables. But just in case, they asked their bureaucrats to study the suggestion during the night.

Wednesday, November 4
7:00 a.m. Jean Chrétien awoke his old friend Roy Romanow in his room at the Four Seasons. He wanted to give him the latest news from the federal cabinet meeting the evening before. But

Romanow was bursting to tell him about the dinner at Mama Teresa's.

"Why don't we get together and talk about it?" suggested Chrétien.

"I'll get McMurtry and we'll be right over," replied Romanow.

8:00 a.m. The "breakfast consensus" went badly that morning. Bill Bennett announced that he was prepared to guarantee the rights of his francophone minority if that's what it would take to reach an agreement with Trudeau. Lévesque was thunderstruck. What the Quebec delegation didn't know was that a month earlier Trudeau had taken Bennett aside at 24 Sussex Drive and appealed to his sentiments: "Language is the essence of my existence," he told him. "You have to give me that."

Trudeau reminded the B.C. premier how his father, "Wacky" Bennett, and he had negotiated a constitutional accord in Victoria ten years earlier. In 1971, Bourassa had been the spoiler. "Don't trust Lévesque," concluded Trudeau, who had just scored a significant point.

Then Blakeney talked about the proposal that his advisers and the Ontario bureaucrats had been chewing over during the night. Finally, Brian Peckford, who had been silent up to then, said he too might have a proposal to submit later that day.

9:00 a.m. Lévesque waded through a series of cameras on his way to the conference room, looking downcast and not saying a word. A Quebec deputy minister, hanging back, told a reporter: "Bennett is slipping through our fingers. Blakeney is crapping on our doorstep, and Peckford is slipping in his shit!"

9:30 a.m. Lévesque had decided, consciously or not, that he could not trust the "Canadians." None of the proposals on the table aroused any great interest, and Trudeau was getting increasingly testy. (In his cabinet he had never liked discussions that dragged on forever. "Your proposal isn't ready yet," he would tell ministers who had not been able to convince their colleagues after fifteen or twenty minutes of discussion.)

That morning Trudeau ordered coffee.

11:00 a.m. Trudeau and Lévesque found themselves face to face before the coffee urn.

"Let's patriate the constitution right now," proposed Trudeau. "If we haven't come to an agreement in two years, we'll settle the

Charter and the amending formula with one roll of the dice, before the people."

Lévesque shrugged his shoulders, a deadpan look on his face, as though he were weighing his options in one of his late-night poker sessions.

When the discussion resumed, Trudeau pulled out a document stamped "Confidential 15/020." During such conferences, documents brought to the negotiating table are numbered and filed by the federal-provincial conference secretariat, a sort of general support group of the sort found at most international conferences.

When Trudeau tabled his document, no one noticed that there had not yet been any document numbered 15/019.

The referendum proposed by Trudeau to test the Charter and the amending formula called for a simple 50 percent plus majority in the country as a whole. As well, the question would have to carry a majority in Quebec and Ontario, in the four Western provinces as a group, and in the four Atlantic provinces as a group. (Trudeau's proposal for a referendum was odd in that he had never approved of such things. The previous summer, during a trip to Stockholm, he had spoken about referendums at length with a reporter. He said that referendums tended to cause needless divisions in families and between friends, and that in a country like Canada it would be difficult to establish a clear rule on just what constitutes a majority. Perhaps Trudeau was remembering another referendum in which he had opposed conscription, and knew that any national referendum would run the dangerous risk of pitting English Canada against French Canada.)

Lévesque pounced on Trudeau's referendum proposal with alacrity, perhaps to avenge himself for what he regarded as that morning's low blows from his Saskatchewan and B.C. colleagues. Or maybe because he was simply in a hurry to get back to Quebec to prepare his upcoming Throne Speech.

12:30 p.m. Lévesque and Trudeau followed each other to the microphones which had been set up for the media in the hallway of the conference centre. The news was spreading across the country like wildfire: "There is a new Canada-Quebec Alliance," the two of them announced.

The federal bureaucrats threw themselves on the Quebec reporters and gushed at them: "Trudeau tried so hard to come to an understanding with Lévesque . . . "

Only Lougheed was still clinging to the idea of a referendum. "We'll fight and we'll win," he declared defiantly.

Blakeney groaned: "The last thing we need is a referendum in the west on francophone rights."

While all this was going on, Sterling Lyon had returned to Manitoba where he was in the midst of an election campaign. (The election was scheduled for the following Monday, and though he didn't know it then, Lyon would lose.) When he heard the news of what was happening in Ottawa on the radio, he flew into a rage and called Peter Lougheed.

2:30 p.m. At the next in-camera session, the first ministers took turns browbeating the idea of a national referendum. Some of them, however, asked for more details. This was the moment Trudeau had been waiting for. He brought out another document, this one numbered 15/019. It would change everything.

Now the proposal was for holding the referendum in six months, not two years, and if even one province refused to sign the accord, Trudeau's original proposal would be adopted without so much as a comma changed. Moreover, Trudeau's "detailed" plan was so complex that even experts like Gérald Beaudoin, the dean of the University of Ottawa law faculty and now a Conservative senator, wondered if it had been drafted in Chinese.

There was consternation in the fifth-floor conference rooms. Lévesque wanted to leave for Quebec immediately, and Trudeau notified the CBC to get ready to go live with the closing session starting at 6 p.m. But then this notice to the national network was also part of the strategy. The rumour spread quickly among the reporters, made its way back to the provincial delegations on the upper floors, and put that much more pressure on them.

It was at this point that Bill Davis suggested knocking off for the night to chew things over.

He knew that Romanow, Chrétien, and McMurtry had been going around since that morning with the sketch of a new proposal that was still in the form of handwritten notes on the back of a telephone message slip. The formula that the three had cobbled together required the agreement of the two clans: the Charter would be hobbled by a "notwithstanding" clause, but there would be no financial compensation for opting out of national programs. There would be no "bonus for separation."

7:00 p.m. The session was adjourned and the Eight promised to call each other in case anything developed.

8:00 p.m. Norman Spector, Bill Bennett's senior constitutional adviser (now head of Brian Mulroney's Federal-Provincial Relations Secretariat), called René Lévesque's suite to remind him about the scheduled breakfast the next morning. Claude Morin took the message. The intergovernmental affairs minister then called a reporter and talked about how pessimistic he felt. Discouraged, he decided to go out to dinner with an aide.

The rest of the Quebec delegation, including René Lévesque, went down to Le Châteauneuf, the Auberge's dining room. There was a lot of wine on the table, but it was more like a wake than a celebration.

8:30 p.m. At 24 Sussex Drive, the senior ministers — Chrétien, Lalonde, MacEachen — and a handful of top-level civil servants were preparing a statement conceding failure. But Chrétien, who felt he had reached an agreement with his two provincial counterparts from Saskatchewan and Ontario, insisted that Trudeau should phone Davis one last time.

9:40 p.m. As he hung up the phone, the Ontario premier confided to a small group gathered in his suite at the Four Seasons: "Remember this moment, it could be historic."

What had happened was that Trudeau had, for the time being, suspended his threat of a referendum and accepted the provincial amending formula, as long as it did not include automatic compensation. Davis did not talk to him about the now-famous "notwithstanding" clause.

11:00 p.m. Lévesque retired to his suite and called his wife. At the time she was helping out with a United Way fund-raising campaign in Chicoutimi in her native Saguenay-Lac St. Jean region. There were no messages for him, and he let it be known that he expected to be back in Quebec early the next morning.

11:30 p.m. The negotiations which had been going on since the beginning of the evening were coming to a head. There was a parade of premiers to Allan Blakeney's door at the Château Laurier: Peter Lougheed, Brian Peckford, and Angus MacLean (who had to be hauled out of bed). McMurtry was there as well, keeping his master, the premier of Ontario, informed. John Buchanan was reached, *in extremis*, at the Ottawa airport where he was waiting to catch the last flight to Halifax. His mother-in-law had died and he was hurrying home to be with his family.

In Bill Davis's suite, Bill Bennett and Richard Hatfield were poring over the new plan, while Roy Romanow was keeping the line open to Blakeney's room. Michael Kirby was keeping an eye on the operation over Davis's shoulder.

Midnight. Chrétien called Roy Romanow to find out where the negotiations with the other provinces stood, but the Saskatchewan minister did not return his call. An anxious Chrétien hardly slept at all that night, which, according to him, explained the dark circles around his eyes the next morning.

"I never took part in the negotiations the night of November 5," he claims today.

Nor did Trudeau seem to be a leading player during what has become known, in Quebec at least, as "the night of the long knives." What happened is that both sides of the negotiating table knew what they wanted. While Trudeau and Lévesque slept in their beds, the English Canadians cut a deal among themselves at Quebec's expense.

Thursday, November 5

1:30 a.m. The negotiations were almost complete. The rough draft of the agreement was given to secretaries who typed up a two-page version. Copies of the document were slipped under the doors of a number of the premiers and ministers. Allan Blakeney called Ed Broadbent at home and read him the proposed agreement over the phone.

7:00 a.m. When René Lévesque got up that morning, nothing had been slipped under his door. He called his wife and left for the daily breakfast consensus. Yes, he had slept well, he told her, and no, nothing had happened since the previous evening.

At 24 Sussex Drive, the limousines began pulling up: first Michael Pitfield, then Michael Kirby, and finally Jean Chrétien arrived.

"Jean, I could just kiss you," Trudeau told him.

Shortly after 8 a.m., René Lévesque arrived a little late at the Château Laurier suite where his colleagues were just finishing their scrambled eggs.

"We have something for you," Peckford told him casually. (To neutralize him during the course of the night, Blakeney had offered the Newfoundland premier the honour of proposing the compromise solution: "Newfoundland was the last province to enter Confederation, so it's normal after all.")

"What's this now?" Lévesque said just as casually.

He began to read, and he continued reading as his eggs congealed and his coffee grew cold. Six of the members of what used to be the gang of eight tiptoed out of the room. For close to twenty minutes Lévesque sat alone with Peter Lougheed. The Albertan felt badly about having betrayed him. This time it was Lévesque who felt "like throwing up."

10:00 a.m. The eleven first ministers met for one last time in the fifth-floor conference room.

"I don't like this notwithstanding clause," groused Trudeau. "Why not limit its effect to five years? That way the premiers would have to assume the blame for overriding their voters' rights every five years . . . "

"That's a good idea," said several of the premiers, anxious to get this over with.

Bill Davis tried one last time to find some common ground for Trudeau and Lévesque to stand on. But the Charter would have the effect of cutting his language law, Bill 101, to pieces. There was no way Lévesque could accept. "Never," he said. "There would be riots in the streets of Montreal."

Trudeau offered Quebec financial compensation for constitutional amendments affecting culture and education.

Lévesque countered with one last plea for his referendum idea.

Lougheed murmured to Chrétien: "I don't want anything to do with an arrangement that takes away Lévesque's jurisdiction over language."

"That's between us Quebeckers," Chrétien assured him.

11:00 a.m. The eleven first ministers returned to the great conference hall where the television cameras awaited them.

"This macabre farce will remain an incontestable historic event," declared Lévesque. "In the tissue of our collective life, we will never, ever accept the effects of this stab in the back."

4:00 p.m. On the way to the Gatineau airport, where the Quebec premier's plane had been symbolically standing by ready to depart throughout the conference, Lévesque called his wife once more.

"We've been screwed," he said.

"He was crushed," recalled Corinne Côté-Lévesque. "He kept it inside himself, just as he did after the referendum, but his voice gave him away. I've never seen him so low, not even after the referendum."

Part Five

Trudeau Bides His Time
(1982–   )

"We have to realize that Canada is not immortal, but if it is going to go, let it go with a bang rather than a whimper."

21

First, Deal with Bourassa

"We are going to make history," Trudeau told Quebeckers a week after the constitutional accord was signed.

But in Vancouver, on November 24, 1981, he added that his work was not yet done. "If we don't want to see this country broken up by centrifugal forces, we have to stop the pendulum before it swings too far."

Once again the federal government would try to shift the precarious balance of powers over to its side. This time it had nothing to do with constitutional formulas or individual rights, but with the economy. The government had serious work to do.

The decorations had barely been taken down after the 1982 New Year's celebrations when Trudeau took everyone by surprise by announcing the creation of a new department of regional industrial expansion, whose initiatives would be channelled through a system of "regional councils." These would be staffed by federal bureaucrats who, like veritable commissars of the new Trudeau republic, would henceforth meddle directly in regional development without so much as a nod to the provincial governments.

This administrative reform was drafted in great secrecy by Michael Pitfield at the very time Pierre Trudeau was making conciliatory overtures to the English provinces to get them to sign the constitutional patriation accord. Another architect of this was Bob Rabinovich, today a senior policy adviser to Jean Chrétien.

"The old kind of federalism," explained Trudeau, "whereby we gave money to the provinces, only to get a kick in the teeth in return because it wasn't enough, and then had to watch them spend it and take the credit . . . That kind of federalism is finished."

This is what it all boiled down to: not only did the federal government want to decide the future of the regions, but it wanted to have a high political profile while it did so. In part this was motivated by the re-election of the Parti québécois on April 13, 1981, which took the federal Liberals by surprise.

They thought they had brought René Lévesque to his knees once and for all in May 1980. The federal strategists may have dismissed it as a myth, but the general impression that the PQ was running a good government was undiminished by the referendum result, allowing the separatist phoenix to rise again from the ashes of the "yes" campaign. What really got the goat of the Trudeau Liberals was that Lévesque had managed to get himself re-elected despite the fact that they held all but one of the federal seats in the province.

"They take the money and they don't even say thank you," complained Trudeau's Quebec MPs, who were never invited to cut the ribbon at factory openings, even when the project had been financed by the federal Treasury Board.

But while Michael Pitfield and his acolytes may have been experts at conceiving government systems, they were not nearly as good at managing the kitty. The grand plan was unveiled just as the country was approaching a full-blown recession, and the federal government discovered that it didn't have the money for its new Regional Development Fund. Ministers who wanted to achieve a high profile could only do so by talk, not action.

In December 1981, Trudeau opened up another front when he accused René Lévesque of betraying the Quiet Revolution. "Quebec must turn a deaf ear to those who preach that it should withdraw behind its borders."

But Trudeau was like a pot calling the kettle black. His government used the Senate as a roundabout route to bring in legislation aimed directly at some of the Quiet Revolution's achievements. This time Trudeau had Hydro-Québec and the Caisse de dépôt et placement (the Quebec pension fund) in his sights.

Marc Lalonde, energy minister at the time, gave his National Energy Board the power to expropriate a corridor across Quebec if Newfoundland would finance, with American help if need be, a new large-scale hydro development in the Churchill Falls basin.

It was such a brazen move that no one really took it seriously. To push its power line across the province, Ottawa would once again have to send in the army.

At the same time the government wanted to put pressure on Saskatchewan, which was refusing to let Manitoba build a power line across the province so it could sell some of its hydro power to Alberta. But the principal target was Quebec. It was such a sledge-hammer approach, however, that no government, not even Pierre Trudeau's, had the temerity to apply it.

At the same time, Quebec had been put on the alert, and the incident served as a dress rehearsal for what was to come.

A few months later, André Ouellet, minister of consumer and corporate affairs, quietly had a bill (S-31) introduced in the Senate. Its aim was to block the development of the Quebec pension fund.

The fund, which managed Quebeckers' public old-age pension contributions, had been created in 1963. On April 20, 1966, Quebec benefited from the opting-out concept of Canadian federalism for the last time in its history when it set up its own old-age pension system. In succeeding years, the Caisse grew even faster than its architects had calculated. In 1966, they predicted that the fund would reach $4 billion within twenty years. In fact, by 1982 it already had $15 billion, and since then it has more than doubled to make it the largest single pool of investment capital in the country.

In 1982 English Canada asked Trudeau to put the Caisse in its place: eighteen years after he wrote his manifesto on "functional politics," he would put it into practice.

Or at least he would try.

The chairman of Canadian Pacific, Fred Burbidge, personally asked Trudeau to limit the percentage of shares that the provinces could acquire in firms involved in interprovincial transportation.

At the time, the Alberta government had recently acquired Pacific Western Airlines using its Heritage Fund, and had moved to transfer its headquarters from Vancouver to Calgary. The government's official line was that it wanted to prevent Alberta from doing a repeat performance by taking over Canadian Pacific and moving its headquarters from Montreal to Calgary.

But before long the cat was out of the bag, particularly because the minister assigned to sell the bill was André Ouellet, one of the most hamfisted members of Trudeau's cabinet. Across the country

he was best known as the minister who had foisted urea formal-
dehyde insulation on a legion of unsuspecting homeowners. In
Quebec he was renowned as the minister responsible for doing
Pierre Trudeau's dirty work in the province. Brian Mulroney and
the Conservatives would later zero in on him as their prime target.

The Caisse was already a major shareholder in Canadian Pacific,
with about 10 percent of the shares. Paul Desmarais, of Quebec's
Power Corp., controlled another 12 percent of the CP shares, which
meant that close to a quarter of the Canadian transportation giant
—which included CP Rail, CP Air, CP Shipping, and Smith Trucking, etc. —was in Quebec's hands. A dangerous situation.

Moreover, since the election of the PQ, and the appointment of
Jean Campeau as Caisse chairman, the pension fund had become an
increasingly high-profile player on the Canadian investment scene.

"It amounts to letting in nationalism by the back door," protested
Ouellet. "It's socialism in disguise. And Campeau is nothing but a
puppet in Parizeau's hands."

"In the national interest, I would rather put my faith in private-
sector firms than in the provinces," said Transport Minister Jean-
Luc Pépin.

Fred Burbidge mobilized opinion in English Canada against the
"provincialization of a national enterprise by a government dedi-
cated to separatism."

But the Quebec finance minister at the time happened to be
Jacques Parizeau, who, in 1963, had conceived the Caisse for Jean
Lesage as "an instrument of economic development for the province
of Quebec."

Parizeau caused a sensation when he assembled the leading representatives of what he called "the rising guard" of Quebec's business
community to back him up en masse at a Senate committee hearing
on a controversial bill. The fact that Parizeau was appearing before
a parliamentary committee in Ottawa was an event in itself, but the
lineup of Quebec business leaders he brought with him was even
more impressive. The group included Jean Campeau of the Caisse;
Jean-Claude Lebel, head of the province's general financing corporation; François Lebrun, of the Quebec Industrial Development Corporation; Paul Bourassa of SOQUEM, the Quebec mining corp.;
and Pierre Martin of SOQUIP, the oil and gas agency.

But the assault squad on Bill S-31 was not limited to PQ tech-
nocrats. Pierre Lortie, chairman of the Montreal Stock Exchange,

mustered an impressive contingent from the private sector, and Conservative Senators from Quebec like Arthur Tremblay, Martial Asselin, and Jacques Flynn provided covering fire from the other side of the committee table.

The government had been hoping to get the bill passed quietly, in the somnolent atmosphere of the Senate chamber. "When the police raid your house, they don't warn you first," said André Ouellet by way of explaining the government's decision to introduce this key piece of legislation late one afternoon before a handful of Senators.

In fact, most of the members of Trudeau's cabinet were not even aware of the bill. "The introduction of Bill S-31 was the kind of decision Trudeau tended to make within his inner circle of associates," said Francis Fox, who was in the cabinet at the time. "The rest of us wouldn't have a lot to say about it."

Trudeau would finally back down on November 23, 1983, when the government withdrew the bill. But considerable damage had already been done. Bay Street was wary of the Caisse, which was obliged to turn to American financial markets. With the value of the Canadian dollar falling, it was not a time for sloganeering. But once again, Trudeau had put his obsession with separatism, and his need to wage guerilla warfare with the PQ, before the national economic interest.

(How ironic little twists of history can be. In 1989, Marc Lalonde happened to find himself on Steinberg's board when the Caisse de dépôt was backing Quebec-based Socanav's takeover of the Quebec food retailing giant. Socanav was a shipping conglomerate that had grown out of oil transportation and gasoline retail outlets. Its chief executive, Michel Gaucher, is one of Quebec's leading new entrepreneurs. Michael Pitfield, then vice-chairman of Power Communications, referred to the Caisse as gangrene that was rotting Quebec's private sector. And since the Caisse also had a substantial block of shares in Provigo, another large provincial food retailer, the "three hawks," now declawed of any real power, were reduced to sneering at the "grocery-store nationalism" overtaking Robert Bourassa's "Provigo state.")

Right after Pierre Trudeau withdrew his Bill S-31, he lost another fight: this time against Robert Bourassa.

In 1969 the federal Liberals had considered sending Jean Marchand back to Quebec to block Bourassa's rise to the Quebec Liberal leadership. In 1983, with Bourassa poised to make a stunning
comeback after his disgrace in 1976, Trudeau decided he would
get involved personally this time.

"I guess my greatest disappointment is my inability to get the
provincial Liberal Party, first in Lesage's day and then in Bourassa's
day, to be very strong federalists," Trudeau told his official biographer. "There are still too many Liberal leaders who go on the
conventional and intellectual wisdom that somehow 'Quebec City
is our government.'"

Pierre Trudeau had never been on good terms with Claude Ryan,
and when Ryan resigned from the provincial Liberal leadership,
Trudeau put his troops on alert.

"I'm sure that there were doubts about my faith in federalism,"
says Bourassa with a knowing smile. "In Ottawa they were convinced that my concept of federalism wasn't the same as theirs."

In 1982, Marc Lalonde got word to Bourassa that Trudeau was
prepared to offer him a plum appointment. To get him out of the
way perhaps?

But Bourassa wouldn't bite, and throughout the summer of 1983
the federal Liberals desperately cast about for an acceptable candidate who could beat Bourassa at the provincial convention.
"They tried André Ouellet, Marc Lalonde, Jean Chrétien. They
went down a whole list of names," remembers Bourassa. "They
knew perfectly well that I was aware they were trying to block me."

But the only candidate who had a remotely serious chance of
beating Bourassa was Raymond Garneau. Trudeau had first spotted him in 1964 during a get-together at the home of Quebec
businessman Georges Bussières. Garneau and Lévesque were
engaged in a lively discussion over what direction the provincial
Liberal party should take.

"Quebec nationalists should carry on their fight within the federal structures," said the young Garneau.

"Godammit, Garneau, you little shit," Lévesque exploded.

Trudeau, who had been observing the scene from the other side
of the room, came over and tapped Garneau on the shoulder. "I
think you've won," he said. "When René Lévesque starts to swear,
it means he's lost."

From then on, Garneau was the federal Liberals' protégé in the provincial party. His federalism was considered more orthodox than either Ryan's or Bourassa's. In 1979 Marc Lalonde had offered him the solidly Liberal Quebec City seat of Louis-Hébert, left vacant by the death of Albanie Morin. But Garneau demurred. "I don't see myself playing sixth, seventh, or eighth fiddle in Ottawa," he said.

In 1983 he was president of the Montreal City and District Savings Bank, earning more than $300,000 a year. But he also knew that the next leader of the provincial Liberal party would inevitably become premier of Quebec and he was seriously tempted, though his wife Pauline wanted nothing more to do with politics.

The anglophone element of the party, the business sector, the federal Liberals, and a good portion of the provincial organization centred around Quebec City, which was controlled by Marc-Yvan Côté, were prepared to support his candidacy. He decided to talk it over openly with Robert Bourassa, who, after all, was still a friend.

"I've prepared myself for this," Bourassa told him. "I don't see why I should have to withdraw. If you can prove to me that I'm hurting the party, I won't stay five minutes longer. But to the extent that I'm helping the party, I'm free to do what I like. I have experience. I've been premier for seven years, and I can be premier again. Don't expect me to back off now . . . "

Despite the groundswell of support, Garneau wasn't doing very well in the polls. It was then that Pierre Trudeau decided to intervene personally. Near the end of the spring of 1983, he invited Garneau and his wife to 24 Sussex Drive.

"Raymond's wife was quite hostile to the idea of him going back into politics," remembers Bourassa, "and Trudeau tried to convince her to let her husband run against me for the leadership. I found Trudeau's zeal, and the way he got involved personally, quite unusual. His summoning a candidate and his wife like that convinced me that he was out to block me.

"Knowing Pierre Trudeau to be so haughty, so above it all, made it an even more extraordinary gesture on his part."

It almost worked. Raymond Garneau was sorely tempted, and his wife was no doubt flattered by the prime minister's insistence.

But Henri Dutil and some other businessmen from Quebec City commissioned a poll that showed Bourassa was far out in front in the preference of Liberal party supporters.

During what seemed like an interminable weekend, Garneau and his brains trust—Pierre Lortie and Marc-Yvan Côté, among others —weighed their chances. Marc Lalonde called a number of times, raising the stakes with increasingly generous offers of support.

Finally, at two in the morning, when he was at last alone with his wife, Raymond Garneau decided he would not run against Robert Bourassa.

"There was panic in Ottawa," chuckles Bourassa. "They knew that if I were to be elected, I'd be able to do whatever I liked. I didn't owe them anything, and they said to themselves: 'He's not going to help us.'"

At the time there was no such thing as a Meech Lake accord. "But they knew there would be one," says Bourassa. "And there was one. The federal Liberals knew there was a price to be paid for Quebec adhering to the Canadian Constitution. A price they weren't too ready to pay then, and still aren't ready to pay."

After Trudeau's resounding "success" in the constitutional wars in 1981, he proceeded to lose all his battles against the separatists and even the Quebec federalists. He was now into his political decline; soon he would end up as a sort of national Maurice Duplessis, saddled with a reputation as a tyrant at the head of a corrupt administration.

There was widespread astonishment when he sympathized with General Jaruzelski, who had just imposed martial law in Poland. But some of his former victims, like Gérald Godin, remembered October 1970: "Our first federalist's haste to bestow his blessing on the Polish version of the War Measures Act leads me to conclude that within our *Cité libriste* lurks a warmonger. That secretly, he dreams of soldiers and tanks. And that 1970 was more than a passing phase of military fever."

There was worse to come. The Trudeau years drew to a close amid a veritable orgy of patronage.

The years during which Robert Bourassa had popularized the concept of "profitable federalism," followed by the PQ victory, convinced the federal strategists that Quebec would remain loyal to the federal regime only if it was clear to them that they were cashing in directly on its largesse.

With this in mind, Marc Lalonde had, over the years, developed a system of distributing federal contracts that involved much convoluted red tape, and was so subtly programmed into the computers at the departments of Regional Industrial Development, Supply and Services, and Public Works, that even the auditor general, and, to a greater degree, Brian Mulroney's Conservatives, were unable to figure out how it worked.

If the government needed architects, entrepreneurs, engineers, or lawyers, the contracts always went to friends of the party in power.

Every Thursday morning, in a room at the parliamentary restaurant, half a dozen Quebec ministers would match names to the lists of available jobs submitted by Marc Lalonde's aides.

During his years in office, Pierre Trudeau named 108 people to the Senate. These included close friends like Jacques Hébert; senior associates like Michael Pitfield and Michael Kirby, the architects of his constitutional battle plan; loyal retainers like speechwriters Jean Le Moyne and Philip Gigantès; his faithful parliamentary lieutenant, Allan MacEachen; and his former fisheries minister, Roméo Leblanc.

Just before leaving, he arranged for seventeen more appointments that would end up hanging like an albatross around John Turner's neck for the duration of the disastrous Liberal election campaign of 1984. There were those who compared it to the last days of Duplessis, a sad end for the *Cité libre* polemicist of yesteryear.

When he pulled his last pirouette on the stage at the Ottawa Civic Centre at the 1984 leadership convention before heading for the wings with his three sons, he got a last standing ovation.

But there were no cries of "Trudeau, Canada," as there had been the evening of April 6, 1968. No one felt "like an orphan," as on the morning of November 21, 1979. Instead, there was a vague sense of uneasiness in the air.

Before leaving, Trudeau had made the Liberal delegates one last promise, or one last threat . . .

"Political reality is such that a Canadian government that tries to oppose the collective and widespread sentiments of Quebec will not be in power for long, and will be replaced by a government that is more respectful of Quebec . . . "

22

"Wounds to Heal in Quebec"

March 3, 1980, was "transition" day in Ottawa. On that day, Pierre Trudeau's staff returned to the offices in the Langevin Block on Wellington Street that they had turned over to Joe Clark's retinue nine months earlier.

In the elevator that went up to the prime minister's office, some joker had stuck up a piece of paper that said simply: "No more '74!"

It was a reference to 1974 when, after two years in the purgatory of minority government, the Liberals had regained their majority, and their old arrogance, in one fell swoop. This time, after nine months in opposition, the suggestion was that previous mistakes should be avoided.

But in the February 18, 1980, federal election, the Liberals had also won seventy-four of Quebec's seventy-five seats. At the time, no one, least of all the likes of Marc Lalonde and André Ouellet, who were going around English Canada boasting about their powerful "red machine" in Quebec, could have imagined that "No more '74" would have a different, far more sinister connotation for the Liberals in September 1984.

When Trudeau announced his impending departure on February 29, 1984, the Quebec question was carefully swept under the carpet by his own party. There was not even a "Quebec candidate" to succeed him. And this despite John Turner, who had previously been elected in a Montreal riding in 1962; Jean Chrétien, who posed as French Canada's candidate; and Donald Johnston, the MP for St. Henri-Westmount who shared Trudeau's anglo-Montreal heritage.

There were only two occasions during the race to succeed Trudeau when Quebec's interests surfaced, albeit timidly. The first was when Turner put his foot in it at the news conference where he announced his decision to run. Politically rusty after nine years in the boardrooms of Bay Street, he suggested that minority language rights were none of Ottawa's business. The other also came at the very beginning of the leadership campaign, when Marc Lalonde let it be known that it was not a French Canadian's turn for the party leadership because in keeping with the party's convention of alternation, the leadership should go to an English Canadian. Pierre Trudeau, dismayed that his heirs were already attacking each other, personally intervened in caucus to urge Chrétien to run.

As for the rest, they were mostly interested in finding a winner. They wanted power for power's sake, and the only thing that interested the Liberal party in Quebec was how to maintain enough of a voting block to cling to power.

As for the "74" Quebec MPs, the idea of negotiating their support for the future leader against something like a veto, for example, never entered their minds. Roch LaSalle had their number when he'd called them wet noodles.

Things were different for the Conservatives.

On February 22, 1976, at a Conservative leadership convention in Ottawa, English Canada had ganged up against a Quebec in which loyalties were divided between Brian Mulroney and Claude Wagner, so the job fell to most people's third choice, Joe Clark.

The Tories would go on to pay dearly for their folly in the 1979 and 1980 elections when they were all but wiped off the map in Quebec, and shut out in areas of the country with a strong francophone presence, like the Acadian areas of the Maritimes, the northern and western areas of Ontario, and St. Boniface, Manitoba.

During the constitutional negotiations that followed the referendum, Brian Mulroney supported the Ottawa leader he most admired: Pierre Trudeau. At the time he talked like a fairly orthodox federalist. He lived in Westmount, and he endorsed the hard line against René Lévesque. When he was asked if he was prepared to compensate Quebec financially for programs from which it had opted out, Mulroney's response was straightforward: "Before I asked

Canada to give René Lévesque a cent," he said in a debate televised by Global TV, "I would ask him what he's ready to do for Canada."

Pierre Trudeau took note of this declaration, and for him at least, the message was clear: "I have the impression that Mr. Mulroney has deep loyalties toward Canada, and that this will put him in contradiction with Quebeckers who want to move towards independence. . . . He pleased the delegates from the other provinces when he said he was against financial compensation for Quebec. Those are my positions."

But Brian Mulroney also offered a proposition that seduced the English Canadian Tories: "For 116 years the party has never had a French Canadian leader," he said. "Given that there are eight million francophones and that they have good reason to reject our party, it seems that the time has come to elect a leader who will be able to appeal directly to French Canadians."

Brilliant political strategist that he is, Mulroney adopted the rationale that the Liberal party, Jean Chrétien in particular, had relied on so long: there are 102 ridings in the country in which French Canadians, representing more than 10 percent of the electorate, for all practical purposes elect their chosen candidate by voting *en bloc*.

In 1980, this type of arithmetic worked out to two seats in all of Canada out of the 102 for the Progressive Conservatives.

Brian Mulroney was finally elected leader of the Conservative party with a clear mandate to win the battle of Quebec. But it was not something that worried Trudeau. "I have the feeling that Mr. Mulroney will try to be closer to my positions [than Joe Clark], that he will go to the people rather than to the provincial premiers."

The message that Brian Mulroney read in Quebec's soul during the summer of 1984 was startling in its clarity: "Quit arguing about the Constitution and create some jobs."

Raymond Garneau also sensed that Quebeckers were looking for a way to get revenge on Pierre Trudeau. At the beginning of the 1984 election campaign, Garneau surprised everyone, including his leader, by announcing that he would go to Ottawa to "regain Quebec's veto right."

"A waste of time and energy," sniffed Gil Rémillard, then a Laval University constitutional law professor. Two years later, as Robert Bourassa's intergovernmental affairs minister, he would be only too happy to find an ally like Garneau in John Turner's camp.

But Garneau made a mistake when he also attacked the Parti québécois for having traded away Quebec's veto for "a mess of pottage." It was a mistake because Quebeckers had it in for Pierre Trudeau, not for René Lévesque. This became obvious when Turner's Liberals tried to ignite a separatist witch hunt during the 1984 campaign by pointing the finger at some of Brian Mulroney's Quebec candidates who had voted "yes" in the referendum. They managed to pin down three, but in fact there were several dozen.

An extraordinary historical about-face took place that summer: the party of Laurier and Pierre Trudeau became the *"mange canayens,"* (francophone-bashers) and the Conservatives, the party that had hanged Louis Riel, suddenly stood as the defenders of the "race."

In one stroke, Brian Mulroney had assembled the most formidable coalition a federal leader could hope for in Quebec. Not only did the 1.5 million "yes" supporters fall into line behind the Conservatives, but the Créditistes, the remnants of the Union nationale, and the provincial Liberals did the same. And a substantial segment of the "no" vote, who had not got quite what they had expected in the way of constitutional renewal, seized the opportunity to get back at the federal Liberals for the way Trudeau had suckered them during the constitutional negotiations.

This "rainbow coalition," as it was called at the time, allowed people of varying political hues to forget the wounds inflicted on May 20, 1980. At this point Quebec's national reconciliation began, and the Liberal party realized it could not win against a Quebec that was showing a united front.

"There are wounds to heal in Quebec," said Mulroney to his north shore constituents. "There are worries to calm, enthusiasm to be revived and ties of confidence to be re-established. After the referendum, Quebeckers suffered a collective trauma. Quebeckers love Quebec and they are proud of Canada. Their hearts are big enough to embrace both allegiances."

For Mulroney, it was no longer simply an electoral calculation. As Senator Arthur Tremblay said, "He too is Québécois in his bones." The *"petit gars de Baie-Comeau"* was helped in his conversion to Quebec nationalism by his university pal, one Lucien Bouchard.

On September 5, 1984, at about 1:00 a.m., slightly dazed by the jubilant clamour in the packed Baie Comeau sports centre, seduced as much as converted by Arthur Tremblay's arguments and Lucien Bouchard's passionate appeals, his voice ravaged by fatigue and two months of campaigning, Pierre Trudeau's successor addressed the nation: "We must imbue our federalism with the spirit of fraternity and creativity which gave it birth. What unites one region to another, one ethnic group to another, one language to another, is the sacred link of heart, mind, and soul." That night, as Wilfrid Laurier would have said, Quebec had no opinions, only emotions.

For Brian Mulroney, it was a reprise of the coalition of Sir Wilfrid Laurier's French Canadians and Sir John A. Macdonald's English Canadians against the ultranationalists of Toronto and the denizens of Montreal's "Golden Square Mile."

Robert Bourassa, commenting on the transition from Trudeau to Mulroney, said: "The political chessboard has been altered, but there is still a 'Quebec power' in Ottawa, a very strong Quebec presence."

It was no coincidence that Robert Bourassa spoke of "Quebec power" in Ottawa rather than "French power." For it was with Quebec's government, rather than with the Quebec population, that Mulroney wanted to negotiate. And Trudeau had been wrong in thinking that Mulroney would seek to ally himself with the people instead of with the provincial premiers.

Even René Lévesque let himself be carried away by the charms of what he called *"le beau risque"* (the beautiful risk) of Mulroney federalism. Less than a week after he was sworn in as communications minister in the new Tory cabinet, Marcel Masse boarded a plane and started a lengthy series of federal-provincial consultations on all manner of items that had been "frozen" by the previous administration.

"We have to turn over a new leaf," said Masse after his first meeting with his Quebec counterparts, Communications Minister Jean-François Bertrand, and Cultural Affairs Minister Clément Richard.

Above all, however, Brian Mulroney was a shrewd and prudent political operator. He knew that René Lévesque's party was in decline, and that the government was on its last legs. Had he been a sentimental man, loyal to the memory of Daniel Johnson, with whom he used to have drinks in the Château Frontenac bar during the sixties, he might have tried to strike a deal with Johnson's son

Pierre-Marc, who had become the new PQ leader in the spring of 1985.

But he decided to wait, for he had nothing to lose. Robert Bourassa was as coldly realistic a political leader as himself, and he offered a constitutional program that was "saleable" in English Canada. He no longer even talked about the notorious "veto right" that had so upset the west.

And where was Trudeau in all this?

For a while, he was almost completely forgotten in Canada. He was invited all over the world to give speeches or to attend international seminars. He was honoured with prizes and medals, and he came within a few votes of a Nobel Prize for his "pilgrimage for peace."

He joined a law firm in Montreal where he was reunited with some old acquaintances: Roy Heenan, a specialist in labour-management relations who had built a reputation as a hardliner at the start of the 1970s during the United Aircraft dispute on Montreal's south shore; Peter Blaikie, an anglo-Montrealer who was close to the Conservatives, who had previously served as party president and unsuccessfully contested the party leadership in 1984, and was one of the leaders of the court fight against Bill 101; and Donald Johnston, a loser in the leadership race and the foremost champion of "Trudeauist" orthodoxy within the Liberal party.

Pierre Trudeau travelled a great deal, using the contacts he had made as prime minister to present the interests of several Montreal businessmen: Paul Desmarais of the Power Corporation in China, for instance, and Bernard Lamarre of Lavalin in the Soviet Union.

Bit by bit, in Ottawa as in Quebec, people became convinced that he had lost interest in politics once and for all. But there was one "incident" that reminded Pierre Trudeau that Quebeckers were not yet ready to forgive him his strong-arm tactics.

According to tradition, former Canadian prime ministers have their portrait painted by the artist of their choice. Trudeau let it be known that he would like a portrait of his three sons by the renowned Québécois painter Jean-Paul Lemieux. But the old man of Ile aux Coudres, downriver from Quebec City, refused for "personal reasons." A Nova Scotia painter, Tom Forrestall, finally did the portrait.

Trudeau barely twitched an eyebrow in 1985 when the Quebec Liberal party demanded a preamble to the Constitution that recognized Quebec as the home of a distinct society and the cornerstone of the francophone element of Canadian duality. No one, especially not Trudeau, who had seen the failure of so many constitutional conferences, believed that the issue could be so quickly settled, particularly in light of the ambitious scope of the party's program.

(The Quebec Liberals also wanted a veto on all constitutional matters; clearly defined limits to federal spending power; increased jurisdiction over immigration; and a say in the nomination of Supreme Court judges. Along with the clause recognizing Quebec as a distinct society, these were Quebec's "five conditions" for becoming a full partner in Confederation.)

Robert Bourassa's return as premier in a provincial election in December 1985 also left Trudeau indifferent. "I don't know if the new improved Robert Bourassa will conform to my idea of a leader of the Quebec Liberal party," he said. "He may possibly have a certain number of clear ideas about where he wants to go, but that was certainly not the case during his first period in office."

Bourassa knew very well where he wanted to go. And he even decided to talk to Trudeau about it.

The two met for lunch at a restaurant on St. Denis Street in Montreal. The meeting had been arranged by Rémi Bujold, a former MP under Trudeau and now Bourassa's chief of staff. Officially speaking, Trudeau and Bourassa were simply going to touch on the major domestic and international issues. "I talked to him about Quebec's five conditions for signing the 1982 constitutional accord," said Bourassa. "He disagreed with me, but we were still at the beginning of the negotiations, and we didn't know if we would ever wind up with an agreement."

The Quebec premier was careful not to say that he had asked Raymond Garneau to convert the federal Liberal party to the virtues of the distinct society. A few weeks later, Trudeau would learn from Serge Joyal that John Turner had bought Quebec's five conditions almost without reservations, and that he was already en route to an important interview with *Le Devoir,* during which he would announce his conversion. He added that the Quebec federal Liberals would propose recognition of Quebec as a distinct society at the party's national convention in November.

Pierre Trudeau felt betrayed. Brian Mulroney was surprised.

Negotiations continued in deep secrecy between Quebec, Ottawa, and the English-speaking provinces. Mulroney and Bourassa did not want to upset any apple carts, and above all they did not want to provoke a national debate. The Liberal conversion had eliminated a potentially important bastion of opposition.

On April 30, 1987, at 10:45 p.m., a horde of journalists headed up the dirt road leading to Wilson House, an old stone manor perched on a Gatineau hillside, just above Meech Lake. The lights from the TV cameras and the photographers' flashes pierced the inky darkness that enveloped the pine trees crowding either side of the road.

Since shortly before noon, the eleven first ministers had been closeted in a first-floor meeting room. There were only two observers present, a federal civil servant and one from Alberta representing the provinces. The two sat apart from the first ministers, taking notes but not joining in the discussion.

When the eleven emerged from Wilson House, they were brandishing two sheets of paper.

The next day the Quebec newspapers headlined: "Canada says yes to Quebec: Mulroney keeps Trudeau's promise of May 1980."

It was intolerably provoking to Trudeau. To be reminded that he had "deceived" Quebeckers when he put the heads of his Quebec MPs on the block.

"I have to do something," Trudeau said to Gérard Pelletier. "But how?"

"You could write something for a major Quebec newspaper — for *La Presse*," Pelletier answered. "But you'll have to keep a lid on your hostility," he added, knowing perhaps that his former *Cité libre* colleague had trouble restraining himself once he took his stiletto pen in hand.

Several days later, Gérard Pelletier contacted Michel Roy, who was publisher of *La Presse* at the time. Roy had known Trudeau since the 1950s, and over the years they had maintained an amicable relationship. "Trudeau and I are concerned about this Meech Lake accord," said Pelletier. "We can't let it pass. We want to launch a debate and to do it we want to start with a big bang. Will *La Presse* run Trudeau's statement?"

"Will we ever!" said Roy without a second's hesitation. Roy had become the editor-in-chief of a large newspaper, but he still had the reporter's instinct for a scoop.

A few days later, it was Trudeau himself who called Roy at *La Presse*.

"I'd like to write something in the style of *Cité libre*, something very polemical," he told Roy. "I can't stomach this Meech Lake accord and I want to give it all I've got."

When Michel Roy got the first draft of Trudeau's text, he blanched at some of the personal attacks it contained. He found the conclusion particularly hard to take: "Alas, only one eventuality had not been foreseen," wrote Trudeau, "that one day the government of Canada might fall into the hands of a wimp. It has now happened. And the Right Honourable Brian Mulroney, P.C., M.P., with the complicity of ten provincial premiers, has already entered into history as the author of a constitutional document which — if it is accepted by the people and their legislators — will render the Canadian state totally impotent. That would destine it, given the dynamics of power, to be governed eventually by eunuchs."

"I told Mr. Trudeau that certain parts in his text went a little too far," remembers Michel Roy. "He had been prime minister himself, and the position, whoever may hold it, calls for a certain respect. There was a long silence at the other end of the line."

The next day Trudeau himself brought the definitive version of his text down to the offices of *La Presse*. He hadn't changed a word.

The English version, published the same day in the *Toronto Star*, was translated by an employee at Trudeau's law firm. "I didn't want to do the text in English," confided Trudeau, as though he wanted to reserve his polemic vitriol for French Quebeckers.

Normally a newspaper piece of such length, with such a high-profile by-line, is worth a small fortune to North American newspapers. The standard payment for such a piece is worth more than $1,500.

Was Trudeau paid for his "*Cité-libre*-style" freelance piece? At first Michel Roy thought that a cheque had been mailed out to Trudeau, but after checking the paper's books, he corrected himself. "I was wrong," he said. "We didn't pay Trudeau anything for his contribution . . . though we know the man isn't indifferent to such details."

23

The Final (?) Charge . . .

" A re you happy?" asked Jack Webster, the crusty reigning monarch of B.C. talk shows, a crowded and competitive field in this part of the country where a disproportionate number of ex-cabinet ministers wind up as hotline hosts. Though Webster normally spent much of his on-air time denouncing Pierre Elliott Trudeau and everything he stood for, Trudeau would happily appear on his show because he found his sessions with Webster a bracing workout. But for once, this time, they weren't sparring.

"I hope I'll be happy when I retire," replied Trudeau. "And as to whether I'll rate, as you say, a footnote in history, I don't know. It will depend on who writes the history, I guess."

Pierre Trudeau had never been fond of explaining himself. He liked apologizing even less. "When you make a mistake, you live with it," he told Jacques Hébert one day.

But then Trudeau had every reason to be happy, with himself and the world, on this 30th day of June 1984. He was at the wheel of his now vintage Mercedes, and the top was down. He was driving up to the Gatineau hills with a twenty-four-year-old blonde on the seat beside him. He had just regained his freedom.

Canada had at last been "decolonized." The fundamental rights of all Canadians, of francophones outside Quebec, of anglophones within Quebec, native peoples — Indians, Inuit, and Métis — and women, had been forever protected against any future legislation by an oppressive Parliament, or any provincial administration with jackboot inclinations.

The principle of equalization, the redistribution of wealth between rich and poor provinces had been clearly defined. A new amending formula, more flexible and without the "bonus for separation" opting-out formula, had been worked out and locked into place. True, there was the odious "notwithstanding" clause, that last-minute wrinkle of such enormous implications; but even it had a five-year sunset provision. All this had been protected, enshrined, carved in stone.

But Brian Mulroney, and Trudeau's own successor, John Turner, along with a host of Quebec commentators, were already beginning to chip away at his accomplishments. "That's not the way to write history," he protested.

During the summer of 1988 his former principal secretary, Tom Axworthy, persuaded him to oversee the editing of a book on the "Trudeau years." He wrote the conclusion himself, putting a lid, as it were, on the pressure cooker he had stoked up during nineteen years of political confrontations. The book was published in both French and English in March 1990.

In 1989 Richard Nixon's former secretary of state, Henry Kissinger, also suggested to Trudeau that he should begin writing his memoirs.

"I don't like to write, and I don't have the time," said Trudeau, shrugging his shoulders.

"But that's not how it works," Kissinger told him. "First you get a million-dollar deal from a publisher. Then you hire five or six of your former aides whom you trust and they write the book for you."

Trudeau was frankly tempted. Not by the money, which would, after all, have to be shared with the hired hands, but by the opportunity to write history himself and to select the place he thought he deserved.

The problem was that when he had broken into print, with the "Cité-libre-style" polemic published in French in *La Presse* and in English in the *Toronto Star*, it stirred up a tempest that threatened to sweep him away along with his opponents.

After publishing the piece in his paper, Michel Roy solicited a reply from Claude Ryan, and welcomed those of others—notably Senator Lowell Murray, Brian Mulroney's minister of federal-provincial relations, and Maurice Blain, a former *Cité libre* contemporary, now a law professor at the University of Montreal. Blain wrote: "*Cité libre* would probably not have run this last provocation, not only because it is arrogant but also because it is antidemocratic."

Even so, Trudeau was not completely isolated. A number of commentators, such as Marcel Adam and Lysiane Gagnon in *La Presse*, the troop of "Trudeauites" who regularly write in *The Gazette* and the *Toronto Star*, and Liberal parliamentarians already nostalgic for the Trudeau years, agreed with his suggestion that the constitutional accord concocted in the space of ten hours at Meech Lake looked decidedly slap-dash when examined closely.

Michel Roy then offered Trudeau more space so he could "pursue his polemic" and respond to his detractors. But Trudeau never took him up on it. By then his friends in the House of Commons and the Senate were offering him an even better pulpit.

On August 27, 1987, at 6:28 p.m., Pierre Trudeau began his presentation to the joint Senate-Commons committee studying the Meech Lake agreement. It was in the historic Railway Committee Room, just down the corridor from the Library of Parliament. The room was filled with young Trudeauites, mostly anglophones recruited in Montreal and Toronto.

(The former prime minister was discreetly reminded that he no longer exercised control over the course of events when Brian Mulroney deliberately chose the same day to announce an important cabinet shuffle. This meant Trudeau would have to share the headlines with his successor the next morning, and he let it be known that he didn't like it.)

Essentially, Trudeau said two things: that English Canada had paid too dearly to make peace with Quebec, and that the truce would be short-lived. Worse yet, the Meech Lake accord would rot the very foundations of the Canadian state: its executive power, its legislative power, and its judicial power.

Apart from the reaction of sycophantic Robert Kaplan, one of his former ministers from Toronto, Trudeau encountered nothing but criticism. None of the "French Canadians" who joined in the two-and-a-half-hour debate, not even Franco-Ontarian Jean-Robert Gauthier (Liberal), or Franco-Manitoban Léo Duguay (Conservative) ventured to endorse Trudeau's pessimistic view.

But in another parliamentary appearance, this time in the Senate, on March 30, 1988, Trudeau once more poured out all his contempt for the Quebec intellectuals. (And just by coincidence,

Brian Mulroney had another cabinet shuffle to announce that day!)*

Trudeau was there to set the record straight because, as he said, it "distressed him to see the way some people were allowing themselves to rewrite Quebec history."

In the august red chamber, the benches were filled by many of his former colleagues, whom he had himself appointed and who would sit there until they reached the age of seventy-five. Before this audience, the former prime minister betrayed his anguish at being rejected by the élite of a society from which he had become more and more removed, even though he had chosen to spend his final years in Quebec and to raise his three sons there.

Trudeau recognized that it was becoming increasingly difficult to back off from Meech Lake; to withdraw the promise made to Quebec on April 30, 1987: "There will be quite a fuss in Quebec if it turns out that Meech Lake is rejected. I think that in the short term we will see a strong wave of indignation in Quebec, and not only among the opinion leaders. But I would say to Quebeckers that this is not the first time something like this has happened. . . . And if the media say so, instead of emitting great cries of indignation, I believe that Quebeckers will turn the page and look to see who won last night's hockey game." No doubt this is what Trudeau was hoping they would do on the night of November 5, 1981 . . .

As for the intelligentsia of his native province, the "General Jaruzelski" of Quebec — as Gérald Godin called him — always complained bitterly that they liked him no more than he liked them. He took the opportunity to settle one last score: "Naturally," he sneered, "it is nice to benefit from special treatment, and this is why the Quebec intellectuals have been so silent about the Meech Lake accord.

"Quebec writers, artists, musicians, and poets will no doubt succeed if they have talent, whether Quebec has special status or not. But if they are less gifted, the Québécois writers, poets, artists, and musicians will have a better chance for success in Quebec because

---

* Editor's Note: On the same day the author was ejected from the Senate press gallery when he protested Mr. Trudeau's extensive use of English during his presentation.

they do not have to compete with the rest of the country. This is why federalism has always seemed such a wonderful system to me, because it makes Quebeckers do what they are quite capable of doing: competing with others, like those people in Nova Scotia who think they are God's gift to mankind. They can show them that we are just as good. This is how we improve ourselves. If we confine ourselves within a special status, with its own powers, there will only be other members of the clan to compete with, which will be much easier."

It was the same argument, almost word for word, that Trudeau had used in his *Cité libre* articles thirty years before.

But in the meantime, Quebec had changed considerably, and a number of his former disciples openly recognized the fact.

"It's a good thing that some members are defeated in elections," said Francis Fox. "In a way it's like sending players to the bench."

The former MP for Argenteuil-Deux-Montagnes and a minister in Trudeau's cabinet was one of those who was buried by the Conservative landslide that rocked Quebec's political landscape on September 4, 1984. When Fox returned to his law firm in Montreal's Place Victoria, his colleagues freely told him off for his arrogance in office, and particularly for the way Quebec had been treated during the constitutional patriation exercise.

"When you come back to Montreal as I did, you notice that this is a dynamic society, that it's changing," said Fox. "And if a society is dynamic, its institutions have to change as well. Quebec is obviously a distinct society. It is not only desirable but essential that Quebec have a French countenance. I've seen the Europe of 1992 in the making—a major change, maybe even a revolution. But here you get the impression that if you change anything, it'll be the end of the world."

Serge Joyal, another Trudeau disciple, went even further, asking if the Liberal party has a Quebec problem: "Quebeckers have at least gained one thing from all these years of broken dreams. They have discovered they have at least one common value: language. They share it, and it holds them together, protects them, and makes them different from others.

"Quebeckers have lost their heroes: Drapeau, Lévesque, Trudeau. They have lost their political faith, their family faith, their religious faith. They have now sublimated their linguistic unity."

*   *   *

Pierre Trudeau, like Joyal, Fox, and many others, also came back
to Montreal in 1984, but he no longer moved in the same professional circles. With the exception of a few diehard loyalists like
Gérard Pelletier and Marc Lalonde, it was mostly anglo-Montrealers
and the Toronto élite who still fawned over him.

As such he realized that he would have to refurbish his intellectual wardrobe. "Until I got into politics, I spent the previous fifteen
years accumulating ideas about how society should be run, keeping
up on all the literature . . . reading what was written about it, and
so on. In a sense, that baggage of acquisitions, intellectual and
other, that I had when I came into the party, I'm not able to renew."

Brian Mulroney and David Peterson tried to get Trudeau to
moderate his statements. Former associates in the senior civil service tried to explain the implications of Meech Lake to him. Some
were disturbed by his stubbornness and his tenacious refusal to
recognize the distinct character of Quebec society. Others were
infuriated. His extreme positions isolated him, and perhaps caused
him pain. "Trudeau feels abandoned," says Paul Tellier. "People he
thought were his disciples, like Fox and Joyal, are no longer there."

Those of his former ministers who would still have lunch with
him from time to time in one or another of Montreal's trendier
restaurants no longer dared bring up the Quebec question with him
because it always ended in an argument. "Because of his position
on Meech Lake," said one of them, "Trudeau no longer feels at
ease in his own party."

Like a wounded old lion, Trudeau gritted his teeth and decided to
fight to the finish.

In November 1987, John Roberts, one of his former ministers,
met him in Montreal. Speaking in Trudeau's name, he announced:
"The battle will be fought in the provincial legislatures, and we
will try to obtain the support of Liberals in this fight."

To this end the "patriarch" made himself available to receptive
provincial Liberal leaders like Frank McKenna from New Brunswick and Manitoba's Sharon Carstairs. His great hope was in Clyde
Wells, the new premier of Newfoundland, a former minister under
Joey Smallwood, whose attitude had been summed up in his declaration: "For Quebec? Nothing! Nothing! Nothing!"

Wells had the power to undo this agreement which had been
concluded in spite of the opposition it raised and in spite of Tru-

deau's efforts. During the summer of 1989 Marc Lalonde, for one, predicted that the Newfoundland premier would have the audacity to sink the accord at the very last minute, just before the June 23, 1990, ratification deadline. Indeed, on March 22, Wells rescinded the approval of his own legislature.

But it was mainly in the national Liberal leadership race that Pierre Trudeau decided to fight his last battle. At the time of his first short-lived retirement in 1979 he had said: "I would like to assure myself that this party does not fall into the hands of someone with a very different orientation from my own."

He had more or less stayed out of the race to succeed him in 1984. No doubt he suspected, as did many others, that no matter what happened in his own party, Brian Mulroney would succeed him as prime minister. And had he not said that the positions held by "the little guy from Baie Comeau" were in many ways close to his?

But having declared that Mulroney was now acting like a "wimp," and having dismissed David Peterson, Robert Bourassa, and all their colleagues as "eunuchs," he had only his own party left to beat.

"In the summer of 1989 he called Marc Lalonde and offered him his services," said someone who is close to both men. "Trudeau said he was ready to do for Lalonde what Lalonde had done for him in 1968."

At the same time, several influential Liberals, mostly from Montreal, offered Lalonde their support. "If Lalonde runs, I'm behind him," said a number of former MPs and ministers who had already indicated support for either Paul Martin, Jr., or Jean Chrétien.

Though Lalonde was without doubt Trudeau's most brilliant heir, he had made himself many enemies in the party. As he got older, however, Trudeau's political enforcer from the seventies had softened his approach somewhat. He began to turn on the charm, and his intellectual superiority was as seductive as ever. But deep down he had lost none of his arrogance, and he knew all too well that he stood little chance against Jean Chrétien's folksy manner and populist style.

After Lalonde had turned down the opportunity to carry the torch of "Trudeauite" orthodoxy, Trudeau turned to his number two choice, his eternal relief pitcher, Jean Chrétien. He got in touch with Chrétien during the summer of 1989, and set conditions for his support.

"The little guy from Shawinigan" would be the last to back off from a fight with the Quebec intellectuals, who had always shunned him as well. But deep down he dreamed of a reconciliation with them, and as such his criticism of Meech Lake had been fairly muted. In fact, he had only one disagreement with the Meech accord: that the Canadian Charter of Rights and Freedoms should always take precedence over the laws passed by Quebec's National Assembly, distinct society or no distinct society.

But this was not enough for Pierre Trudeau, who obliquely threatened Chrétien: "My support is not unconditional," he reminded him. So, on January 16, 1990, Chrétien announced his support for the "five conditions" of Quebec, but stated that they would never be ratified without amendments, a statement ambiguous enough to keep Trudeau silent.

The candidates for the Liberal leadership knew that Pierre Trudeau's dream of Confederation was still deeply embedded in the hearts of English Canadians and those of millions of new Canadians who had chosen "Trudeau's Canada" when they left their homelands for the new world.

In Quebec, on the other hand, "there has been almost a complete changing of the guard," observed Francis Fox, who had the thankless task of scouring the Quebec countryside for candidates to run as Liberals under John Turner. "Quebec reacts more and more as a single entity," he said. "The mass and the élite are now on the same wavelength."

Trudeau's ferocious determination to destroy the Meech Lake agreement was similar to Sir John A. Macdonald's determination to hang Louis Riel a century before, and it threatened to have the same effect on the Liberal party that Macdonald's decision had had on the Conservatives.

In a last double-or-nothing wager, Pierre Trudeau was making his own party choose between himself and Quebec. But if the Liberals were to weigh the proposition, as he would have done, with "reason over passion," they would conclude, as did one of their number: "We have to realize that Trudeau is not immortal. But if he is going to go, let him go with a bang rather than a whimper."

Epilogue

So Long, Monsieur Trudeau

*"But he died before I ever got into any open
conflict with him."*

Must there be a conclusion? Any conclusion might be the
wrong one. Or it might let Trudeau get away without admitting he was wrong.

June 24, 1968; October 16, 1970; November 15, 1976; May
20, 1980; November 5, 1981; August 27, 1987 . . . From the
heights of Parliament Hill, Trudeau spent two decades in public
life defying Quebec.

In Ottawa, the windows of the prime minister's office faced
north, the Great North where he so loved to escape, and west, to
English Canada and Ontario. Between Trudeau's desk and his
fellow Québécois, there was always Parliament, which he knew
how to use to serve his purposes, be it to build a just society, to
send in the army, or to lock the country into English majority
rule.

Was he arrogant? If so, he was arrogant with everyone: the
Atlantic fishermen, the Orangemen from Ontario, the prairie farmers, the loudmouths from British Columbia, Richard Nixon and
the Americans, and Charles de Gaulle and the French.

Was he a traitor? "No!" protested Pierre Vadeboncoeur. "Contrary to a lot of things that have been written about him, I can say
without the least hesitation that Trudeau was not a traitor. On the
contrary, he was scrupulously faithful to his own thinking, which
may have been rigid, but it was also as straightforward as it was
in a way, narrow."

In any case, how could he betray a cause whose legitimacy he always denied?

It could be said that he was a difficult child. Torn between two cultures, deprived of his father during his adolescence, and constantly being urged by his mother to travel as a way of pushing him out of the nest and making him spread his own wings.

When Trudeau spoke of his father, he sounded just like any Quebecker: "He wielded some authority; that made me respect him and during the last years of his life, probably also challenge him from time to time, as adolescents do."

There was something in Trudeau's tone that suggested that the premature death of his father had robbed him of a stage in his development during which he could have resolved the normal adolescent conflicts most boys have to work out with their fathers. He admired him without having the opportunity to show him that he was better; he respected him without ever being able to prove to him that he could manage without his advice; he was jealous of his father's success before he succeeded in his own right.

Perhaps Trudeau suffered from not having experienced this initiation rite, this confrontation, which would have consecrated him as a member of "the tribe." A precocious adult, rather than a child prodigy, Trudeau transferred his aggression to a Quebec that was then still in its own adolescence, expressing hatred for this "disgusting race of blackmailers," and heaping scorn on French Canadians, a people who spoke "lousy French," who let themselves be indoctrinated by the Church and bought out by the English.

Trudeau travelled as though fleeing a society huddled in its wretchedness, a society to which he refused to belong. Like a father who is always away from home, he did not see Quebec grow up and free itself. He wasn't there to measure himself against it.

When there was nothing left to discover elsewhere, Trudeau returned home. And, as though he still wanted to cut himself off from a people to whom he refused to belong, he ensconced himself in power to say, "No!" Alone, remote, impatient with those who did not understand him, scornful of those who refused to follow him.

He was always the "*enfant terrible*," spoiling for a fight, throwing down challenges, always saying, "No!"

As a "*Cité libriste*," his attacks on Quebec had limited impact. But as prime minister, his blows marked Quebec's collective destiny. And his "No" was endorsed by a majority of his people.

In the great psychodrama of Quebec history, from the aftermath of the "dark ages" to the 1980 referendum and even in days to come, should Trudeau be moved to return to affairs of state, he has always been a "negative spirit."

Between René Lévesque's "Yes," and Pierre Trudeau's "No," Quebec has confronted its contradictions with heart-rending intensity. "The confrontations between Lévesque and Trudeau," observed Roger Marcotte sadly, "hurt both men, and the people they wanted to serve." After all, there is something profoundly schizophrenic in electing Lévesque in Quebec and Trudeau in Ottawa on the basis of the same gut reaction.

It is a sad fate for a people who can no longer choose, since Lévesque is dead and Trudeau is still saying, "No!" Quebec certainly did a lot of growing up since Maurice Duplessis's death. But Trudeau still addressed the province like a prodigal child, like the delinquent in the family who has to be turned in to the police and put in prison.

"But he died before I ever got into an open conflict with him," Trudeau said of his father.

The orphaned Pierre-Philippe became Pierre Elliott and corrected his French-Canadian accent, as though he wanted to shake off the dust he had picked up from the land of his ancestors.

So what was Trudeau suffering from? He must have been suffering, because it seems unlikely that anyone so cruel could be a happy person.

With his considerable erudition, he must have come across the lesson of Julian the Apostate. During a trip to Greece, this former Roman emperor fell under the influence of neo-Platonism and renounced the Christian faith he had inherited from his father, Constantine. It was, he said, "a religion for slaves, incapable of inspiring noble and heroic souls." He became obsessed with eliminating all traces of his father's religion, to the point that he would spend a long time every morning vigorously scrubbing his face, as if to erase the stain of the holy oils with which he had been baptized.

There was something of the apostate in Trudeau, who rejected what he called "the Québécois box" with such hatred. But in the end, he isolated himself to the point where he found himself imprisoned in his own box.

He was like a dethroned prince, still attended by a lingering clutch of courtiers who would remind him of the splendours of power. And he clung to current political affairs as though fearful of finding out during his lifetime what his place in history would be.

Trudeau, who spent most of his career using his emotions like a sledgehammer, now found that his passion for his country had become his last remaining weapon. Against the hyprocrisy of an English Canada that no longer fears his indictments, and against the adolescent crises of a Quebec that still needs spanking.

Like a modern-day Ptolemy, he carries his country's history on his back, hoping that it will finally judge him to have been right, and let him pass into legend.

What goes through Trudeau's mind when English Canada spits a contemptuous "No!" in Quebec's face? Is he happy, at least, to see his people seek a special place at the family table and suffer the humiliation of being refused? Like a father provoking his son to the point of tears, Trudeau never stopped berating Quebec.

Yet he has chosen to return to Quebec, to imbue his sons with a sense of their roots. And to die there . . .

Unless it is simply that Montreal is a city like any other, pleasant enough to live in and English enough for Justin to feel at ease. A way of proving, to the end of his days, that one can be Canadian and still live in Quebec.

Did Trudeau applaud when his son Michel played Molière in the school pageant? Would he applaud if one of his sons had a part in a play by Michel Tremblay?

But then anything might happen. Did René Lévesque not prove that when he hauled out Maurice Duplessis's larger-than-life statue after fifteen years in a storage closet and planted it on the National Assembly's front lawn?

One of these days, the president of an independent Quebec might think of erecting a statue to Trudeau as well.

"He was Québécois, after all," people would say.

The people of Quebec would cheer. And Trudeau would not be there to protest, or to say, "No!"

Bibliography

Journals
Cité libre. June 1950 (No. 1) to October 1965 (No. 80).
Le Brébeuf. Journal published by the students of Collège Jean-de-Brébeuf, 1938-1940.
Le Quartier latin. Journal published by the students of the University of Montreal, 1941-1944.
Parliamentary Library. Press clippings (62 volumes). Ottawa, 1962-1984.

Books
Bourassa, Robert. *Bourassa Québec*. Les Éditions de l'Homme, 1970.
Chrétien, Jean. *Straight from the Heart*. Seal Books, 1986.
Collectif. Le Québec et le Lac Meech: Un dossier du Devoir. Guérin littérature, 1987.
Fournier, Louis. *F.L.Q.: The Anatomy of an Underground Movement*. NC Press, 1983.
Fraser, Graham. *P.Q.: René Lévesque and the Parti Québécois in Power*. Macmillan, 1984.
Gingras, Pierre-Philippe. *Le Devoir*. Libre Expression, 1985.
Godin, Pierre. *Daniel Johnson (Book II)*. Les Éditions de l'Homme, 1980.
Gwyn, Richard. *The Northern Magus: Pierre Trudeau and Canadians, 1968-1980*. McClelland and Stewart, 1981.
Johnson, Daniel. *Égalité ou indépendance*. Les Éditions de l'Homme, 1965.
Laurendeau, André. *Witness for Quebec*. Macmillan, 1973.
Lévesque, René. *Memoirs*. McClelland and Stewart, 1986.
MacDonald, Ian. *Mulroney*. McClelland and Stewart, 1984.

McCall-Newman, Christine. *Grits: An Intimate Portrait of the Liberal Party.* Macmillan, 1982.

McKenzie, Robert. *Pierre Trudeau.* Toronto Daily Star, 1968.

Morin, Claude. *L'Art de l'impossible.* Boréal, 1987.

Morin, Jacques-Victor. *Les Années de "grande noirceur."* (Inédit).

Nielsen, Erik. *The House Is Not a Home.* Macmillan, 1989.

Pelletier, Gérard. *Years of Impatience: 1950-1960.* Methuen, 1984.

Pelletier, Gérard. *Years of Choice: 1960-1968.* Methuen, 1987.

Radwanski, George. *Trudeau.* Macmillan, 1978.

Sheppard, Robert and Valpy, Michael. *The National Deal.* Fleet Books, 1982.

Simpson, Jeffrey. *Spoils of Power.* Collins, 1988.

Stanké, Alain. *Pierre Elliott Trudeau.* Stanké, 1977.

Stewart, Walter. *Shrug: Trudeau in Power.* New Press, 1971.

Trudeau, Pierre. *The Asbestos Strike.* Lewis and Samuel, 1974.

Trudeau, Pierre. *Federalism and the French Canadians.* Macmillan, 1977.

Trudeau, Pierre. *Réponses.* Éditions du Jour, 1968.

Trudeau, Pierre. *Approaches to Politics.* Oxford University Press, 1970.

Vadeboncoeur, Pierre. *La Dernière heure et la Première.* L'Hexagone-Parti Pris, 1970.

Westell, Anthony. *Paradox: Trudeau as Prime Minister.* Prentice-Hall, 1972.

General Reference

Debates. Official transcripts from the House of Commons and the Senate (Hansard).

Lacoursière, Jacques et Vaugeois, Denis. *Canada-Québec.* Éditions du Renouveau Pédagogique, 1978.

Liberal Party of Canada. *Pierre Elliott Trudeau: A Biography*, 1981.

McInnis, Edgar. *Canada; A Political and Social History.* Holt, Rinehart and Winston, 1982.

Office of the Prime Minister. Speeches and transcriptions of interviews.

Rémillard, Gil. *Le Fédéralisme canadien (Tableaux synoptiques).* Québec-Amérique, 1985.

Index

Index